THE FIRST DESTROYERS

Hardy in 1897. See page 83.
(National Maritime Museum,
London: G5303)

The First
Destroyers

David Lyon

Plans and cutaway drawings by John Roberts

MERCURY BOOKS

First published in Great Britain in 1996 by Chatham Publishing.

This soft back edition published in 2005 by Mercury Books
20 Bloomsbury Street, London WC1B 3JH
ISBN 1 845600 10 X

British Library Cataloguing in Publication Data
A catalogue record for this book is available from the British Library.

Cutaway drawings and plans by John Roberts

Designed by Roger Lightfoot
Cover Design by Open Door Limited

Typeset by Dorwyn Ltd, Rowland's Castle, Hants
Printed and bound by C.T.P.S. Hong Kong

Contents

Introduction

'This I have firm so keep it quiet, Obadiah, keep it quiet' . . . '*The* invitation to tender has come from the Admiralty.' In two successive letters sent three days apart one partner in a shipbuilding firm wrote to another about the culmination of a campaign to persuade the Admiralty to build a new kind of warship. This book is a documentary selection with linking commentary, plus a series of data tables, telling the story of the very first destroyers, the Torpedo Boat Destroyers, or TBDs as I have chosen to call them here. The book covers the so-called '26-knotter' prototypes, two each built by the main torpedo boat specialists, Thornycroft and Yarrow, plus another pair ordered somewhat later from Laird's. These were followed by the group known as the '27-knotters' ordered from a total of fourteen firms. Over a number of years the more successful of these firms went on to build the larger versions of their designs known as '30-knotters'. At the same time three high speed 'Specials' were building, to be followed somewhat later by three turbine-powered TBDs. A break was then marked by the ordering of larger, sturdier vessels, which put less emphasis on high speed on trial. These were the 'Rivers', and they will not be covered in the present book, though I hope to write a follow-on volume about this group. However, several years later, two modified versions of the '30-knotter' type were purchased from Palmer's who had built them 'on spec' – and this pair are included in the book.

This book is not a complete history of these early destroyers, though it is, I hope, a step in that direction. It is the story as told by quotation, direct or indirect, from the main series of technical documents of the Royal Navy, and supplemented by reference to the records of one of the main firms concerned in the development of the type, Thornycroft's, as well as by reference to the more obvious secondary sources. In other words this is the story told from the records available in the National Maritime Museum, where I worked for thirty years, for the majority of them in charge of the ship plans and technical records used here. A complete history would require investigation of other shipbuilders' records – for example those of Yarrow's, Thomson's, and Fairfield which survive under the control of the Scottish Record Office. These would have to be supplemented by further investigation of the surviving Admiralty records in the Public Record Office.

A further limitation of this work is that it is primarily concerned with the history of the development of the type, from the technological angle and as seen by the DNC's department and the firm that was one of the two pioneers of the type and which, unlike the other pioneer, continued to build TBDs for the Royal Navy until they were about to be superseded by more advanced designs. It does include a good deal of reporting back to the designers and builders by the men who had to operate these vessels, but is not primarily concerned with either the theory or the practice of operating TBDs. Even on the technical side I have refrained from venturing too far into the structural and theoretical concerns of naval architects, still less the technology of machinery and boilers.

What I hope I have provided is some of the interest and excitement of investigating those splendid documents, the

Daring photographed in No 3 Basin at Portsmouth in 1895 with the battleships *Revenge* (left) and *Majestic* (centre) behind her. The triangular structure behind her boat is a pair of dockyard sheer-legs. She is fitted with her pair of deck tubes, and shows the very uncluttered appearance of the earliest TBDs, before extra superstructure, canvas dodgers and so on made their appearance a little less spare. (National Maritime Museum, London: G10207)

Admiralty Ships' Covers, whilst removing at least some of the frustrations of trying to identify where a particular entry fits in to the story, or what it means. I have also tried to sort the material into a somewhat more accessible and meaningful shape. The main illustrations, which are major documents in their own right, are the Admiralty plans, the majority of which are 'as fitted' – showing the vessel in great detail as built and/or as altered one or more times after completion. A number of design plans have also been included. The plans are complemented by photographs, showing how the vessels actually appeared in three dimensions, whilst the recognition drawings of the late Richard Perkins give a nearly complete record of visual changes during the vessels' careers. Particular thanks are due to Bob Todd of the NMM, who in his inimitably cheerful and helpful way made these available to me.

Sorting out the large numbers of variants can be done in two separate ways. The approach can be purely chronological, dealing with each successive annual programme in turn. Alternatively, the TBDs can be separated according to builder, as each builder constructed its own design and modified that design from year to year to a greater or lesser extent, but usually made no radical changes. My policy here has been to describe the ordering of the vessels year by year first, and then to describe each builder's designs in detail one by one. The chapters covering the builders start by considering the two specialist torpedo-vessel firms who built the prototypes, Thornycroft and Yarrow, followed by Laird's and then all the other TBD builders in the order in which they received their contracts. The remaining eight destroyers were 'odd men out' and each group is given a chapter to itself – the three 'specials' intended to make 32 or 33kts, the three turbine-powered TBDs and the final pair purchased from Palmer's in 1909.

Having dealt with the building history and the designs of the particular groups of TBDs, the final section is a series of sections relating to general aspects of the TBDs, starting with how they were built, trials, seaworthiness, machinery, armament, boats and so on.

The book concludes with a list of available plans.

This photograph shows *Success* at Portsmouth in October 1901 with the cruiser *Spartiate* and the battleship *Resolution* behind her, and with the ram bow of another large warship nearly cutting off our view of her bow. (National Maritime Museum, London: G10210)

TBD Terminology

In May 1892 the DNC, writing to the Controller, referred to 'Designs for large sea-going TBs'[1] and the original conditions for TBDs of 1892 described the type as a 'Sea going TB of high speed'. Slightly later 'Instructions to the Firms relative to construction of hull' called them 'High Speed Torpedo Boats' and then inserted 'Sea-going' after the word 'Speed'.[2] On 30 July 1892 there is a reference to the 'Torpedo boat catchers' recently ordered.[3] At much the same time, whilst discussing the two different armament 'mixes' to be carried, the states are referred to as those for a 'Gunboat' ('destroyer' substituted in pencil) and 'torpedo catcher' ('torpedo boat' in pencil).[4] Whilst in the same month yet another document refers to 'fast sea-going torpedo boat catchers'.[5] However, it did not take long for the official name for the type to be 'Torpedo Boat Destroyer', inevitably abbreviated to TBD, an abbreviation which remained in use until the First World War. From the start this was competing with the term 'destroyer' which was eventually to be accepted as the standard name for the type.

'Destroyer' had been used before, for example to describe the 125-ft torpedo boats of the middle 1880s in their (not much used) gun-armed anti-torpedo boat version. Also the torpedo gunboat-type vessel built by Thomson's Clydebank yard for the Spanish Navy was called *Destructor* (which translates as *Destroyer*). However, the idea of shortening 'Torpedo Boat Destroyer' to 'Destroyer' probably came from either 'Jackie' Fisher or, even more likely, W H White, the DNC.[6]

In this book I refer to all the early destroyers (up to, but not including, the 'River' class) as *TBDs* to differentiate

Firm	92–3	93–4	94–5	95–6	96–7	97–8	98–9	00–1	Total
Thornycroft	2	3	4	2	3+1[1]	1	–	–	16
Yarrow	2	3	–	–	–	–	–	–	5
Laird	2	3	4	6	1[2]	1	2	–	19
Armstrong	–	2	–	–	–	–	–	1[3]	3
Barrow (NC & A)	–	3	–	3	1	–	1	–	8
Clydebank (Thomson)	–	3	–	4	1+1[4]	–	–	3[5]	12
Doxford	–	2	–	–	2	1	1	–	6
Earle	–	2	–	–	2	–	–	–	4
Fairfield	–	3	–	–	3	1	2	–	9
Hanna, Donald & Wilson	–	2	–	–	–	–	–	–	2
Hawthorn Leslie	–	3	–	–	2	1[6]	3	–	9
Palmer	–	3	–	6	2	1	3[7]	1[8]	16
Thames Iron Works	–	1	–	–	–	–	–	–	1
White	–	3	–	–	–	–	–	–	3
TOTAL	6	36	8	21	19	6	12	5	

1. 'Special' intended for high speed (32kts).
2. 'Special' intended for high speed (33kts).
3. Turbine boat – built 'on spec'.
4. 'Special' intended for high speed (32kts).
5. All 'stock' boats, building 'on spec' and purchased when nearly ready for launch.
6. Turbine boat – Parsons was the main contractor.
7. One of these was a 'private venture' boat already building and purchased on the stocks.
8. 'Stock' boat, building 'on spec' and purchased.

Notes to table: No destroyers were ordered for the 1899-1900 Programme. The 1892-1893 Programme vessels were the so-called '26-knotter' prototypes, the 1893-1894 orders for 27-knotters, subsequent years orders for 30-knotters except when indicated otherwise.

There is confusion over the 1895-1896 Programme and that for the following year, as to whether the total for both years was twenty, rather than the figures given here.

Three vessels were purchased after the last financial year in this table, the turbine vessel *Velox* building as a joint venture by Parsons and Hawthorn Leslie and the Palmer 'stock' boats *Albacore* and *Bonetta*, the latter bought in 1909.

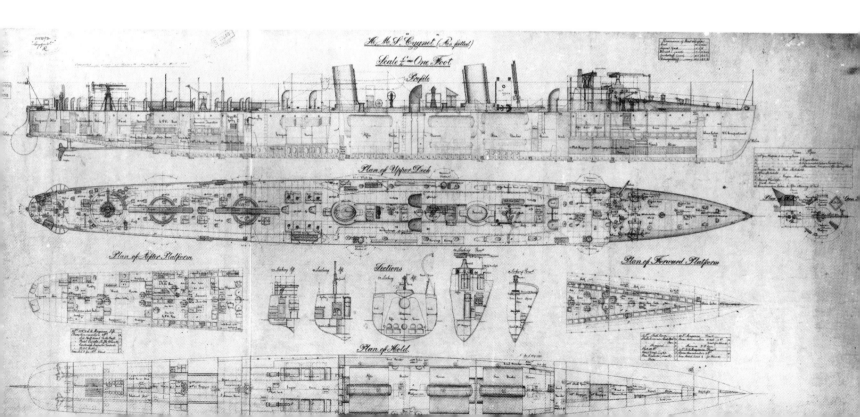

Armstrong's constructional sections plan for their *Swordfish* shows the characteristically light construction of these craft. The problem was always to combine lightness with strength. Armstrong's were to build what was probably both the lightest and the worst-built TBD in the shape of the ill-fated and short-lived *Cobra*, though whether that lightness of construction caused or merely contributed to her loss is still a matter of controversy. (National Maritime Museum, London: 33225)

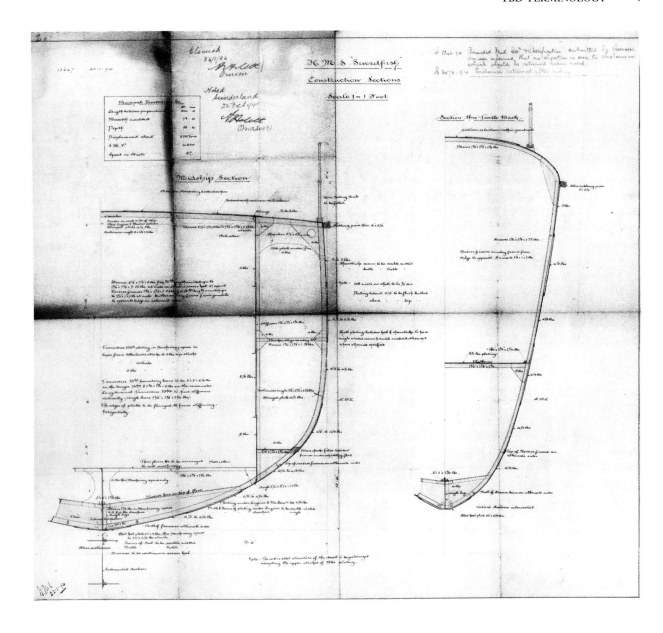

Left, Cygnet as built and as altered up to 1917. Note the lowering of the after 6pdr gun, the addition of a wireless office between the mast and fore funnel, and the removal of the shield to the after steering position as well as the modifications to the conning platform. (National Maritime Museum, London: 105492)

them from the later *destroyers* ('River' class on, except for the special case of *Albacore* and *Bonetta* – which were updated versions of the 30-knotters). This is solely a matter of convenience. 'Destroyer' is used in the Covers for what I call TBDs almost as often as 'Torpedo Boat Destroyer' or 'TBD', and later covers for many years use the three terms indiscriminately.

There are some indications that there were at least occasions when some at least of the TBDs were referred to in classes designated by a ship's name. W H White referred in a minute of 6 July 1893 to the '*Boxer* Class' when he could be referring either to Thornycroft's 27-knotters or to the first order for 27-knotters, or to all the 27-knotters.[7] To confuse matters, however, at least some of the 27-knotters were referred to as the *Ardent* class (an exact sister of *Boxer*!) in a document[8] which also mentions the *Charger* class – and therefore refers (I would suggest rightly) to the Thornycroft and the Yarrow 27-knotters as

separate classes. For the 30-knotters there is a general reference[9] to all the first TBDs of this type as the *Desperate* class. However there is also a reference[10] to separate *Quail* (Laird 30-knotter), *Whiting* (Palmer 30-knotter), *Janus* (Palmer 27-knotter) and *Rocket* (Thomson 27-knotter) classes. Despite this evidence I have distinguished between the different classes and groups of TBDs by date of order (which was done in the annual Estimates – or Programmes – which ran from the beginning of April to the end of March of the following year to tie in with the government's financial year) and by builder. The major groupings were as follows. The differences between the '26-knotters', the '27-knotters' the '30-knotters' and the various 'Specials' built by a particular firm tended to be comparatively large, but the alterations from year to year between the '30-knotters' built by that firm tended to be minimal – with the exception of Thomson's of Clydebank.

Sources & Acknowledgements

The principal sources that this account of the TBDs is taken from are the so-called 'Ships' Covers'. A 'Cover' in this context is a large, hardback binding into which are collected a series of government files. The files, in this case, are those of the Department of the Director of Naval Construction – the documents concerned with the design, construction, and subsequent alterations to a class of vessels. They include letters, memoranda, written discussions, reports, filled-out forms relating to, for example, trials, as built dimensions or stability data. There are also the occasional plan and diagram. Most of the extensive quotations which form the bulk of this work are taken from these Covers.

These 'Covers' are public records, now held as part of the Admiralty Collection at the National Maritime Museum, Greenwich. They are associated with the ship plans, some of which have been used to illustrate this book, and the relevant ones of which are listed as an appendix.

Covers List

The first column in this list is the DNC Cover number, the original, and meaningful, reference number of these documents and the one that I have used throughout this work. After that, in brackets, I have given the Public Record 'Admiralty 138 series' reference number. These are followed by the subject and the title.

128 (Adm 138/129)	26 & 27kt Torpedo boat destroyers: *Daring, Decoy, Havock, Hornet, Ferret, Lynx*
128A (Adm 138/130)	26 & 27kt TBDs: 'TBDs'
128B (Adm 138/131)	26 & 27kt TBDs: '*Swordfish* etc.'
128C (Adm 138/132)	'TBDs 26–27kts (old)'
142 (Adm 138/154)	TBDs: '*Ariel* class.' 1894 (30-knotters)
154 (Adm 138/224)	Turbine destroyers: *Cobra, Viper, Velox, Eden*
160 (Adm 138/210)	Torpedo boat destroyers: *Coquette* class (30-knotters)
165 (Adm 138/165)	Torpedo boat destroyers: 30-knotters 1898-1905
165A (Adm 138/166)	Torpedo boat destroyers: *Albacore, Bonetta* etc
165B (Adm 138/167)	Torpedo boat destroyers: 30-knotters 1908-1919

References are given in this work using the Cover (not the 138 series) number in the following form. 'Cover 128/25' when 128 is the Cover number and 25 is the 'folio' number. Individual pages are usually not numbered, but the individual files ('folios') within the cover are numbered consecutively. There is one Cover number missing entirely from the sequence in this period – which would seem to coincide with the missing papers for the 1895-1896 and 1896-1897 programmes.

Admiralty Ship Plans Collection

The 'Covers' are associated with the Admiralty collection of ship plans which have been useful sources for some of the data given in this work, have been used as illustrations, and the more significant of the relevant ones of which are listed as an appendix. These are also now held at the National Maritime Museum.

Thornycroft Collection

Another collection held in the National Maritime Museum is that of the shipbuilder John I Thornycroft & Sons, one of the two pioneers of the TBD type and a firm which continued to develop the destroyer in subsequent years. The letters, technical documents and plans of that firm have also been used in the compilation of this book and have been extensively quoted from and listed here.

Printed sources

What follows is merely an indication of the works I have used and (usually) found useful. It is not a complete listing of all the relevant books.

Very few serious attempts have been made to write up the TBDs after their first appearance. So, although there is a great deal about them in such trade journals as *Engineering* and in Brassey's *Naval Annual* for the years in which they were entering service, there is not much of later date which can be referred to. Unfortunately the one attempt to write a comprehensive history of the destroyer in the Royal Navy, Edgar J March's *British Destroyers* (London 1966) is poor, unreliable and better ignored even on the later destroyers. It is particularly bad on the TBDs, completely failing to sort them into any rational order, and, though based mainly on the Covers, commits far too many sins of omission and misunderstandings to be remotely reliable. T D Manning's book of the same title, *British Destroyers* (London 1961) was written by someone of much greater knowledge and understanding but is very little more than a listing with photographs and some comments and is better on the later destroyers..

The present author made an attempt to make some sense of the TBDs by listing them and their immediate successors, the 'River' class destroyers, in the British torpedo craft section of *Conway's All the World's Fighting Ships 1860-1905* (London 1979). As will be seen in some of the later sections, a closer look at the sources has made me alter some of the data and attributions given there. I also contributed the general chapter on 'Underwater Warfare and the Torpedo Boat' in *Steam, Steel and Shellfire*, the relevant volume in the 'Conway's History of the Ship' series (London 1992) which is useful for background.

For a lively and light-hearted account of what it was

like to be aboard the TBDs before the First World War, told from the officers' point of view and full of anecdotes see Lionel Dawson, *Flotillas* (2nd ed, London 1935).

The story of destroyers during the First World War, including that of the surviving TBDs, was written up by an officer who himself had commanded vessels of this type both before and during the war. *Endless Story* by 'Taffrail' (Captain H Tapprell Dorling) (London 1931) is an excellent account, and very much more than just a collection of eyewitness stories. It is all too short, but what there is is an invaluable mixture of eyewitness report and careful research as well as being balanced and well written.

On the background to the designers and builders of these vessels there are two invaluable works. David K Brown's *A Century of Naval Construction: The History of the Royal Corps of Naval Constructors* (London 1983) is a fascinating account of the department whose records form the basis of my book. On the relationship between the Admiralty and the shipbuilders, see the chapter by Hugh Lyon in Brian Ranft (ed), *Technical Change and British Naval Policy 1860-1939* (London 1977). I also owe much to both David and to my brother Hugh for much useful information and discussion over the years. There are two reasonably useful books about the firms which built the pioneer TBDs – Lady Yarrow's life of her husband (London 1929) and Kenneth C Barnaby's *A Century of Specialised Engineering* (London 1966) which is a centenary history of Thornycroft's.

On the operational reasons behind the ordering of the first TBDs see A Cowpe's essay on 'The Royal Navy and the Whitehead Torpedo' in the volume edited by Brian Ranft referred to above. However, this essay is of little technical interest: an author who writes on this subject and is clearly unaware of the existence of the first British torpedo vessel, *Vesuvius* (he refers to *Polyphemus* as the first such vessel), and who can attribute the whole development of the TBD to Yarrow cannot be regarded as adequate in this field. There is also some all too short but characteristically shrewd comment in Ruddock Mackay, *Fisher of Kilverstone* (Oxford 1973).

Probably the best general history of the Royal Navy in this period is still A J Marder, *British Naval Policy 1880-1905* (London 1940), later republished as *The Anatomy of British Seapower*, but this is long overdue for replacement. Some of the ammunition for this is provided in Jon Sumida's *In Defence Of Naval Mastery* (London 1989) but this is more concerned with the opening years of the twentieth century than the closing ones of the nineteenth. An excellent and lively account of international naval rivalries in the period is Peter Padfield's *The Battleship Era* (London 1975).

On the development of foreign vessels of the kind see H Fock, *Schwarze Gesellen*, Band I (Herford 1979). This is meant to be an international history, but where it is valuable is, as one might expect, on German vessels. The standard French account is H Le Masson, *Les Torpilleurs Français* (Paris 1963). On the Italian experience see Ufficio Storico Della Marina Militare, *I Cacciatorpediniere Italiani* (Rome 1969). Norman Friedman's *US Destroyers* (Annapolis & London 1982) is characteristically lively and thoughtful. I know of no detailed account of the early development of Russian destroyers. There is an excellent history of Swedish destroyers, Borgenstam *et al*, *Jagaren* (Karlskrona 1989), but it is written in that language.

Acknowledgements

I would like to acknowledge the help, stimulus and encouragement I have received on the subject of destroyers and other matters covered in this book from conversations and correspondence with many friends, including Philip Annis, Stellan Bojerud, David K Brown, Ian Buxton, Norman Friedman, Andrew Lambert, John Lambert, Nicholas Lambert, Hugh Lyon, Iain MacKenzie, the late George Osbon, Alan Raven, John Roberts, David Sambrook, Bob Todd and the late David Topliss. David K Brown very kindly let me see the relevant extracts from his forthcoming book on this period as well as sending many valuable comments. I would particularly like to thank my old friend and colleague Antony Preston; we started talking destroyers within minutes of his arrival to work in the National Maritime Museum and have never really stopped. My friend and publisher Robert Gardiner has as always been a most knowledgeable and intelligent sounding-board on this as on all other maritime subjects; my especial thanks to him and to Julian and Stephen for their patience, and best wishes for their new venture.

I would also like to thank the members, past and present, of the Historic Photographs and Ship Plans sections of the National Maritime Museum who have provided me with the material and illustrations for this book.

For hospitality beyond the common run whilst in the final throes of this work, many thanks to Monica, Nils, 'Skrutt' and all their splendid relations

Finally, thanks to Leo for companionship, interest, and unselfish encouragement, and above all for giving me the delightful opportunity of mentioning her in such a context.

All credit to those mentioned above (and anyone I have inadvertently omitted – to whom my apologies) for their generous and manifold contributions; the responsibility for error is mine alone.

David Lyon
Isle of Dogs, King's College, Cambridge and the Stockholm Archipelago
Midsummer 1996

Glossary of People, Offices, etc

This listing gives brief definitions or details on a number of words and people who appear a number of times in this book and may be unfamiliar to the reader.

Admiral Superintendent. The Naval Officer in charge of a Royal Dockyard.

Arnold-Forster, H O (1855-1909). Politician – Secretary of the Admiralty in 1901 – later as Secretary of State for War reorganised the War Office.

Barnaby, S W. Chief naval architect to Thornycroft's, son of Nathaniel Barnaby who had been Director of Naval Construction. S W Barnaby's son, K C, was to follow him as chief naval architect of Thornycroft's and was to write the centenary history of the firm.

Beaumont, L A. Captain of HMS *Vernon* around 1892.

Berthon, Edward Lyon (1813-1899). The designer of the folding lifeboat which bore his name, and which was carried by most TBDs (see Boats section).

Biles, Sir John (1854-1933). Naval architect, had been involved (not altogether successfully) in shipbuilding at Southampton, but was much more successful as chief designer to Thomson's. Set up the Department of Naval Architecture at Glasgow University. Acted as the chairman of the TBD Enquiry of 1903.

bp. (Length) between perpendiculars.

Catcher (ie '*Torpedo boat catcher*'). A designation used occasionally for the first TBDs, but more often associated with the earlier TGBs.

Controller, the. The naval officer in charge of the design, construction and maintenance of the ships of the Royal Navy. He was the Third Sea Lord on the Board of Admiralty. At the time the TBD was conceived the position was filled by John ('Jackie') Fisher, who played a crucial part in the ordering of the type.

Cover. Bound file or files (literally inside a pair of hard covers); in this context the 'Admiralty Ships Covers', the files of the DNC's department on the design, construction and subsequent alterations to a class or group of ships. See the introduction for further details and a listing of the relevant ones.

Cunnah, Wright & Co. Builders of the 'unsinkable' reindeer hair lifeboat adopted for TBDs about 1893-95 (see Boats section).

Deadman, H E. Naval Constructor in charge of destroyers for the DNC's department. Sketched the outline design for the first TBDs. Became Assistant Director of Naval Construction (ADNC).

Destroyer. The word which evolved from 'Torpedo Boat Destroyer' (TBD) and was initially used indiscriminately with 'TBD' to describe the type we are looking at in this book. However, I have used it (except when quoting directly from a contemporary document) only to designate the later vessels from the 'River' class on, bigger, more seaworthy and more heavily armed, and nearly all of which had raised forecastles rather than the 'turtleback' forecastle which characterised the first TBDs we are dealing with here.

DNC. The Director of Naval Construction – the chief naval architect of the Royal Navy and the senior technical officer of the Admiralty. In this period the post was filled by W H White and then P Watts.

DNO. The Director of Naval Ordnance, the officer in charge of the development of guns, mines, torpedoes and other weapons for the Royal Navy.

Domville, Sir Compton. DNO around 1893.

Donaldson, John. Brother-in-law and partner to John Thornycroft. He provided the business skills and acumen to Thornycroft's whilst his brother in law got on with technical matters.

Durston, Vice Admiral Sir John. Engineer-in-Chief 1889- after 1905.

Ellis. Naval Constructor who seems to have done much work on TBDs.

Engineer-in-Chief (EinC). The chief marine engineer of the Navy, the professional head of the engineering branch and the third member of the triumvirate (with the DNC and DNO) backing up the Controller in the design and building of ships for the service.

ext. Extreme (depth).

First Lord of the Admiralty. The political head of the Navy.

First Sea Lord. The professional head of the Navy, responsible to the First Lord for the running of the service.

Fisher, J A. Admiral of the Fleet, Baron Fisher of Kilverstone (1841-1920). The best known naval officer of his period. Controller 1892-1897 and bore a large share of responsibility for originating and ordering the TBDs. He went from this post to become Commander-in-Chief of the Mediterranean Fleet.

Goschen, G J. First Lord of the Admiralty 1895-1900 (also 1871-1874); became 1st Viscount Goschen in 1900.

Hall, W H. Captain in 1892 (the founder of the Naval Intelligence Department).

hp. Horsepower.

ihp. Indicated horsepower.

May, Admiral of the Fleet Sir William H. Controller 1901-1905.

Metacentric height. A measure of the stability of a ship. The greater this figure, the more stable the ship.

mld. Moulded (depth).

NMM. The National Maritime Museum, Greenwich, where the Admiralty and Thornycroft Collections are held which provide the main documentation for this book.

oa. (Length) overall.

Overseer. DNC's representative overseeing and inspecting building of a vessel.

QF. Quick-firing. Denotes a gun firing ammunition where shell and propellant charge are combined.

Richards, Sir Frederick W (1833-1912). First Sea Lord 1893-1899, and excellent in this post, his part in the re-generation of the Royal Navy after the 'dark ages' of the 1870s and early 1880s has been obscured by the achievements of the more publicity-conscious and spectacular Fisher, but should not be forgotten.

rpm. Revolutions per minute.

Spencer, Lord (1835-1910; Fifth Earl Spencer). First Lord of the Admiralty 1892-1895.

TB. Torpedo Boat.

TBD. Torpedo Boat Destroyer – basically an enlarged TB – and the origin of the word 'Destroyer'. In this book I have used TBD specifically to indicate the group of vessels described here, whilst 'destroyer' has been used to indicate the larger, sturdier and more powerful vessels from the 'River' class on.

TGB. Torpedo Gunboat.

Thornycroft, John I (1843-1928). Founder of the firm named after him, specialist in the design of fast light craft, especially torpedo vessels.

Torlesse, Arthur W. First commanding officer of *Hornet*.

Turtleback. The rounded, semi-conical forecastle which characterised the later Torpedo Boats and the TBDs I have described here, which are often referred to in subsequent accounts as 'turtleback destroyers' to differentiate them from the raised forecastle destroyers which came later.

Vernon, HMS. Torpedo school, Portsmouth (the, less important, equivalent at Plymouth was HMS *Defiance*). *Vernon* was the Navy's centre for development of torpedoes, mines and electricity ('A mysterious fluid invented by Captain Fisher [an earlier captain of this establishment] and perfected by Commander Wilson,' according to one examination answer by a trainee torpedoman). At the beginning of the period she was still a hulk, but by the end of it the transformation to a 'stone frigate' (shore establishment) had begun.

Watts, Sir Phillip. DNC 1902-1912.

White, Sir William H. DNC 1885-1901.

Wilson, A K. Admiral of the Fleet 1842-1921. Had served as Captain of *Vernon* As a Rear Admiral was in charge of the destroyer force in the 1895 manoeuvres. Nicknamed 'old 'ard 'eart' by the lower deck (the sailors), and later First Sea Lord.

wl. Waterline.

Yarrow, Sir Alfred F (1842-1932). Founder of the firm that bears his name, specialising in light fast craft, particularly torpedo vessels. Both a clever inventor and a very successful businessman.

Tables: Ship dimensions are given as Length × Breadth × Depth in hold + Draught.

Machinery statistics are given as No. of Shafts, Cylinder Diameters × Length of Piston Stroke, Pressure, IHP.

Part I: Development

The Prehistory of the TBD

There are two different lines of development of the British Torpedo Boat Destroyer. One is the purely technical – the progressive development of the torpedo boat in speed, size and fighting power until it becomes a different type entirely.[1] This is also the story of the specialist builders of this type of craft. The other is the development of a tactical need against the background of Anglo-French naval competition in the English Channel. As is usually the case, the two strands interweave

Whitehead's invention of the locomotive torpedo in the late 1860s, followed by its rapid adoption by the navies of Europe in the early 1870s, immediately raised the question of how the new weapon should be taken into action. The British Torpedo Committee, in its carefully thought-out report of 1873 gave among its conclusions two answers which formed most of the prehistory and early history of the TBD as a type. These were to build specialised seagoing torpedo craft on the one hand, and the development of fast light torpedo launches for inshore and coastal work on the other. The two lines of development were finally to merge in the destroyer, a vessel which was, in a neat and slightly paradoxical way, both the nemesis of and the replacement for the torpedo boat. It did this also by filling the gap left by what was perceived as the failure of the unfairly neglected torpedo gunboats, and thereby merged the separate lines of development of the torpedo boat and torpedo vessel.

From the launch of the RN's first torpedo vessel *Vesuvius* in 1874, through the 'torpedo-ram' *Polyphemus* of 1882 and the *Scout* and *Archer* class torpedo cruisers, the emphasis had been on torpedo attack alone, with little or no consideration for the need to protect the core of Britain's maritime strength, her battlefleet, against torpedo attack, either by escorting that fleet, or chasing and destroying the increasing numbers of torpedo boats building for Britain's chief maritime rivals, France and Russia. In the mid-1880s the growth in the French torpedo flotilla, and the possibility of war with Russia (which would entail sending a fleet into the Baltic in the same way that had brought an end to the Crimean War thirty years earlier) focused attention on the need for 'torpedo catchers'. W H White designed the *Rattlesnake*s, basically miniaturised cruisers armed with quick-firing guns and torpedo tubes, whose primary function was in the anti-torpedo boat role, but could also serve as high seas torpedo vessels. These were the first 'Torpedo Gunboats'. There were to be three subsequent classes, the *Sharpshooter*, the *Jason* (or *Alarm*), and the *Dryad* (or *Halcyon*) classes. They were the victims of two particular problems. One was a problem with their machinery (see below), which prevented them achieving their intended top speed. The second followed on from this, and was basically a problem of perception. Their failure to obtain top speed meant that they were not successful in 'catching' torpedo boats in the light weather in which the latter operated best. In fact the TGBs made reasonable fleet escorts, and in even slightly heavier weather were perfectly capable of running down their smaller opponents. However, they were marked down as a failure. Ironically twenty years later the 'River' class destroyers had in size, armament and emphasis on sea-speed reached very much the same level as the TGBs, in what, with improved technology, represented an excellently balanced design. They had however reached that position by following the other route of incremental growth from the original torpedo boats. The TGBs were a false start, but not, in the long run, a mistaken one.

The Royal Navy's series of torpedo boats started with *Lightning* (*TB No 1*) of 1877 – an armed version of Thornycroft's fast river launch designs, and with all the obvious disadvantages that entailed. Range was short, and seaworthiness less. Only capable of use in sheltered water or very calm conditions, and with a weapons system as delicate and short-ranged as herself, she and her immediate successors were basically experimental craft requiring careful tuning and nursing if any reasonable results were to be obtained. It was to be nearly a decade before there was a substantial increase in size and seaworthiness. This increase owed much to the specialised torpedo boat builders, Thornycroft and Yarrow, who had been steadily improving their designs for the foreign navies who ordered such craft from them in numbers. The Russian crisis of the mid 1880s led to large orders for the 125-footers which were intended at first to have two alternative armaments. The first was a gunboat armament of quick-firers so that they could accompany the fleet to areas such as the Baltic and tackle enemy torpedo boats, a role which was on at least one occasion described as 'torpedo boat destroyers'. In practice, and because the crisis died down, these vessels were all fitted in the torpedo boat mode. At much the same time an even larger version of a torpedo boat design was purchased from J S White who had built her 'on spec' as the *Swift*. *TB 81*, as she became, was also intended to have an alternative weapons-fit in the 'torpedo boat catcher' mode. She could be considered a prefiguring of the TBD concept, but in practice what she actually did was to herald a further increase in torpedo boat size, power and seaworthiness.

This takes us to the end of the 1880s, the period of naval expansion which caused and was reinforced by the 1889 Naval Defence Act. The French, partly as a defensive reaction to the British predominance in battle-ships and particularly what Andrew Lambert has called 'coastal offence' ships (*eg* the *Glatton* and the other breast-work monitors) which directly threatened the French bases, partly because of the ideas of the '*jeune école*', and partly because of the pressure of technological factors to make torpedo boats bigger and better, were already producing large numbers of sea-going ('*haute mer*') torpedo boats. These would be a serious menace to the British fleet in the narrow waters of the Channel.

The TGBs had apparently proved to be inadequate for anti-torpedo boat work, and were admitted to be so even by their designer W H White. For several years the two main specialist builders of torpedo boats had been pressing the Admiralty to build enlarged versions of their torpedo boat designs which could be used in the TGB role. The times were auspicious and the factors which would produce the TBD were coming together.

At the beginning of 1892 J A Fisher, an officer already noted for his energy and his, usually well-informed, technological enthusiasms, was appointed as Controller and Third Sea Lord, in charge of providing new ships for the Navy. He appointed a committee which investigated the problem and suggested building vessels fast and powerful enough to catch and destroy torpedo boats. He had already reached that conclusion in February 1891 when, as Director of Naval Ordnance, he produced a paper on the subject[2] stating amongst other things: 'Since torpedo boats necessarily have a limited range of operations, a moderate coal supply and radius of action suffices for the torpedo boat destroyer. The armament may also be of a lighter character than that appropriate to the torpedo gunboat, and inferior sea-keeping qualities and accommodation are permissible . . . [however it] . . . should be considerably larger than a torpedo boat so as to have superior sea-going qualities, together with a more powerful quick-firing gun armament.' Other features compared with the TGBs should be a less conspicuous outline, shallower draft so that torpedoes would pass underneath, and a lower price. He proposed a vessel of about 300 tons and costing about £30,000. Its duties were to include: 'Channel protection . . . hunting down the enemy's torpedo boats and watching their stations . . . [and watching his main bases] . . . when the ordinary torpedo boats could not be depended on to keep the sea, and large cruisers would have to keep off at night on account of torpedo boats . . . [it would be better to build TBDs rather than more torpedo boats] . . . the role of the latter is more offensive than defensive, *and as our real line of defence lies on the French side of the Channel* and France has no trade [*ie* merchant ships] against which the boats could act, it appears to be expedient to build a larger class of vessel.'

It is clear from this paper, and what subsequently happened, that Fisher's role in the conception and ordering of the TBDs was a major one, though it is also legitimate to wonder how much these were his own ideas and how much he was taking from other people, particularly Yarrow and other shipbuilders, and the DNC and members of his department. Whatever the truth of this matter, it is

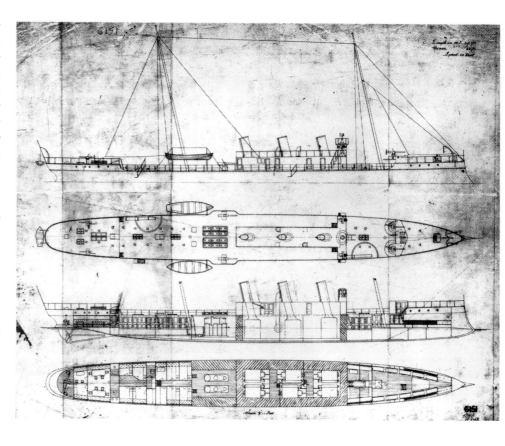

certain that it was Fisher who directly inspired the ordering of the first TBDs, though it was W H White who persuaded him to use the specialist torpedo craft builders rather than the Royal Dockyards.[3] The role of Alfred Yarrow in the ordering of the first destroyers is well attested, so much so that he is sometimes given the entire credit. This is to ignore the role played by Thornycroft which becomes apparent on consultation of that firm's records, and by the DNC and his department. The actual armament layout and therefore general appearance of the early vessels was established in a sketch design by the constructor Deadman, who was to become the chief authority on the TBDs. The indications are that White concentrated on the design of larger warships, leaving the TBDs to Deadman and his assistants, when necessary signing the drafts they prepared, but rarely adding anything. Yarrow's chief achievement was to build both a locomotive boiler and a water tube boiler version of the TBD in very short time so that they were both in service considerably before the two Thornycroft vessels were completed. It is also probable that as a very powerful personality Alfred Yarrow made more impact on that other powerful personality, Fisher, than did his quieter rival.

Before moving to consider the ordering of the prototypes, we should consider a number of technical factors which provide some of the explanation for the form these vessels took. They were very much at the cutting-edge of technology of the day, as a new jet fighter would be now. The torpedoes which they were to carry had emerged from the experimental stage during the previous two

One of Thornycroft's designs for a TGB-like vessel – this one dated 1893, by which time the firm was already building its first TBDs. (National Maritime Museum, London: HO 6151)

decades and were larger (18in rather than 16in or 14in), more powerful and more reliable than had previously been the case, though it was not to be until after 1900 that the 'air heater' engine and controlling gyroscope made for a really radical increase in range. The previous decade had seen the introduction into service of the quick-firing gun, including the ubiquitous 12pdrs and 6pdrs with which the TBDs, in common with so many other vessels, were to be armed.

The steady development of marine engineering had already produced the triple expansion engines with which these ships were fitted, though the torpedo boat builders had evolved their own versions to cope with the extreme high speed which had to be combined with extreme lightness, strength and (it was hoped, though not always achieved) both reliability and (relative) lack of vibration. A large number of TBDs were to be fitted with triple expansion engines which had four cylinders, the low pressure steam being shared between two separate cylinders. This was done to make the engine better balanced in an attempt to avoid the terrible vibration which all too often affected these reciprocating engines. In the long run it would be the rotary engine which became the obvious power plant for such fast craft, but 1892 was five years before the Engineer-in-Chief of the Navy invited Charles Parsons to bring the *Turbinia* to the Diamond Jubilee Review.

The years when the TBDs were building were also the years of the 'battle of the boilers'. The standard boilers used aboard torpedo boats were locomotive boilers. These were also used aboard the majority of the TGBs and were the chief source of their troubles. This was because the locomotive boiler became unreliable when forced to the limits of its performance to produce higher pressure steam to drive a faster or larger vessel. The alternative was the water tube boiler, various versions of which were advancing from experimental status to practical use just as the first TBDs were ordered. In 1892 it was sensible to 'hedge bets' by ordering one locomotive boiler TBD and one with water tube boilers from Yarrow. The greater speed achieved by the latter was a straw in the wind. The next trio of TBDs ordered from the same builder, and a number of the other 27-knotters, were built with locomotive boilers, but the Yarrow trio were refitted within a couple of years with water tube boilers. The next year's programme, the first in which 30-knotters were ordered, saw the total abandonment of locomotive boilers for TBDs – all future vessels being ordered with water tube boilers. The TBDs in a sense were a laboratory for trying out different types of water tube boiler, and proving the general concept.

This was the era of speed, high speed for its own sake. This had really started with the torpedo boats, each new design attempting to reach a higher speed than anything before. There seems to have been little rational discussion of why high speed was necessary for torpedo attack. Speed was seen as a good thing in itself. It became a subject for international competition. The specialist torpedo boat firms all competed for the fastest speed on water. Everything was subordinated to achieving high

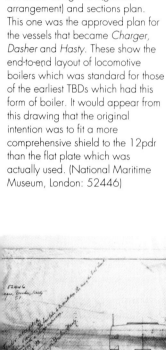

A Yarrow design GA (general arrangement) and sections plan. This one was the approved plan for the vessels that became *Charger, Dasher* and *Hasty*. These show the end-to-end layout of locomotive boilers which was standard for those of the earliest TBDs which had this form of boiler. It would appear from this drawing that the original intention was to fit a more comprehensive shield to the 12pdr than the flat plate which was actually used. (National Maritime Museum, London: 52446)

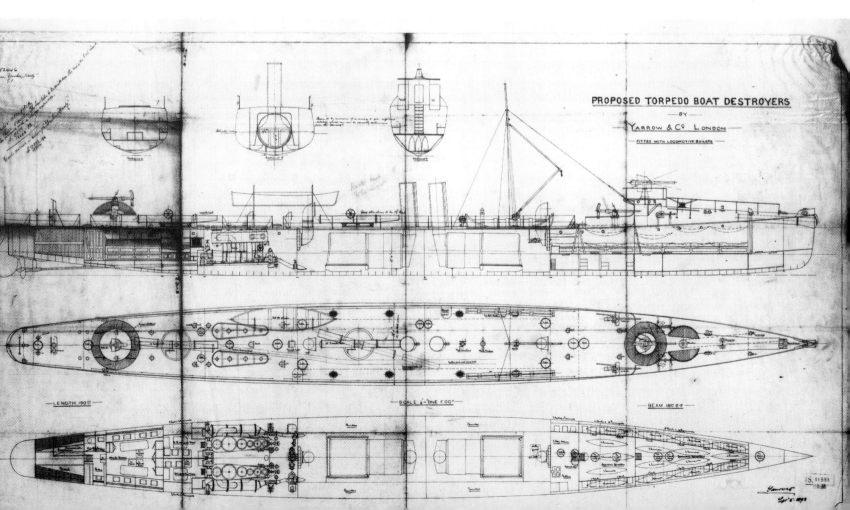

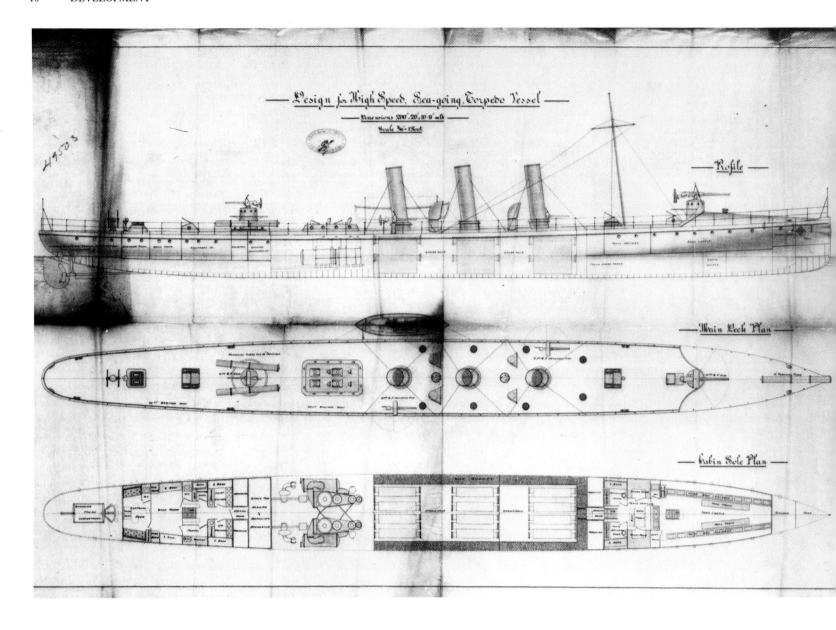

Design for High Speed, Sea-going, Torpedo Vessel

Profile

Main Deck Plan

Cabin Sole Plan

speed on trial. Special courses were used which later re-search would show were exactly the right depth to pro-duce an enhanced and unrealistic top speed. Trials were run in calm water, with specially trained crews of stokers and, literally, hand-picked coal. Very often the forced draft (blowing air by fans into boiler room or directly into the fireboxes to make the fires burn more fiercely and provide steam at higher pressure, thus producing con-siderable increases in speed) was so fierce and the strain on the machinery so great that there was permanent damage. Even without such damage trial speeds could never be repeated in service. As we will see later very few of the '30-knotters' could make more than about 26kts, if that, in service and this was only in calm conditions. With any sort of sea speed dropped off rapidly.

To obtain high speeds the vessels had to be very lightly built, and the same applied to their machinery. They were easily damaged, unreliable and a worry in bad condi-tions. The plans of the 'Specials' show just how much of the hull volume had to be devoted to engines and boilers in an unsuccessful attempt to reach 32 or 33kts (and still only carry a standard TBD armament). The absurdity reached a peak with the first turbine destroyers which could only approach their intended speeds with enor-mous stoking gangs which could not be accommodated aboard. It is not surprising that there was a reaction in favour of larger, sturdier, more reliable vessels with an adequate sea speed that they could actually maintain in service conditions. This reaction produced the 'River' class, the first true destroyers. For the first time in a quarter of a century the relentless pressure to drive tor-pedo vessels ever faster was replaced by the need to produce what was simultaneously the true torpedo vessel and the best type of fleet escort.

This general arrangement plan is J Samuel White's 1892 design for a TBD with that firm's characteristic 'cut up' stern. Three water tube boilers feed three funnels. (National Maritime Museum, London: 49503)

Ordering the prototypes – 26-knotters, 1892-1893 Programme

The first order for TBDs was for two from Thornycroft (*Daring* and *Decoy*) and two from Yarrow, the latter being subdivided into one with locomotive boilers (*Havock*) and one with water tube boilers (*Hornet*). Both these latter were to be completed well before the two Thornycroft boats. A later order was placed with Laird's for another two boats (*Ferret* and *Lynx*). These six prototypes are occasionally referred to as '26-knotters' and, though in fact the Admiralty requirement was for 27kts, this is the designation adopted for convenience here to distinguish them from the succeeding, very large, group of 27-knotters ordered under the next year's programme.

In March 1892 the Controller, the redoubtable 'Jackie' Fisher, had informal discussions with the heads of the two specialist torpedo boat firms, John Isaac Thornycroft and Alfred Fernandez Yarrow. Although previous accounts have given Yarrow greater importance in the birth of the destroyer (following Lady Yarrow's somewhat partial account in her biography of her husband), it is clear that Thornycroft was just as much involved. Out of these discussions grew the idea that an enlarged and faster torpedo boat was perfectly possible. So on 12 April 1892 the Admiralty asked a number of firms to submit designs and tenders for 'large sea-going torpedo boats' and all had done so before the end of May[4] as the DNC informed the Controller: 'in the enquiry letter special attention was devoted to 200-ton vessels. Several firms have sent in 300- and 400-ton designs, but in accordance with the wishes of the [Admiralty] Board report is restricted [so] that the highest possible speed shall be obtained, and, unless the clauses as to penalties for non-attainment of speed are stringent it will really pay any contractor to accept the Penalty and content himself with the lower speed. Probably if these penalties are inserted, the Contractors will urge the association with the penalties of premiums for higher speed than 27kts. Of the firms asked to submit amended offers Messrs Thornycroft, however, stand alone in asking premiums, and we should prefer not to have any premiums for higher speed if they can be avoided. As far as we can judge on a review of all the circumstances, the speed of 27kts is the most which we can reasonably hope to obtain under present conditions with the load specified; and if any firm desires to guarantee a higher speed with that load there is nothing to preclude them from doing so, associating their offer with an increased price . . . All firms should be sent papers C & D [the detailed conditions] except Hanna Donald & Wilson, and tracings showing layout of armament, and inform them that only 200-ton [vessels are] wanted at present. Their Lordships want submission of amended designs and tenders strictly in accordance with conditions; [the matter is urgent, 14 June suggested as delivery date.] Messrs Thornycroft and Messrs Yarrow to . . . be informed that their designs are in the main considered satisfactory. They should be asked to quote for one or two boats. Yarrow should also be asked to tender for tubulous [water tube] boiler as they suggest for [their] second boat and to state speed. The other firms concerned were to be told of the deficiencies of their designs in the case of Thomson's, Palmer's and White's, whilst Messrs Hanna, Donald & Wilson have submitted a design which cannot be recommended for acceptance . . . ' (Details of these designs can be found in the chapters on each firm.)

The Admiralty already had decided on the armament of one 12pdr for use against the French *haute mer* boats, one 6pdr and an 18in bow torpedo tube. In addition either two more 6pdrs or a pair of revolving torpedo tubes.

The table (left) gives the available data on the 200-ton designs. (HDW = Hanna Donald Wilson, the data for the Thompson design, unfortunately, is concealed by a fold in the page of the original document.)

The detail conditions (the Appendix C referred to above) ran as follows: 'The boat is to be built and completed in her hull, masts, rigging, propelling machinery, auxiliary machinery – consisting of evaporating and distilling, steering, air compressing, electric light engine and dynamos of 100 amps, 30 volts – fittings and Machinery

	Palmer	HDW	White	Laird	Thornycroft	Yarrow
DISPLACEMENT	205t	–	220t	185t	–	–
LENGTH	190ft	184ft	200ft	175ft	180ft	–
BREADTH	18ft 6in	15ft 6in	20ft	17ft 6in	18ft 6in	
DEPTH	9ft	9ft	–	6ft	6ft	
TRIAL SPEED	–	26kts	26kts	26½kts	27kts	24kts
TRIAL IHP	4200	–	–	2700	3200	–
NO. OF SCREWS	2	1	2	2	2	2
RPM	350	400	–	–	–	–
PRESSURE	165–175lbs	180lbs	–	–	210lbs	–
NO	5	2	–	–	–	–
SURFACE GRATE	155	90	–	–	–	–
SURFACE HEATING	5320	3300	–	–	–	–
COAL, TONS	19	20	15–20	12	–	50

MACHINERY: Palmer's – Triple 4-cylinder inclined, 2 cranks opposite with Du Temple boiler/Hanna, Donald & Wilson – 20in.32in.52in × 18in locomotive, dry bottom boiler/White – Maudslay engine similar to *Seagull*, water tube boiler of new design/Laird – Not stated about machinery, but in the larger boat proposed to use tubulous boilers with 200lbs/Thornycroft: Triple expansion engines, 4 cylinders 16in.24in.25½in. 25½in × 15in water tube boiler/Yarrow 24in. 37½in × 15in [??] dry bottom locomotive boiler.

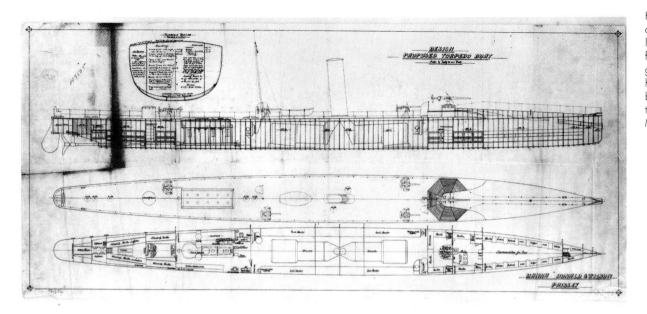

Hanna, Donald & Wilson's 1892 design for a TBD. The end-to-end locomotive boilers feed one very tall funnel (the higher the funnel, the greater the natural draft). This design has only one shaft and only one boat. There are four 6pdrs but only the bow torpedo tube. (National Maritime Museum, London: 49505)

spare gear, in all respects – except where otherwise stated – ready for service at the expense of the Contractor.

In addition to the fittings relating to the Hull, pumping and draining arrangements, ventilating, messing, sleeping and cabin arrangements for 40 officers and men, magazines, armament fittings, etc. the following articles of outfit are to be supplied by the Contractors: Corticene for upper deck, watch bell, chart table, signal lockers, chronometer and compass boxes, galley and cooking utensils. coal box, cooks tables, larder etc. Awnings and fittings complete. Tanks for drinking water to contain at least 400 gallons. All necessary oil and store tanks. Cordage reels. log reel and fittings. Fittings for patent taffrail log – the log will be supplied by the Admiralty. Boats – 24ft

Whaler of light construction, two Berthon boats 20ft in length. Boats' davits complete with griping spars, blocks, falls, grips, etc. Canvas covers for boats, torpedo tubes, guns, compasses etc. Lifebuoys two in number. Night lifebuoy, Whitby's patent two (?) in number. Compasses will be supplied by the Admiralty but all necessary supports, fittings, etc., to be provided by the Contractor. Lockers for stokers' dirty clothes and wash deck gear. Fittings for mast head, anchor and bow lights. The lanterns will be supplied by the Admiralty. Relieving tackles for steering. Two steering stations to be provided. The steering wheels are to be available for either hand or steam gear. Anchors 2 × 6cwt, 2 × 2cwt without stock. Cables 100 fms [fathoms]. ¾in cable complete with shackles

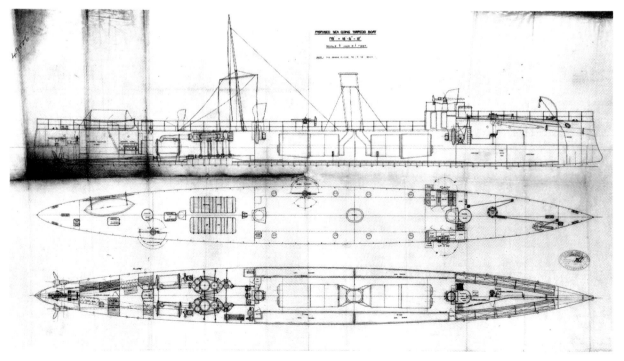

J & G Thomson's 1892 design for a TBD is, not unsurprisingly, somewhat reminiscent of their *Destructor* built for the Spanish Navy. It is, with its ram bow, cruiser stern, raised forecastle and greater freeboard, more in the TGB style than the enlarged torpedo boats which would actually be built. The two locomotive boilers are arranged end-to-end so as to feed a single funnel, which separates the two stokeholds. (National Maritime Museum, London: 49506)

swivels etc 100 fms 3in flexible steel wire rope with swivels. Hawse pipes, bollards, riding bitts, bow stopper, transporting chocks, catheads, ground chains, catting chains, towing arrangements etc, complete. Deck pipes, slips, clenches, wire rope compressor. Reel for wire rope fitted with brake attachments. Chain lockers etc. Capstan with all necessary cranks etc and arranged to work with cable and wire rope. Gun stands, supports, platforms, all necessary strengthening to hull etc. Holding down rings, mountings and guns will be supplied by the Admiralty. Torpedo tubes and racers will be supplied by the Admiralty, but all necessary fitting to boat, bow cap arrangements, locking bar etc, is to be done by Contractors. All necessary torpedo davits fitted with Baskerts winches, wire pendants, etc, fittings for stowing torpedo warheads and exercise heads. The electric light projector will be supplied by the Admiralty but all leads, supports, holding down rings, resistance cutouts, terminal boxes etc are to be supplied and fitted by the Contractors. Stowage is to be provided for two spare torpedoes. The lamps for internal lighting will be supplied by the Admiralty, but all fitting is to be done by the Contractor . . . FURTHER CONDITIONS The Bunker capacity of between 40 and 50 tons to be provided. The metacentric height to be guaranteed with all weights on board to be not less than 2ft. This will be tested by an inclining experiment at the Contractors works; all necessary fittings and assistance for this purpose to be provided by the contractor . . . '

Six general points were made[5] to all the firms submitting tenders, including that armament fittings were to be tested by firing trials on receipt and any defects to be made good by the contractor. All sketches required by the overseer for submission to the Admiralty were to be prepared by the contractor. Material was to be manufactured by approved firms and under Admiralty supervision.

By July 1892 the decision had been made to order from Thornycroft and Yarrow, but there was still the question of whether to build to the designs of Laird, White or Palmer – though the latter was described as unsatisfactory and was therefore dismissed from consideration. The DNC reported:[6] 'The following we submit for consideration. – (1) With regard to Messrs Lairds' statement that their facilities are such that they can proceed with two vessels as easily as one – whether they should be entrusted with more than one, seeing that they have not to our knowledge, had any extended experience in building vessels of this type; further, we should not recommend placing an order for more than one vessel with Mr White in view of the experimental form of boiler proposed. (2) If any tender is accepted the firm to be informed that while it is desired to give them as free a hand as possible, it will be necessary for them to submit details of construction for approval, and that any addition or modification required must be carried out without extra charge. (3) Should contractors be called upon to furnish guarantee for return of money if the boats are rejected, say by insurance, or should the risk not be accepted by the Admiralty . . . '

1893-1894 Programme Order – the 27-knotters

The initial order for 27-knotters was placed with the two specialist torpedo boat firms only, Thornycroft (*Ardent, Boxer, Bruiser*) and Yarrow (*Charger, Dasher, Hasty*), with three vessels each. However, this was soon followed by a series of follow-up orders. The Admiralty was making a deliberate attempt to involve as many shipbuilders as possible in this effort and, besides including the firms whose designs had been turned down the previous year, added several others. There were two from Doxford (*Hardy, Haughty*), three from Palmer (*Janus, Lightning, Porcupine*), two from Earle (*Salmon, Snapper*), three from Laird (*Banshee, Contest, Dragon*), three from White (*Conflict, Teazer, Wizard*), two from Hanna, Donald & Wilson (*Fervent* and *Zephyr*), three from Fairfield (*Handy, Hart, Hunter*), three from Hawthorn Leslie (*Opossum, Ranger, Sunfish*), three from Thomson (*Rocket, Shark, Surly*), three from Naval Construction & Armament, Barrow (*Skate, Starfish, Sturgeon*), two from Armstrong (*Spitfire, Swordfish*) and one from Thames Ironworks (*Zebra*). In the end thirty-six vessels were ordered for this programme from fourteen separate firms.

The DNC proposed on 27 July 1893,[7] as six additional TBDs were provided for in the 1893-1894 Estimates, to write to Thornycroft and Yarrow for tenders for three TBDs each which 'in all essential particulars will closely resemble the two [already building]'. However, the space for accommodation of the crew would be somewhat larger. Four 'separate' training torpedo tubes, 'also to be provided for, will involve some extra length'. It is not clear whether this was a question of having four totally separate tubes, which seems unlikely in view of the room available, or two twin mountings, which seems more likely. In fact there would only be two separate tubes fitted in this group of vessels and their immediate successors. 'Great importance attaches to the rapid construction of [the] vessels. The dates named for delivery should be such as can be guaranteed under the conditions of practise and in view of experience. Their Lordships, while recognising the good work done by your firm in the construction of torpedo vessels, consider it desirable to encourage other firms in undertaking work of this class. It must be understood therefore that Their Lordships

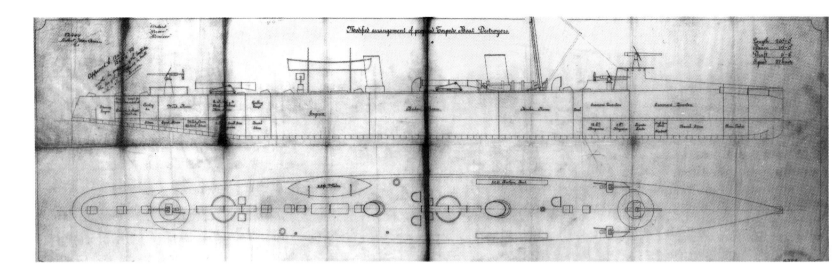

consider themselves entitled to make use of information in their possession respecting the torpedo boat destroyer type as may appear necessary in the public interest.' This was to cause some trouble, especially with Yarrow, and may have been part of the reason why that firm (admittedly very happily employed building and designing destroyers for foreign navies) built nothing more for the Admiralty for nearly a decade after the trio ordered at this time.

The Admiralty Board had already, on 1 July, decided to call for tenders for at least eight TBDs from other firms. In the 1893-1894 Estimates a sum of about £651,000 had been set aside for payments on fourteen vessels. It had been anticipated in framing those Estimates that orders would not be placed at an early date, not, in fact, until the first prototypes had satisfactorily completed their trials, and that provision was to be made in the next (1894-1895) Estimates to complete the payments. However, the First Class cruiser programme (*Terrible* and *Powerful*) was postponed to January 1895, in order to push on the TBDs, allowing twenty-five new boats to be ordered this year instead of fourteen and the sixteen others contemplated to be begun in 1894-1895. This would give thirty-one completed TBDs by the end of 1894-1895 with others in hand, though the completion dates would prove to be over-optimistic in all cases, grossly so in many.

The firms asked to tender in 1892-1893 were to be asked to do so again except: 'Pending trial of vessels now building by Laird, we submit not to place further orders with that firm, the class of work being novel to them, propose to add: Naval Construction & Armament Co, Hawthorn Leslie, Earle's, Fairfield, Thames Iron Works [for the hull with Penn or another firm providing the machinery], Armstrong Mitchell (hull), Humphreys & Tennant or other approved firm (machinery) and Doxford. Each firm to be sent conditions of instalments, machinery specifications, conditions of tendering, outline drawing showing accommodation spaces, general features of the vessel and disposition of the armament. Particular attention [is] drawn to speed conditions.'

The August 1893 printed conditions for tendering[8] included the following conditions. 27kts trial speed to be guaranteed for three hours, measured on six consecutive Measured Mile runs, and a 12-hour 10kt coal consumption trial to be carried out. Trial load 30 tons to be carried. The penalty was £250 per ¼kt or fraction [thereof] between 27 and 26kts and £500 per ¼kt between 26 and 25kts with a liability to rejection below 25kts. There was to be a penalty of £15 per day late. Bunker capacity should be at least 60 tons. Metacentric height guaranteed not less than 2ft with 30-ton load. To have good manouevring power and both steam and hand steering. To have a 'turtleback' forecastle. The conning tower plates to be at least ½in thick. The lower deck forward was to be watertight as were all magazines below this deck and the flat above the magazines aft: '. . . as free a hand as possible will be given to the Contractors in carrying out the designs for these vessels, for which they will be held entirely responsible, but the details of the scantlings, or the hull and fittings and accommodation, proposed details, particulars and dimensions of machinery and boilers and all necessary drawings must be furnished for consideration before the work is taken in hand, and failure to do this may render such work liable to rejection, and any modifications which may be considered necessary in these proposals will be required to be carried out without extra charge; further no deduction from the weight to be carried on trial can be made . . .'

The machinery was to be as far as practicable in accordance with recent Admiralty practice and should have a twelve-month guarantee. Tenders were to be in by Noon on 3 October.

The designs received are discussed in detail in the chapters on the appropriate builders, but a list of the prices initially quoted is shown in the table opposite.

The tenders of the first five builders only were accepted (on 7 November 1893), the others would have their designs further modified before acceptance.

The Admiralty went to considerable trouble to inform the builders less used to building torpedo craft about the techniques involved. It also seems to have exercised considerable patience with those firms that had difficulty in building vessels which could reach the speeds asked for. As no firm actually came near the over-optimistic delivery

Thornycroft's initial profile and upper deck layout design for their 27-knotters (*Ardent* and her sisters). (National Maritime Museum, London: 52444)

Hanna, Donald & Wilson's design plan for *Fervent* and *Zephyr* showing how the locomotive boilers were fitted end-to-end, thus permitting the uptakes to be trunked into the single funnel which was to be the unique feature of these destroyers as at first completed. (National Maritime Museum, London: 55832)

Builder	Number of TBDs	Hull cost	Machinery cost	In months
Hanna, Donald & Wilson	1	£10,000	£23,919	8
(loco boilers)	2	£19,600	£47,238	23
	3	£29,400	£79,857	28
Palmer's	1	£14,128	£23,932	13
(Du Temple boilers)	2	£27,776	£46,804	15½
	3	£46,154	£69,846	18
J & G Thomson	1	£14,500	£22,252¾	12
(Normand boilers)	2	£27,200	£41,305½	14
	3	£41,000	£60,758	16
J S White	1	£15,540	£23,073	13
	2	£31,080	£46,146	15
	3	£46,620	£69,219	17
Doxford	1	£17,250	£21,900	12
(loco boilers)	2	£32,460	£41,800	13½
	3	£48,300	£62,400	15
Hawthorn Leslie	1	£15,600	£17,600	9
(either loco or water	2	£29,800	£33,600	11
tube boilers)	3	£44,250	£49,950	13
Earle	1	£13,850	£19,100	9
(loco boilers)	2	£27,100	£37,800	10
	3	£40,350	£56,400	11
(water tube boilers)	1	£13,850	£20,850	9
	2	£27,100	£41,200	10
	3	£40,350	£61,400	11
Naval Construction Co.	1	£15,500	£19,100	12–15
(loco boilers)	2	£30,550	£37,650	13–16
	3	£45,150	£55,650	15–18
(water tube boilers)	1	£15,250	£18,850	12–15
	2	£30,050	£37,150	13–16
	3	£44,400	£54,900	15–18

dates originally agreed to there was even greater patience needed over these. Some firms (Hanna, Donald & Wilson, White, Thames Iron Works and, interestingly, Armstrong's) were not to get any more TBD orders, but, as we will find later, other firms which had severe difficulties (including Thompson's and Doxford – see their appropriate chapters) would be given what seems to have been very fair treatment.

30-Knotter Orders

1894-1895 Programme – first orders

The first six 30-knotters were ordered from firms which had built the 26-knot prototype TBDs, from Thornycroft (*Desperate*, *Fame*, *Foam*, with a fourth, *Mallard*, added later), and from Laird (*Quail*, *Sparrowhawk*, *Thrasher*, with a fourth, *Virago*, added later); the other original firm, Yarrow, though tendering, finally did not accept the Admiralty price.

The opportunity to order these first 30-knotters was provided by the considerable delays in completing the majority of the 27-knotters. On 27 July 1894 the DNC sent a note to the Board[9] pointing out a shortfall of about £85,000 on estimated expenditure on TBDs, and reminding them that in the event of this contingency arising, it had been the intention to order some improved vessels. He proposed that Yarrow 'be invited to tender for the construction of two or three TBDs of 30kts speed' and that Thornycroft and Laird also be considered. '. . . Since time will be taken up in a settlement of any new design so that it will probably be well into October before any order could be actually placed . . . [eight vessels could be ordered] . . . but, in view of the new departure as to speed and other novel conditions we think it desirable at this stage not to order more than six.'

Fisher, the Controller, then (27 July 1894) wrote: 'Propose to write confidentially to Yarrow asking for tenders for one, two or three boats, similarly to Messrs Thornycroft for one or two boats and similarly to Messrs Laird for one, naming three months from date of letter for receipt of tenders. This will give them sufficient time to elaborate their designs. It might be advisable to state to the firms that the acceptance of the tenders will be contingent on Treasury sanction . . . It certainly will be of great advantage to have a few boats of improved type well advanced before placing next year's order for TBDs.'

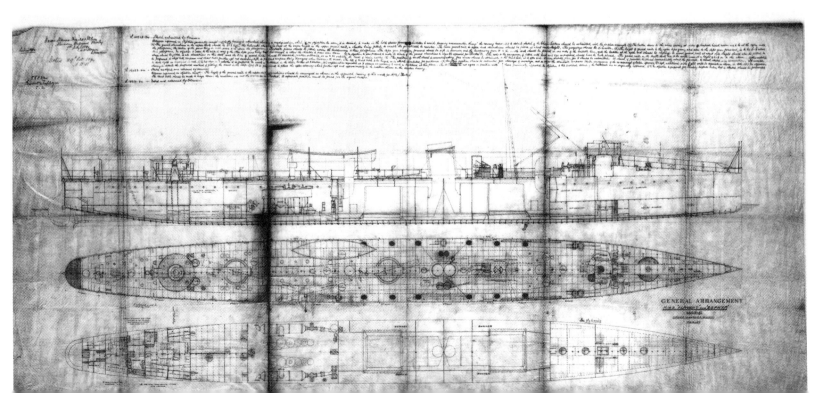

However, it was felt politic not to approach the Treasury until later, although in the meantime the preliminary design steps could be put in hand. Prudence required that: 'Letters to the three firms should indicate that the Admiralty do not bind themselves to giving orders and may not be able to take more definite steps till the next financial year.'

Someone slipped up in sending the letters out to the builders because Thornycroft was inadvertently asked to tender for up to three vessels rather than just one or two. As the firm had already acknowledged receipt of the letter, no action was to be taken, and, as we have seen, the firm did, in the end, provide three TBDs in this particular batch.

Meanwhile, Lord Spencer was querying the Financial Secretary as he was worried about the form of words about the use to be made of firms' designs; all drawings were to be retained by the Admiralty: 'but this wouldn't touch the right of sending the designs of one firm to another . . . some better words than those used in clause five of the letter of 28 August 1893 might no doubt be put together but I feel we cannot finally lay down what we shall do . . . without knowing more precisely than we do what the custom of the private trade is.' He received a very Civil Service reply, suggesting that it might be well not to raise the question at that moment with the firms. Perhaps the Controller would discuss the matter with the DNC and Engineer-in-Chief on his return from abroad.

The printed conditions of tendering for the 27-knotters were altered to fit the new requirements for 30-knotters. The load on trial was to be 35 tons. There was to be a reduction of the price by £250 for every ¼kt below that speed and £500 below 29kts with absolute rejection at 28kts. The penalty per day late was to be £15. The bunker capacity was to be at least 80 tons and metacentric height not less than 2ft. The vessel were to have good manoeuvring powers and both hand and steam steering. The conning tower to be of not less than ½in steel and a turtle back was to be fitted. Stands for four Maxim machine-guns (to be 0.45in ones rather than 1in calibre) and mountings for two 12pdr guns were to be provided, though this armament would be later altered to the famil-

iar combination of a single 12pdr with 6pdrs. Galvanising was to be used and two 8cwt and one 2¼cwt anchors supplied.

In early December the following details were given of the machinery of the three builders' designs. Yarrow's had offered three separate designs, in one of which were alternative arrangements of twin or triple screws, the details here being for Number 2 design, the only one for which full details were given. The Thornycroft design had three shafts, the Laird one two.

	Yarrow	Thornycroft	Laird
ENGINE ROOM WEIGHT	49 tons	68½ tons	62 tons
SHAFTING & PROPELLERS	6 tons	6½ tons	12½ tons
BOILERS & WATER	80 tons	75 tons	82½ tons
TOTAL	135 tons	150 tons	157 tons
IHP	6400	6500	7000
RPM	Ca.420	Ca.390	Ca.400
TRIAL DISPLACEMENT	350 tons	315 tons	309 tons
SPEED	29¾kts	30kts	30kts

'Not one of the designs can be recommended as it stands.' The Yarrow design (2) was rejected on the grounds of caution over the use of aluminium alloy and HT steel (see Yarrow chapter for details). Both the Thornycroft and the Laird proposals could be revised to make them acceptable. Revised tenders were invited after experience with the *Ardent* class seemed to confirm that a 30kt vessel could be obtained on not much more displacement. In view of the satisfactory completion by Laird of *Ferret* and *Lynx*, it was submitted that they should be put on the same footing as other firms and asked to tender for two or three vessels.

Letters were sent to the firms on 15 February 1895 asking them to submit further designs. Admiralty requirements could be met by vessels considerably smaller than at first submitted, and therefore at considerable saving in cost. Laird had submitted proposals for vessels which were practically repeats of *Banshee* and in view of other

Doxford's design plan for their first 30-knotters, *Violet* and *Sylvia*, showing approved modifications. This plan also shows loading positions for the torpedo tubes. (National Maritime Museum, London: 61028)

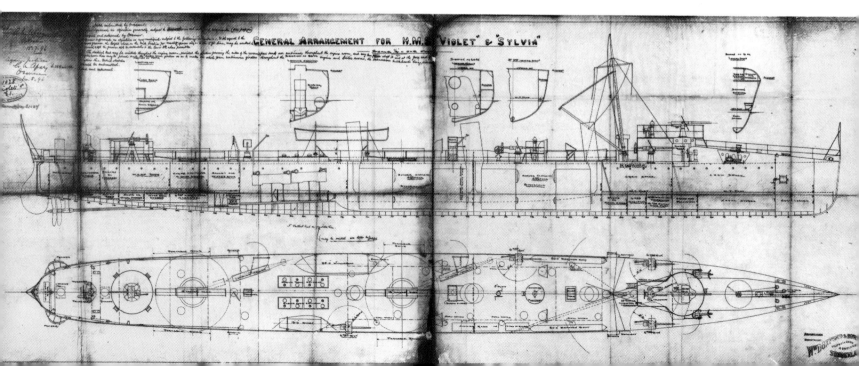

GENERAL ARRANGEMENT FOR H.M. "VIOLET" & "SYLVIA"

nations (France with its 220-ton torpedo boats was mentioned), it was not desirable to build less than 30-knotters.

The printed conditions for tendering were further modified by March 1895: 30kts to be maintained for three hours continuous steaming and tested during the trial by six consecutive Measured Mile runs. A twelve-hour trial would be held, *if required*, to ascertain the consumption of coal at 13kts. Only high-quality Welsh coal, which had the advantage of producing maximum heat with minimum smoke, was to be used. 'As free a hand as possible will be given the Contractors in carrying out the designs of these vessels, for which they will be held entirely responsible, but the details of the scantlings of the hull and fittings and accommodation proposed, details, particulars and dimensions of machinery and boilers, and all necessary drawings must be furnished for the consideration of the Officers of the Controller of the Navy's Department *before the work is taken in hand* and failure to do this may render such work liable to rejection and any modifications which may be considered necessary in these proposals will be required to be carried out without extra charge; further, no deduction from the weight to be carried on trial can be made when such modification involves extra weight.' The machinery was to be guaranteed for twelve months 'but in cases of untried designs of either engines or boilers, or of designs which Their Lordships may have no actual experience, a two years' guarantee may . . . be insisted upon.' The contractor to be responsible for any payment on infringement of patent rights.

On 10 April 1895 the DNC reported to the Controller[10] that the new designs could be accepted as satisfactory with some minor detail modifications, the prices quoted by Laird were very reasonable: 'but those quoted by the London firms are high. In view of Messrs Yarrow's and Messrs Thornycroft's exceptional position as the pioneers of this class of vessel and also of the superior performance of the boats built by the latter firm as regards speed we are of the opinion that they are entitled to some advance on Messrs Laird's prices.' Suggested £4000 a boat reduction.

On the same day Fisher proposed to give three boats to each firm – Laird as offered at £140,250 in fifteen months, Thornycroft and Yarrow conditional on reduction in price and delivery time to fifteen months. The Thornycroft price was about 10 per cent and Yarrow's 7.5 per cent beyond that named by Laird's.

The next year's programme (1895-1896) produced more orders for 30-knotters from Thornycroft (*Angler* and *Ariel*) and Laird (*Earnest, Griffon, Locust, Panther, Seal* and *Wolf* - the last was originally to be called *Squirrel*), in both cases very slightly modified versions of the previous year's designs. To these were added designs by Vickers (*Avon, Bittern, Otter*), Thomson (*Brazen, Electra, Recruit, Vulture*), and Palmer (*Star* and *Whiting* were ordered first, followed by *Bat, Crane, Chamois* and *Flying Fish*).

On 2 October 1895 the DNC noted[11] that of twenty TBDs included in that year's programme only twelve were as yet ordered and it was time for the other eight.

The following firms had completed one or more TBD satisfactorily: Thornycroft, Yarrow, Laird, Thomson, Palmer's, Naval Construction & Armament (Barrow), Fairfield and Earle's. It was noted of the last two firms that: 'The vibration in these boats is not yet satisfactory but this will be overcome.' Thornycroft, Laird and Thomson were thought to have received orders for four boats each (this was not actually so: Thornycroft were supplying two boats and Laird six), Yarrow declined the price offered by the Admiralty which was accepted by another London firm (Thornycroft). As the number of boats was small the invitations to tender should be restricted to Yarrow, Palmer's, Barrow and Fairfield.

On the same day Fisher signed and sent the invitations to tender. The letter included the following points: 'Ventilation will have to be increased beyond that in existing boats. The ventilation to the galley space must be specially attended to and this compartment should not be utilised for messing or sleeping any of the crew. Use of HT (high tensile) steel will be allowed. Displacement on trial not to exceed 300 tons. Proposals for use of higher steam pressures than previously employed will be entertained. Maximum rpm should not exceed 400. Tender to be delivered no later than 5 November 1895.'

The 1896-1897 programme saw three more TBDs ordered from Thornycroft (*Coquette, Cynthia, Cygnet*), slightly lengthened with improved lines but otherwise similar to the firm's previous 30-knotters. Palmer's also were given an order and repeated their very successful design with *Fawn* and *Flirt*. Vickers also built a virtually unaltered version of their previous year's design (*Leopard*). Thomson's had, however, had considerable difficulty in getting their first 30-knotters to make their intended speed and therefore produced a new design with altered lines for the one TBD they built in this programme (*Kestrel*). Doxford (*Violet, Sylvia*), Hawthorn Leslie (*Mermaid, Cheerful*), Fairfield (*Osprey, Fairy, Gipsy*) and Earle (*Dove, Bullfinch*) all received orders for 30-knotters for the first time. This was also the year that three higher-speed 'Specials' were ordered, from Thornycroft (*Albatross*), and Thomson (*Arab*), both of which were intended to make 32kts, and from Laird (*Express*), which had the even more ambitious aim of 33kts. None of them managed to reach the intended speed, and the Thomson boat would not be begun, because of the problems which that firm had during the trials of its first 30-knotters, until much later.

1897-1898 Programme

By the time the orders were being placed for this programme there were already doubts being expressed about the pursuit of speed for its own sake, and no more of the large and expensive 'Specials' were ordered. Instead a small additional series of orders were placed for 30-knotters with the more successful builders: Thornycroft (*Stag*), Laird (*Orwell*), Doxford (*Lee*), Fairfield (*Leven*), and Palmer (*Spiteful*), none of which made more than small alterations to the previous designs they were based on. Barrow, Clydebank, Earle's and Hawthorn Leslie also tendered but were not awarded an order. In the end six TBDs were ordered in this year (two under the original programme and four under a supplementary programme). The additional vessel was, apparently, the first turbine destroyer, *Viper*.

On 6 September 1897 the DNC noted:[12] ' . . . It would appear desirable not to duplicate orders for these vessels of exceptional speed with either of the three firms in question, [Thornycroft, Laird, Thompson] until the vessels already ordered have been tried and proved successful. Of the other builders only Messrs Yarrow, Messrs Palmer and the Fairfield Co are as yet in such a position in regard to speeds obtained as to justify their being asked to submit designs and tenders for vessels of 32 or 33kts. It is possible that Messrs Hawthorn Leslie, Messrs Doxford, the Earle's Company and the Barrow Company may hereafter justify their receiving such invitations, but at present we do not advise it. Another fact, which deserves consideration, is the very large proportionate increase in cost and size involved in this increase of speed: for example, the 30kt destroyers building by Thornycroft cost about £51,500, whereas *Albatross* of 32kts has about one-third greater displacement and costs £66,500. A 30kt destroyer built by Lairds' costs about £47,000 and the 33kt destroyer will cost £62,500. In round figures the increase of two to three knots in speed means an increase of about one-third in displacement and total cost. Again it is now a matter of experience that, under working conditions at sea, where dead smooth water is but seldom met with, the higher contract speed of two knots is not associated in practice with an equal gain in sea-speed. In fact the limit of speed attainable is very commonly fixed by the condition of the sea rather than by the power available in vessels. Another reason for holding our hands with the vessels of extreme speed, until the vessels now on order have been tried, is to be found in the fact that the four destroyers of about 300 tons displacement, which are provided for in the Supplementary Programme of the French Navy for 1897, have the reputed speed of *26kts*. There can be no doubt that this will be exceeded on trial since the designer is M Normand, and the indicated HP stipulated is *4800* in vessels about the size of our 30kt destroyers. It is very doubtful if these French vessels will exceed the speed of 28 to 29kts unless the power developed is increased very considerably. Having regard to the foregoing statement the following course is submitted for consideration:

(1) That invitations to tender be sent to the Firms who have already received orders, or been invited to tender for 30kt vessels; asking them to submit new offers for vessels generally fulfilling the conditions of tendering for 30-knot Destroyers dated February 1896.

If the firms are prepared to guarantee a higher speed than 30kts they are to be at liberty to do so.

We submit that these invitations be *not* [underlined] sent to the Thames Iron Works, Armstrong & Company, Hanna Donald & Wilson and J S White of Cowes.

(2) If thought desirable to repeat the inquiries for the vessels of higher speed we submit that the invitations be limited to Messrs Yarrow, Thornycroft, Palmer, Laird, Thomson and the Fairfield Company. The conditions of tendering for Fast Sea-going Destroyers of above 30kts speed to be associated with these latter invitations.

(3) Tenders to be made by each firm for one or two vessels.' This document was signed by R T Butler for the Engineer in Chief as well as W H White, the DNC, on 7 May 1897.

Fisher added: 'This matter has been carefully considered and discussed and it is suggested (1), (2) and (3) be approved as we in no way commit ourselves by the enquiry under (2) to order the faster vessels.' The First Sea Lord concurred.

Nine firms responded to the tender for 30kt destroyers since Yarrow's declined to tender

1898-1899 Programme

It appears as if the twelve destroyers originally intended to be ordered as part of a supplementary programme under this programme were actually ordered under the next programme (see below).

Goschen, the First Lord of the Admiralty, suggested[13] to the Naval members of the Board on 25 July 1898 that before the next TBDs were ordered they should ask the Engineer in Chief to investigate the apparently high accident rate of the type, expressing a personal preference for a reliable 27kt ship which was less often in dock over a 30kt boat as liable to accidents. A J Durston (the E in C) and W H White (the DNC) replied on 9 August that although the design was largely down to the Contractors, experience showed that the structural strength was adequate under all circumstances; many had survived collision or grounding but safely reached port; several had made long ocean passages and their behaviour and seaworthiness had been most satisfactory even in very severe weather; stronger and more rigid nickel steel was extensively used later vessels and any improved material would be adopted for additional strength and lightness. The only consistent weakness was the propeller bracket of the early 27kt vessels built at Barrow, which were of forged scrap iron, whereas in most later, and all new, vessels they were of cast steel or forged ingot steel. 'The new specifications will embody all our experience and all approved recommendations for alterations up to date both as regards hull and fittings.'

Goschen also wanted to know if any particular firm's machinery was more troublesome than others, but the E in C stated that there was nothing 'of a specially important character'. The DNC proposed sending a similar tender enquiry to that of May to the following successful builders of 30-knotters: 'Thornycroft, Laird, Palmer, Fairfield, Doxford – Yarrow's have also built successful vessels of about this speed for foreign navies and may therefore be added to the list . . . Because of possible employment hereafter of oil fuel, bulkheads should be made oil-tight.' As Hawthorn Leslie had tried two vessels which had worked well, though had not yet attained their contract speed, their name should be added to the list. Vickers 30-knotters had also achieved a 'satisfactory' speed.

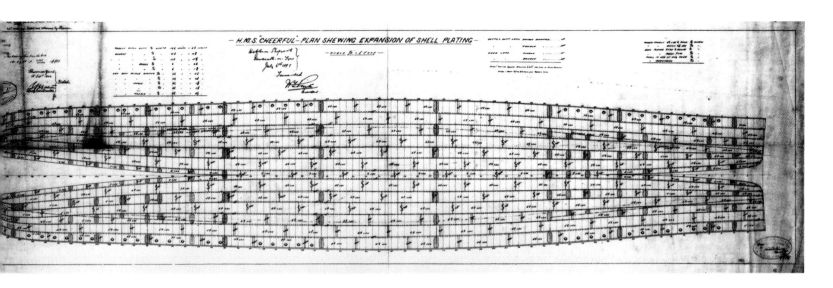

- H.M.S. CHEERFUL - PLAN SHEWING EXPANSION OF SHELL PLATING -

This is a 'shell expansion' plan, of Hawthorn Leslie's *Cheerful* showing how the external hull plating would look if it were ironed flat. This was useful in showing what shape to cut the plates, though the initial working out of this would normally be done on a block model of the hull. (National Maritime Museum, London: 105276)

The DNC's draft letter asked for delivery of one, two, three or four vessels within fifteen, sixteen, seventeen and eighteen months respectively. Arrangements should be made for burning oil only or oil and coal together. The approved letter was sent out to the various builders on 5 October asking for tenders to be in by 16 November. Rapid delivery was of importance. The engines were to be balanced. Yarrow's were tempted with an offer to share the latest information on 30-knotters, but the firm did not put in a tender.

Additional clauses were added on 1 November. The voice pipes from the engine room to the steering stations were to be omitted and mechanical revolution telegraphs were to be fitted. Particular attention would be given to prevent flaming at the funnels, a constant menace and give-away during night time torpedo attacks by TBs and TBDs – if it did appear it would need correction and if it happened in the official trial there would be a retrial.

The tenders from Hawthorn Leslie, Laird, Doxford, Palmer's, Fairfield and Vickers were all allegedly accepted on 30 March 1899, the penultimate day of the government's financial year. However, at least one note in the Cover suggests the date as April, so perhaps there was a small amount of administrative rigging to get the order in the old year rather than the new one, though in the end it appears that the ships were counted in the next year rather than this.

1899-1900 Programme

The twelve TBDs ordered under this programme, or rather all under a supplementary programme, were three from Palmer's (*Myrmidon*, *Syren*, plus their private speculation, *Peterel*); three from Hawthorn Leslie (*Greyhound*, *Racehorse*, *Roebuck*); one from Barrow (*Vixen*); one from Doxford (*Success*); two from Fairfield (*Ostrich*, *Falcon*); and two from Lairds (*Lively*, *Sprightly*).

The preliminary correspondence for these orders is cited above, under the previous programme.

1900-1901 Programme

Four 30-knotters were purchased whilst building under an additional programme, three from Clydebank (*Thorn*, *Tiger*, *Vigilant*) and one from Palmer's (*Kangaroo*). The fifth destroyer, also purchased whilst building this year, was the ill-fated and extremely short-lived *Cobra*

1901-1902 Programme

With this programme the true destroyer appeared for the first time as the Royal Navy altered its requirements to seaworthiness and sturdiness rather than unrealistically high trial speeds as prime requirements with the order for the first 'River' class. Theirs is another story for a later book, but the last of the TBDs still remained to be ordered.

1902-1903 Programme

More 'River' class were ordered this year, but though one of those ordered the previous year was to be powered by turbines (*Eden*), the losses of both *Viper* and *Cobra* had created an urgent need for getting a turbine-powered destroyer into service as soon as possible to gain more experience with this new and promising form of propulsion. Parsons and Hawthorn Leslie were already building a turbine-powered vessel to be called *Python* as a private venture on the general lines of a 30-knotter, with reciprocating triple-expansion engines coupled to the low-pressure turbine for more economical cruising. This was acquired for the Admiralty and became *Velox*.

1908-1909 Programme

Right at the end of this financial year, as the result of the loss of two destroyers, a pair of 'stock boats' which had been built by Palmer's, who were having difficulty in finding a buyer, were purchased as *Albacore* and *Bonetta*. Although differing in some respects from the 30-knotters, their design was still based on this type.

The 'Specials' – 32/33-Knotters, 1896–1897 Programme

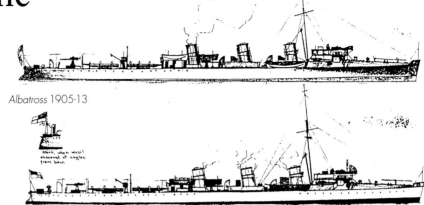

Albatross 1903

Albatross 1905-13

Ordered 21 April 1896 for delivery ?. (Note this is the order date for *Albatross*, known from the Thornycroft records. The other two would have been ordered on or near this date. *Arab* to cost £65,281.)

Thornycroft 32-knotter

	Yard No.	Laid down	Launched	Completed
Albatross	318	27.11.1896	19.7.1898	Jul 1900

DIMENSIONS: (design figures) 227ft oa/225ft wl × 21ft 3in × 14ft 3in + 8ft 4½in

DISPLACEMENT: 380 tons light, 485–490 tons full load, 430 tons navy list

CREW: 69–73

FUEL: 104–105 tons coal

MACHINERY: 2 shafts, 4 Thornycroft water tube boilers, 240 pounds per square inch working pressure, contract speed 32kts

TRIALS: 5.4.1900 (Measured Mile) 382.7 tons displacement/ 31.4kts/7645ihp/311.2rpm
July 1900 (3 hours) 31.5kts/773ihp/378.2rpm

WEIGHTS: (in tons) Hull 114.131, boilers 68.7, engines 101.96, fittings 33.084, woodwork 7.361, spare gear 10.841 = 336.011

FIRST COST: £68,311

Laird 33-knotter

	Yard No.	Laid down	Launched	Completed
Express	629	1.12.1896	11.12.1897	Dec 1902

DIMENSIONS: 239ft 6in (or 239ft 3in?) oa, 235ft wl × 23ft 6.7in ext, 23ft 6in mld × 14ft 8in

DISPLACEMENT: 465 tons light, 540 tons full load

MACHINERY: 4 Normand boilers, 240lbs, 9250ihp

COAL: 130 tons

FIRST COST: £71,797

Opposite below, Laird's modified 1896 design for their 33kt 'Special' *Express* showing that firm's characteristic arrangement with the engines sandwiched between two pairs of boilers, instead of the more conventional position abaft the boilers. This explains why the funnels seem to take up so much of the length of their TBDs. The propeller guards on either side of the stern are particularly conspicuous in the upper deck plan in this GA and sections plan. (National Maritime Museum, London: 62529)

Albatross early in her career (before 1904) in the Mediterranean colour scheme of white hull and yellow funnels. She spent most of her career on the Mediterranean station. (National Maritime Museum, London: G12601)

This profile, decks and sections plan of the *Albatross* is unusually lacking in detail for an 'as fitted' (*ie* as built) plan. The guns are not drawn in at all, and there is a low level of detail compared with most similar plans from this period, or, for that matter, of Admiralty plans from fifty years earlier or even fifty years later. (National Maritime Museum, London: 11474)

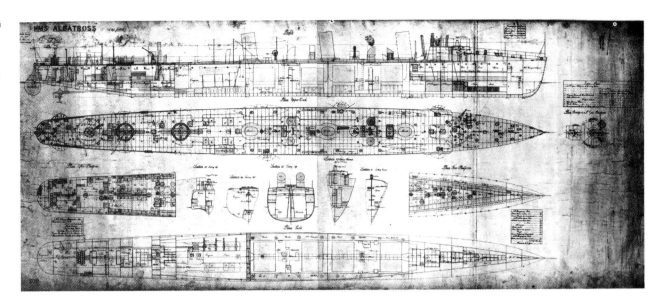

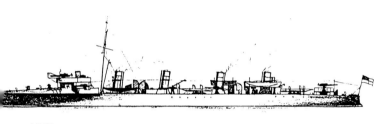

Express 1908

Express 1914

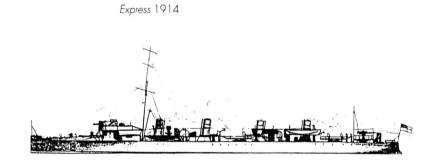

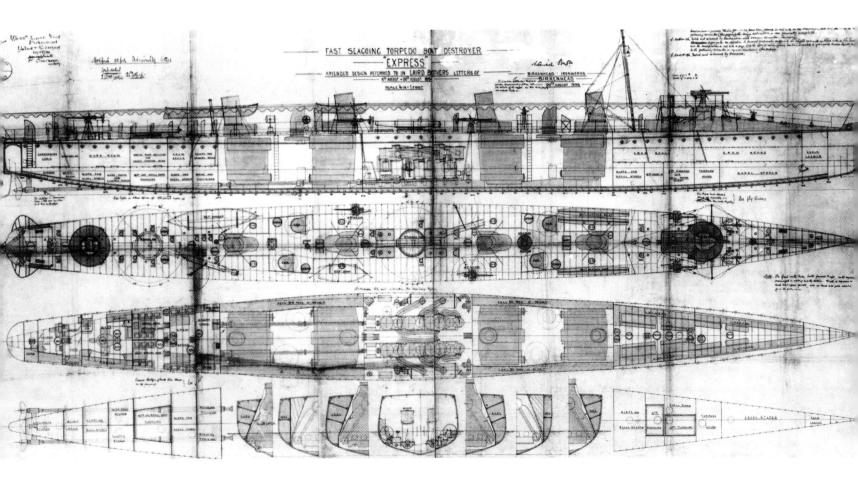

Thomson 32-knotter

	Yard No.	Laid down	Launched	Completed
Arab	299	5.3.1900	9.2.1901	January 1903

DIMENSIONS: 232ft oa, 227ft 6in bp × 22ft 3in mld × 9ft 9in
DISPLACEMENT: 470 tons light, 530 tons full load
MACHINERY: 4 Normand boilers, 240lbs, 8600ihp
COAL: 109 tons
FIRST COST: £67,849

Unfortunately, the original DNC documentation on the ordering of these vessels does not appear to have survived, but clearly the success of the earliest TBDs to complete led to an increased appetite for even greater trial speed and the most successful builders of the earlier TBDs were to be asked to provide vessels which would obtain that speed by enlarging the hulls and increasing the power of the engines of the earlier designs.

By the time came round for the ordering of the TBDs for the next year's programme it was becoming clear that the DNC, amongst others, was having second thoughts about building any more such craft, as recorded in the chapter on the 30-knotter orders for the 1897-1898 programme. In fact no more of these larger and more powerful TBDs were ordered. Instead there was a gradual growth of disillusion as first *Express* and then *Albatross* failed to make their designed speeds and instead spent much time on unsuccessful trial runs.

The *Albatross* was the nearest to success of the three 'Specials', but that was only a relative eminence. In 1902 S W Barnaby (her designer, as Thornycroft's Chief Naval Architect), giving evidence to the destroyer enquiry of that year, stated: 'She was entirely an experimental vessel from beginning to end.' She took two years and three months from the order to the launch and two years from then till acceptance. She went through seventeen sets of

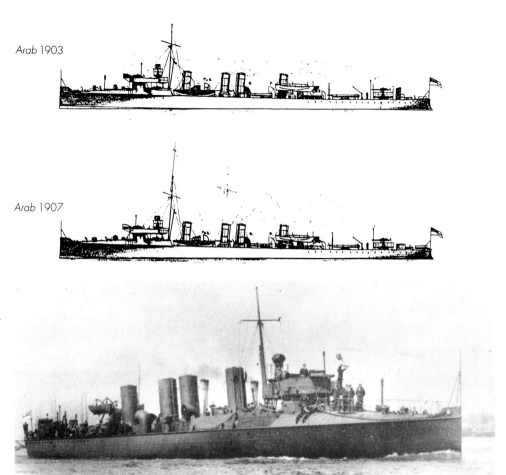

Arab 1903

Arab 1907

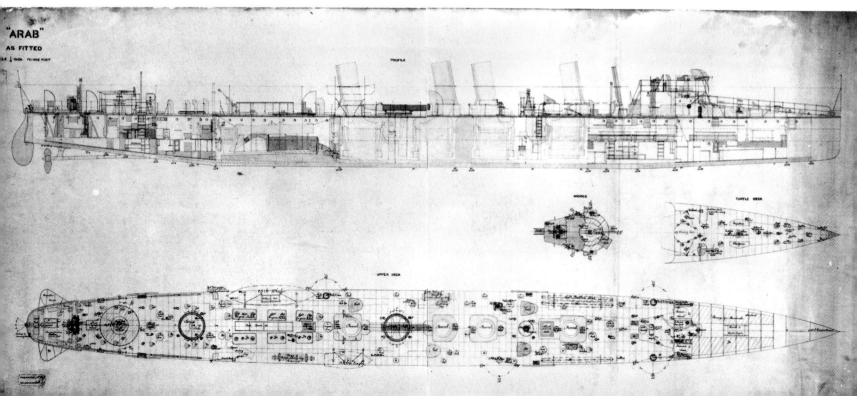

"ARAB"
AS FITTED

Below left, This is Thomson's 'Special' *Arab* pictured in 1904, passing a two-funnelled vessel (perhaps an excursion steamer, or a tug?) with a signaller sending a message by semaphore on the wing of the conning platform. The searchlight is already installed on its own platform immediately ahead of the mast. (National Maritime Museum, London: N2007)

Centre left, the four funnels widely spread out indicate that this is a Laird vessel, the lack of mast and armament that she is on trial, and the extra length that this is the *Express* attempting to reach her designed 33kts on one of the long series of unsuccessful trials she had to undergo in Liverpool Bay. The photo is dated 1900. (National Maritime Museum, London: N2042)

Bottom left, *Arab* as built. Four boilers are arranged so as to be stoked from two stokeholds, hence the uneven arrangement of the funnels. (National Maritime Museum, London: 39113)

trials in all. On one trial she reached 32.294kts with 400 rpm – which was a world record at the time. An Admiralty letter of 31 March offered to accept the vessel 'at a speed of 31½kts in lieu of 32kts, subject however to penalties provided in the contract for such diminution in speed', but on 10 July 1900 Thornycroft's wrote[14] to the Admiralty requesting that, considering the delays occasioned by the engineers' strike and the lengthy and costly trials period of an experimental vessel of a new type, the penalty should not be enforced. Writing to the Swedes about the design, in which they were interested,[15] Thornycroft's stated she carried 3½ tons of drinking water and a distiller. Coal consumption at full speed was 17,977lbs per hour. On her coal consumption trial she steamed for twelve hours at 14.33kts. One ton of coal gave 22.63 nautical miles, a radius of action of 2375 nautical miles. The Swedes were offered one such repeat for £69,500, and two for £68,400 each

On 17 July 1900 Deadman remarked[16] of *Express*'s builder that ' . . . for a period extending over eighteen months they have endeavoured to obtain the speed contracted and have gone to the great expense of fitting new shafts for the purpose of experimenting with two screws on each shaft. It appears hopeless therefore to expect better results than those already obtained, and it is considered that the interests of the Admiralty will be best served by avoiding further delay and taking the official trials at once, the vessel being accepted at the speed actually obtained (if 31kts or over) under the penalties for loss of speed specified in the contract.' He then summarised her builder's trials as shown in the table below.

Different propellers were tried on most trials. In none of these trials did she approach the over-optimistic 33kts which her builders had aimed at, despite the fact that the estimated HP (9250) for the contract speed had been exceeded. It was decided to allow Laird to offer the vessel at 31kts or such higher speed as she might attain – the

contractors hoped to attain 31½kts – subject to the penalties laid down in the contract. Furthermore, the effort to attain this extreme speed was wearing the machinery considerably, so it was decided to stop the trials immediately, but 'In consideration of the great efforts the Firm have made, the penalties in this case be reduced to those due if Messrs Laird had originally contracted for 32kts, the same as Messrs Thornycroft – viz:£500 for every ¼kt or fraction of ¼kt in falling off of speed between 32 and 31kts and £1000 for every ¼kt between 31 and 30kts.'

When, much later, *Arab* began her trials, attempting the less ambitious target of 32kts, she was equally unsuccessful:[17]

Date	Displacement	IHP	Knots	RPM	
11.3.1901	420t	?	26.432	315.5	– last 2 runs
14.3.1901	420t	7280	28.368	339.5	– last 2 runs
18.3.1901	420t	7561	29.514	355	– ditto
27.3.1901	427t	8300	29.316	378.5	– ditto
30.3.1901	429t	8115	30.025	367.7	– ditto
10.5.1901	430t	8370	29.907	359.1	– ditto
14.5.1901	430t	8500	30.072	360.5	– last 6 runs
20.5.1901	430t	8250	30.769	380	– best single run
27.5.1901	430t	8000	29.801	367.1	– last 2 runs

Arab was delivered[18] on 20 October 1902, still not having made her design speed, her estimated and actual costs being:[19] hull and fittings £21,125/£18,125 (£3,000 abated on account of vessel failing to reach contract speed), machinery £44,495/£44,531 gun mountings £833/£828, air compressing machinery £158/£158.

It was not long before the trio were regarded as slightly larger 30-knotters, lumped in with their contemporaries when it came to dividing them into B or C 'classes'. They represented a very poor return for the extra cost and effort lavished on them by Admiralty and builders alike. The answer to obtaining greater speed proved not to be enlarging the size and power of the 30-knotters, but by introducing a new type of engine, the turbine. The three vessels we have just been looking at were an attempt to push contemporary technology a little too far for success.

Albatross had three funnels, equally spaced and in Thornycroft's usual handsome flat sided style, which, combined with a rakish convex bow, made her a particularly handsome ship. The other two were both four-funnelled. *Express* had equally spaced funnels which were high when completed, unlike her 30kt contemporaries by Laird. *Arab*'s middle pair were closely grouped. The latter had a topmast fitted in 1905.

Albatross, having spent nearly all her peacetime service life in the Mediterranean, going out there in October 1902 and returning in 1914 and was sold for breaking up on 7 June 1920 to J W Houston. *Express* served in home waters and was sold for breaking up on 17 March 1920 to G Clarkson of Whitby. *Arab* also served entirely in home waters, being in the local defence flotilla at Scapa Flow early in the war, and was sold for breaking up on 23 July 1919 to Fryer of Sunderland.

Date	Displacement	RPM	Knots	IHP
8.12.1898	394	349	30.97	9363
15.12.1898	394	369.6	31.45	9673
20.12.1898	400	374.3	31.02	9728 – cylinder cover gives out
31.1.1899	395	376	31.11	9542
9.2.1899	379	370	30.95	9480
18.2.1899	397	390	30.94	9917
11.4.1899	401	372.3	29.33	9741
18.4.1899	403	370	31.08	10012
19.5.1899	399	375.5	31.143	9381 – exhaust pipe broke
1.7.1899	399	373	30.29	9314
5.7.1899	401	390	30.28	9679 – trial abandoned – bad results
11.7.1899	403	376.3	31.74	9501
15.7.1899	379	378.2	32.04	9511
11.5.1900	402	355.8	30.38	9266 – double screws
17.5.1900	406	358.6	30.46	9094 – double screws
24.5.1900	402	367.7	31.24	8933
30.5.1900	500	358.4	29.7	9489

The Turbine TBDs

Experience with the 30-knotters and particularly the 'Specials' had shown that the reciprocating engines then in use were unsuited to sustained high speed. The problem of severe vibration had been only partially overcome by balancing the machinery, whilst the failure of any of the 'Specials' to approach, let alone reach, their intended speed emphasised that these engines were being pushed further than was technically desirable or possible. Fortunately the work of Charles Parsons on rotary engines was already coming to fruition. This was spectacularly demonstrated in the famous incident at the Diamond Anniversary Review of the fleet at Spithead when Parsons' yacht *Turbinia* easily outdistanced all the high-speed naval craft. As a result an experimental turbine-powered TBD was ordered.

There were to be continuing problems with the high rotational speed of the turbine shafts, the poor fuel economy and with the impossibility of reversing a turbine. The first caused much trouble with propeller design, cavitation and so on. The second and third meant experiments with various combinations and permutations of machinery to permit better cruising performance and some sort of performance going astern. Also, the higher speed which it was possible not only to reach but also to sustain with turbines brought new problems: namely, the impossibility of meeting its demands with the number of stokers that could be carried.

These problems were not ones that would be solved immediately, the more so because both of the first turbine boats ordered were lost almost before their careers had begun.

Viper, 1898-1899 Programme

ORDERED: 4 March 1898 from Parsons (hull building Hawthorn Leslie) for delivery in 15 months.

	Yard No.	Laid down	Launched	Completed
Viper	366	1898	6.9.1899	1900

DIMENSIONS: 210ft bp × 21ft ext × 12ft 6in
DISPLACEMENT: 344 tons light
MACHINERY: 4-shaft Parsons turbines

On 4 March 1898 the Admiralty wrote[20] to Parsons accepting their amended tender of 12 January 1898 for £53,000 (hull £19,800, propelling machinery £32,000, auxiliary machinery £1200 – delivery fifteen months). Guaranteed speed was to be 31kts, but at its own risk and expense the company undertook to seek the highest speed of which the vessel was capable, which they anticipated would be at least 34kts. The astern motors, on the two inside shafts as designed, were if possible to be transferred to outer shafts, in order to obtain greater manoeuvring powers. All detail modifications required by the Admi-

Viper

ralty were to be carried out without extra charge. Displacement with a 40-ton load would be 344 tons. When inclined at 306 tons displacement her metacentric height was 2.74ft. It is not altogether clear from the documents in the Cover whether the *Viper* had already been begun as a private venture, as some accounts suggest, or whether, as seems more likely from this document, this TBD was building for the Admiralty from the start.

The contract required *Viper* to make 15½kts astern[21] – but did not specify the length of time. By December 1900 she had not done this in a straight line astern, but had made sufficient revolutions astern for the speed whilst going round in circles on contractor's trials. Deadman and White jointly agreed to accept the vessel without further delay to obtain service experience as quickly as possible. The steering engine was to be strengthened and Parsons were to continue working on better steering astern. By this stage she had established herself as the fastest vessel in the world by making 33.57kts on the Measured Mile and 33.838kts on the three-hour run during her full speed trials on 31 August 1900.

Unfortunately, she then ran aground at speed on rocks near Alderney whilst on exercises designed to test her machinery in service conditions. Not everyone saw this as an absolute tragedy, as this extract from a letter[22] to the

Viper in the Solent, taken in 1900 or 1901 between her commissioning and her loss. A forecastle party is either preparing to anchor or moor. (National Maritime Museum, London: N2148)

First Naval Lord from Commander Douglas Nicholson dated 7 August 1901 shows: 'The *Viper* I do not regard as a great loss *qua* Destroyer, her speed is a fraud, her top speed under normal conditions never touched more than 28kts and her coal expenditure was so excessive as to be positively ridiculous. A fair example of her achievements in the coal-eating line may be given by telling you that she was sent from here, Portland, to the Lizard, to take a slight sweep towards the French coast and to average 22kts and return here with news. She started with about 90 or more tons of coal and she returned here with 5 tons left in her bunkers. She averaged 6 tons of coal an hour! The *Spiteful* could have done the same thing at almost the same speed with an average 2 tons an hour.'

He went on to describe the turbine as 'a very pretty toy', but until its economy was improved, the latest Palmer vessels were better destroyers.

This was passed to the DNC and Engineer in Chief for any remarks by W H May (the Controller). Durston (the Engineer in Chief) noted that *Viper* carried thirty-two stokers, when it was estimated that 29kts was her maximum speed; compared to the 28kts maximum speed of *Albatross* & 27kts maximum speed of any so-called 30-knotter. '*Viper* does not seem to compare unfavourably with these.' Consumption per HP increased more rapidly as speed dropped in a turbine boat. The estimate of *Spiteful*'s performance, however, was much too low.

Rather fairer was Lieutenant W Speke, her Commanding Officer, who thought she compared favourably with other ships of her type, with little or no vibration except at very high speeds and even then comparatively little. When making a passage her steering was good, and a given speed could be maintained with accuracy. When picking up a berth or manoeuvring in a confined space the inner screws only being used for going astern made her difficult to turn in a confined space. But considerable advantage was gained by the steady motion by which the ship gathered way either going ahead or astern; also the reversing gear was quick and reliable consisting only of opening one valve and closing another about ¾ turn for full speed.

In manoeuvring with the flotilla a good deal of difficulty was at first experienced in keeping station owing to the comparative slowness in gathering and losing way, and the difficulty in quickly increasing speed which is explained by the large consumption of coal, entailing harder work on the stokers of whom an additional twenty were applied for but permanent accommodation was only possible for five.

This made it impossible to maintain a position for blockading Alderney for more than twenty-four hours, allowing sufficient margin of coal to leave and return to Portland at 20kts.

During the preliminary trials carried out at Portsmouth, stokers in two watches maintained 26kts; working all the stokers gave 31.5kts for a short period, and for half an hour an average of 30.5kts.

This and other reports on the general working of machinery and behaviour of vessel prior to the accident satisfied Durston.[23]

'With turbines of only about sufficient capacity to give the power required Messrs Parsons anticipate slightly greater economy in future designs . . . So far as can be seen from these reports the main turbine machinery appears on the whole to have given satisfactory results, except as regards coal consumption and this especially at low powers. The principal points affecting future designs of machinery are: (1) speed which should be provided for going astern. (2) Whether astern turbines should be fitted on the inner or outer shafts. (3) Whether in order to reduce coal consumption at low powers it is desirable to fit reciprocating engines, and if so what speed they should be capable of maintaining.'

Whilst *Viper* was completing it was decided to acquire another turbine-powered vessel building as a private venture by Armstrong's. This vessel was lost for reasons which are still uncertain, whilst on her delivery voyage so had an even shorter life than the other turbine-powered prototype. This reinforced a naval superstition about giving ships 'snake' names and caused the doubts about the structural strength of these TBDs to come to a head in a major enquiry.

Cobra

ORDERED: (purchased) 8 May 1900 for delivery ? for £63,500.

	Yard No.	Laid down	Launched	Completed
Cobra	674	?	28.6.1899	1901

DIMENSIONS: 223ft 6in oa, 213ft 7½in bp × 20ft 6in mld × 13ft 6in mld + 7ft

DISPLACEMENT: 375 tons light

MACHINERY: 4-shaft Parsons turbines

On 8 May 1900 the Admiralty wrote[24] to Armstrong accepting their offer of the previous 12 December of a 'Turbine-motor TBD' for £63,500 provided that: (a) a speed of not less than 34kts was to be guaranteed; (b) guaranteed maximum coal consumption per hour at full speed with a 40-ton load aboard was to be stated; (c) 'The fore and aft girder plates at middle line under boilers to be straightened and properly stiffened . . . The vibrations in the vessel at any speed must be small and insufficient to render any part of the vessel uninhabitable or preclude accurate practice with the guns.'

An ominous note had already been sounded by a constructor's report on the inspection of this turbine

Cobra

destroyer[25] building 'on spec' at Armstrong's Elswick yard on the Tyne; which pointed out that the stern of the vessel had settled somewhat – not surprising since the ship had no girders under the deck abaft the galley, or longitudinal strengthening of any sort. It is quite evident that the Admiralty was perfectly well aware that they were buying a vessel which was not as strongly built as the TBDs built under contract for it, even though she was somewhat larger than a 30-knotter.

The main overseer's report[26] stated that the Elswick vessel was inferior to *Viper* in the following important particulars: she was a much larger and heavier vessel for the same work; her speed was likely to be about 1½kts less than *Viper*; hull construction, based on that of the 27-knotters *Swordfish* and *Spitfire*, was much inferior to present practice, for instance in the absence of special steel in the construction of important parts of the vessel, inadequate longitudinal strength and stiffening of bow and stern, the shaft brackets and rudder frame were of cast steel instead of forged steel and were of weaker design than in *Viper*, the galvanising of the hull was done by the cold process which had been found unsatisfactory, woodwork was not rendered non-flammable, and the derrick and rigging was too weak for lifting Berthon boats. The torpedo tubes were not of service pattern and several alterations would be required, including a separate compartment for torpedo head stowage.

She was, however, regarded as superior to *Viper* in the following particulars: the crew spaces were more roomy than in *Viper*, but in the second space this was neutralised by fitting dynamo and pump for Tower's platform; the engine room had more head-room; lit throughout by electricity (navy practice was to light only machinery spaces); a larger bridge, fitted with a 24in projector [search light] (not service pattern) on Tower's steady platform (navy practice was to fit a 20in projector on deck). 'It is not considered that this vessel will be so satisfactory as those vessels which have been entirely designed and built under Admiralty Inspection but if it is considered desirable that the vessel should be acquired by the Admiralty to prevent her becoming the property of a Foreign Power no objection is seen to her purchase so far as Hull is concerned . . . '

At first it was proposed to man this vessel like the 30-knotters,[27] but this would soon be revised once the immense appetite of the early turbines became apparent. On 8 March 1901, basing his assessment on the coal consumption trials[28] A J Durston proposed fifty-nine engine room staff, forty-eight of whom would be stokers. He assumed that each fireman would handle about 18cwts of coal and each trimmer 30cwts per hour. (Firemen were the stokers actually feeding the boilers, trimmers the stokers who dug out the coal from the bunkers and took it to the firemen.) Even in two watches, it was arduous work and the full speed could not well be maintained for more than three or four hours starting with the fires in clean condition. Deadman noted that this was twenty-one men more than for a 30-knotter giving a total complement of

eighty-four and he couldn't find room for more than seventy.

In the circumstances the reaction of Prince Louis of Battenberg is understandable – 'As the case now stands Their Lordships possess a Destroyer of unprecedented speed which, however, she apparently will never be able to realise as the necessary personnel cannot be accommodated. Under these circumstances it is thought that a special effort might be made by the DNC to meet the difficulty and provide some additional accommodation. The increase in weight cannot be considered a serious drawback when the first hour's steaming will lighten the vessel by over 13 tons. It is not possible to reduce any of the deckhands.'

The DNC's department replied that accommodation for up to seventy-seven could be provided, but with messing, sleeping and locker areas of some of the men scattered. After delivery to a dockyard it might be possible to work out more. The *Cobra* was never to reach a dockyard, but in the long run the answer would prove to be the use of liquid fuel. There were many good reasons for burning oil rather than coal, but certainly turbine-powered vessels would not have been able to obtain their full potential for sustained high speed cruising without the labour-saving potential of the liquid fuel.

When *Cobra* sank on her delivery voyage the following notes were sent to Deadman on 27 October 1901[30] at Pier Hotel, Southsea: displacement of *Cobra* was 490 tons with bunkers full of 106 tons of coal. The calculated maximum stress with *Havock* at 234 tons displacement was 6.2 tons with the vessel in a wave trough and therefore 7.3 tons maximum if the stress varied in parallel with the displacement. With *Desperate* at 305 tons displacement the stress was 7.62 tons or 8.9 tons at 356 tons displacement. With *Cobra* taking same case but allowing for the manhole cut in the vertical plate to the boiler bearers at the side the maximum stress became 10 tons.

It is clear from the above that *Cobra* had been built with less reserves of strength than any other such vessel built for the Royal Navy. In the circumstances it is not entirely surprising that she split in two on her delivery voyage. This may have been due to just the stresses set up by the action of the waves, though this seems unlikely to have proved enough to break the ship in two. The most recent technical survey of this subject[31] tends towards the opinion that there might be some substance in the survivors' reports of feeling an impact on the vessel's bottom just before she split in two. The shock of striking, say, a substantial item of floating debris such as a spar from a wreck whilst the hull was under sufficient tension from sagging in the trough of a wave could, possibly, cause enough stress for the hull structure to fracture under the strain. Nobody saw such floating wreckage around the area the ship was lost, but it still seems to be the most attractive alternative.

The ensuing panic about the strength of TBDs resulted in a major enquiry which in the end, after extensive investigations utilising the *Wolf* for strength trials, basically gave the type a clean bill of health. Subsequent experience, especially four years of war service, justified this confidence in the strength of the type.

Meanwhile, however, there remained the problem that both of the prototype turbine TBDs had been lost, and the sooner experience was gained with this new form of propulsion, the better. Fortunately Parsons, in conjunction with Hawthorn Leslie, were already building a private venture vessel which the Admiralty to order. She would not prove to be an ideal vessel for the Royal Navy but she was available when needed.

Velox

Ordered (from Parsons, hull being sub-contracted from Hawthorn Leslie): July 1902 to be delivered as soon as possible:

	Yard No.	Laid down	Launched	Completed
Velox	383	10.4.1901	11.2.1902	Feb 1904

DIMENSIONS: 215ft oa, 210ft bp × 21ft ext/21ft mld × 13ft + 9ft
DISPLACEMENT: 445 tons
COAL: 86 tons

On 5 July 1901 Parsons wrote to the Admiralty[32] offering a new machinery layout for a destroyer similar to that for *Viper* but with the heating surface of boilers reduced to 13,000 sq ft and small reciprocating engines added for cruising. The trial displacement was about 350 tons and the firm was prepared to guarantee 32kts and anticipated 33kts, but the vessel could be driven at a higher speed if required; 10cwts per hour at 13kts was guaranteed as the coal consumption. Parsons were also

preparing an alternative design with the same hull but 10,000 sq ft of heating area, smaller turbines, and less displacement, speed and coal consumption for a guarantee speed of 30kts.

Eleven days later they wrote offering the latter design with about 300 tons displacement with 35 tons load. They anticipated 32kts and a coal consumption of 8cwts per hour at 13kts. It was to have about 100 tons bunker capacity and be powered by one High Pressure and two Low Pressure turbines with reversing turbines combined with the latter on the outer shafts

Durston noted that it was evident that the boilers would have to be forced to a greater extent than could be agreed to. Coal consumption in destroyers should not exceed 1.2lbs per sq ft of heating space per hour and Parsons should be informed of this. A four-hour trial was to be adopted. Coal consumption to be guaranteed for twenty-four hours at both 13 and 18kts: ' . . . It appears questionable whether the advantages of reciprocating engines are sufficient to justify the additional complication of weight and space involved.' The proviso was introduced that trials were to be run at full load draft.

W H May, the Controller, wanted to test the turbine thoroughly before widespread adoption so in October 1901 proposed buying the Parsons destroyer, fitting two of the current year's order for destroyers with turbines, and also fitting one of the Third Class cruisers and a torpedo boat; this was agreed by Spencer, the First Lord.

The investigation of the fresh designs went on for some time. On 25 October the builders replied[33] to questions raised in the Admiralty letter of 26 August on their earlier four-shaft design. The speed they would be prepared to guarantee on a four-hour trial with displacement at about

Velox 'as fitted'. Note the small reciprocating engine shown at the forward end of the engine room, just abaft the aftermost boiler. (National Maritime Museum, London: 57821)

Velox

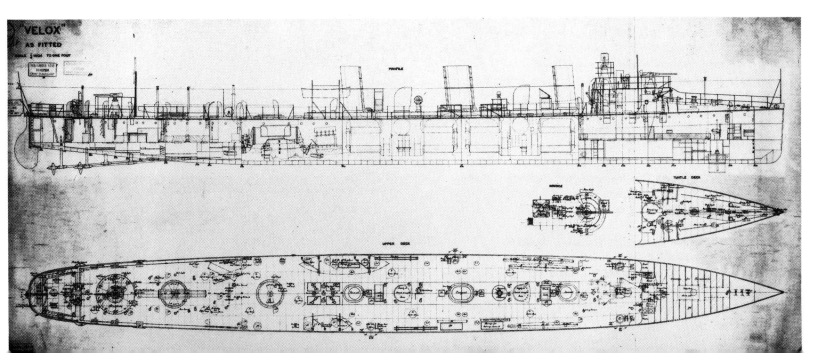

440 tons was 28kts. For a speed of 13kts they estimated an ihp about 650 and coal consumption of 13 tons for twenty-four hours. At a speed of 18kts they estimated 1650ihp and 54 tons in twenty-four hours; this would be without the reciprocating engines working. For 28kts coal consumption they hoped for 2.25lbs per ihp. The proposed additional pair of reciprocating engines would be of 230ihp each with cylinders 9in/13½in/20in × 9in stroke. These engines would be kept working up to about 500rpm with a corresponding speed of about 15kts. The astern speed guaranteed was 11kts without a bow rudder (it would be greater if one were fitted). The alternative three shaft design would be guaranteed at 27kts and with coal consumption figures which would be slightly more favourable.

The DNC's department noted[34] that the machinery of Parsons four shaft design (A), if placed in present 30-knotters would give a speed of 28kts with vessel fully equipped and bunkers full; which would be an advance in speed of one knot in practice over the 30-knotters. The three shaft arrangement (design B) would be equivalent as regards power to the 30-knotters and provided for a maximum speed of 27kts. 'If the two turbine destroyers to be ordered this financial year are to be on the lines of the new design with long forecastle [ie like the 'Rivers'], increased accommodation and of more substantial build the displacement will be increased much beyond the 440 tons which Parsons have assumed and the anticipated speeds will be modified. Bow rudders had never proved satisfactory but they were prepared to let Parsons try in the pursuit of a higher speed astern with full steering control.

The Engineer-in-Chief added on 5 November that *Greyhound* and *Roebuck*, fitted with similar boilers to those proposed, had on twelve-hour trials made 503ihp with consumption of 1.83lbs of coal per ihp per hour and 0.41 tons of coal per hour at 13kts. The fitting of reciprocating engines would probably lower coal consumption by at least 50 per cent compared with *Cobra* and *Viper*. The estimated coal consumption per ihp at 18kts should be about 30 per cent more than with *Syren*, the only TBD to run consumption trials at this speed. This would be with turbines only and would appear to represent added economy over *Viper* and *Cobra*'s experience. About half the total power would be available for manoeuvring. The reciprocating engines were not fitted with reversing gear and were understood to be enclosed and fitted with automatic lubrication therefore capable of greater speed than ordinary open engines (not in fact fitted); but it was doubtful whether their highest speed could be maintained.

Parsons proposed a modified design on 11 November 1901 with two small High Pressure and Intermediate Pressure turbines which would be permanently coupled to the main Low Pressure shafts. At speeds up to 15/16kts the steam would pass through the two turbines in series and then to main turbines. At higher speeds additional boiler steam would be turned into the main turbines or into the intermediate cruising turbines.

Later the same month Durston[35] commented that this removed the objection to the high number of revolutions entailed by using turbines and therefore avoided disconnecting the cruising machinery at high speeds as was necessary in previous combination designs. The arrangement of this new design was with three shafts (as for B) but with the heating surface and full speed as in A. This would mean a slight increase in estimated coal consumption at 13kts which would be accentuated at lower speeds, but a considerable reduction at 18kts. The speed with Low Pressure turbines only would be about 24½kts and 11kts astern. Some alterations were needed to the design but Durston was basically in favour of it.

Meanwhile, the investigation of the TBD Parsons and Hawthorn Leslie were building as a speculation, and which was to become the *Velox*, continued. In reply to an Admiralty enquiry of 6 November 1901, Parsons sent details the following day, stating that the boat should be ready for trials during next spring. The boilers were of the improved Yarrow type and of similar construction to those fitted in HMS *Viper*, with a total heating surface of 13,000 sq ft. It would probably be six to eight weeks before the launch could take place, provided no alterations were made in the scantlings, which were those of the Japanese Navy – about 5 to 10 per cent in excess of those of *Viper*. It is not clear whether this means that the vessel was being built with the intention that the Japanese Navy would buy her, or merely that these scantlings were adopted as a convenient standard.

The engines were duplicates of the *Viper*'s except that the Low Pressure turbines and the astern turbines had been incorporated in an arrangement like that found successful in the *King Edward*, the Clyde excursion steamer which was the first merchant ship built with turbines. The space saved by this alteration was used for two reciprocating engines of 150ihp each, in line with and coupled to the extension of the Low Pressure turbine shafts; these engines to be used for cruising purposes at around 12kts and below. The condensers and water circulating

Velox in 1911, with the extended bridge incorporating the searchlight and the wireless fitted by this date. The sided 6pdr emplacements are completely covered by a combination of weather cloths and awnings. (National Maritime Museum, London: N8792)

arrangements were much improved with a view to securing superior economy in fuel. Four feed-water heaters were being fitted and also turbine instead of the usual heavier fan engines. A small bow rudder was fitted, to be worked with hand gear, and only to be used in the case of going astern; when going ahead it was retracted out of harm's way.

Although of 20 to 25 tons less displacement than the *Viper*, chiefly owing to the smaller boilers, steam pipes, etc, the company expected their vessel to at least match the *Viper* for speed at the same loading, while at cruising speeds around 12kts, fuel consumption should be about half that of the *Viper* and probably less than the 30-knotters. She would be considerably stronger than *Viper*, without any alteration, but the company planned some strengthening of the deck and longitudinal beams and stringers, albeit causing some delay and increased cost.

The company preferred to guarantee low figures of 12kts astern and 32kts ahead, carrying a load of 40 tons, but anticipated in reality 14 to 16kts and 33¾kts, and with hard driving a knot or two more. They believed that the vessel was worth £70,000.

Assistant Constructor Ball and Mr Winsom, an RN Engineer Inspector were then directed[36] to survey, respectively, the hull and machinery of this stock vessel. Wisnom reported that the machinery could be accepted with slight modifications; though the combination of turbine and reciprocating machinery was not as satisfactory as the all-turbine design that Parsons were proposing for the new destroyer. The boilers, built by Hawthorn Leslie as slightly modified versions of those fitted to *Greyhound*, were of 13,200 sq ft heating area as opposed to 15,044 in *Viper*. More powerful reciprocating engines with larger working parts and bearing surfaces would have been preferable, as would enclosed ones rather than open engines with forced lubrication.

On 13 February 1902 Deadman submitted the hull report. One strake of the bottom plating and also the coamings were thickened. This meant that, compared to *Viper*, there was a considerable increase of strength, especially as the displacement was less; and there was no indication of weakness in *Viper* in the first place. The price was high at £70,000 plus £3000 for alterations against £53,000 for the somewhat more powerful *Viper*; or £60,000 for one of the last 30-knotters; but it was suggested that the firm be asked to carry out all alterations for their asking figure.

The vessel was launched on 11 February 1902, and ten days later Parsons were continuing[37] what was to be a very long-drawn out haggle over terms. They were by this time prepared to guarantee 27kts at full displacement and with coal consumption not exceeding 1.2lbs per sq ft per hour. This was because the Admiralty had decided to carry out trials with the vessel fully equipped and bunkers practically full. This made for a load of about 120 tons instead of the 35 usually carried on 30-knotter trials – which was why the contract speed had been fixed at 27 not 30kts. By 17 March[38] Palmer's were prepared to reduce their price to £67,000 in return for rapid acceptance

(and hence payment). They were offering rapid delivery, but the experienced Deadman was sceptical about the proposed date.[39]

Two days later the Controller was prepared to accept £67,000 provided Parsons made the necessary alterations and additions without any further charge, but the DNC wanted to wait until full information was available about the boat's structural strength and stability. Parsons acknowledged[40] the order of 7 April, but pointed out their reduced price of £67,000 did not take into account the extra modifications they had to make. They also had not taken into account the Admiralty's demand for twenty-four hour trials at 13 and 18kts whilst tendering and proposed these be at the Admiralty's expense. On 13 September 1902 Watts suggested adding £275 of extras above the £67,000 agreed including £45 for lengthening the 12pdr platform to take the searchlight. Bilge keels were not to be fitted. In addition the Admiralty would pay for the 13 and 18kt twenty-four hour trials, which seems fair enough as these were a new departure.

Over a month later (23 October 1902) Deadman with a, surely excusable, air of satisfaction was quoting the original Parsons declaration that the 'ship would be ready for trials in May or June last. The office estimate was that the vessel would commission in December next. The firm now ask six months after the delivery of armament and stores, although the work on the ship has proceeded in the ordinary way during negotiations . . .' He wanted them told in no uncertain fashion that this was unacceptable.

The moment of truth for Parsons' estimates on coal consumption came when, on 8 January 1903, *Velox* ran her official four-hour trial,[41] an hour doing Measured Mile runs at 27.249kts then three hours at a mean of 27.142kts. At the end of this trial there was hardly anything left of the 40 tons of coal which had been put aboard, representing an average consumption of nearly 10 tons per hour. Parsons was described, understandably, as being 'very concerned'. Another full speed trial was run on the 24th[42] at a mean speed of 27.076kts with a rate of 9.825 tons of coal per hour burnt. As the contract figure was 7.07 tons per hour this was very worrying. New propellers were to be tried to get greater economy. Matters did not improve on the twenty-four hour 13kt trial[43] where the firm anticipated burning 13 tons whilst the actual consumption was 19¼ tons. Allowing for their difference in displacement this represented about 80 per cent greater consumption than the 30-knotters. On the other twenty-four hour consumption trial she burnt 15.96 cwts of coal per hour at 13kts – about 48 per cent more than the firm's estimate. In fact these consumption trials represented much the same results as *Viper* and *Cobra* – in other words no gain at all from the reciprocating engines or any other 'improvements'. However, the bow rudder seems to have worked – after turning trials the captain remarked[44] that it 'is of assistance in turning in a narrow channel – though great disadvantage is it is not possible to personally observe if it is put over correctly'.

By late 1907 the clearly useless reciprocating engines were being replaced by cruising turbines.[45] Despite this alteration *Velox* does not seem to have been much of a success in service. The final blow to her serving in an active flotilla came in May 1909[46] when there was a report of her unsatisfactory behaviour on passage Campbeltown-Portsmouth. Off Lands End she experienced a port engine breakdown and then began running out of feed water for the boilers thanks to rolling which prevented the badly-situated feed water inlets keeping a steady flow of water to the condensers. She was in danger of being totally immobilised just off a particularly nasty lee shore. The senior officer present pointed out that her margin of safety was low, and that the conditions that suited her, 'fine weather and an open sea are conditions which are not invariably obtained in the ordinary course of destroyer work'.

Tyrwhitt, then a Captain, reported that 'I have always considered *Velox* to be a most unsatisfactory destroyer when worked in combination with a Flotilla for the following reasons: – (1) Excessive coal consumption. (2) Inability to go astern at more than 5kts speed (at any time) and also not being able to go astern at any time without previously warning the Engine Room. (3) General unhandiness, chiefly due to (2). (4) Unseaworthiness, due to the condensers being fitted above the water line. I would therefore submit that the *Velox* is a great source of anxiety to the officer in command and also to the commander of the division to which she is attached and I would suggest that she may be permanently turned over to the *Vernon* as an Instructional vessel in Torpedo and Wireless telegraphy which duties would not necessitate her going to sea in anything approaching bad weather.' This was approved.

Further comments on the ship were that only the two central shafts were used for manoeuvring. The excessive coal consumption was at least partly caused by the turbo motor fans in the boiler room. These were a constant source of trouble and it had been decided recently to remove them and replace by the ordinary type. The liability to overheating of the condensers had always been a defect. The circulating arrangements had been much improved but it was impossible to place the pumps below the waterline with the arrangement of condensers and turbines, so there was always a danger of the pumps failing with much rolling

The Director of Naval Intelligence suggested she should be put in the same category as *Lynx* and *Daring* at Devonport, both of which were prototype 26-knotters, and which were no longer considered fit to go to sea with a destroyer flotilla. *Velox* in fact lasted till the end of the First World War in active service, but it was to be later turbine-powered destroyers which proved that system of propulsion in naval service.

The two 12pdrs mounted side by side on a more substantial bridge show that this is a picture of the two modified versions of the 30-knotters purchased from Palmer's, in this instance *Bonetta*, taken in 1910. (National Maritime Museum, London: N2028)

The Last 30-Knotters

Several years after the last 30-knotters had entered service in the Royal Navy, two modified and updated versions of the design were purchased to fill the gaps left by the loss of the *Tiger* and of a 'River' class destroyer, the *Gala*. These two had been building as speculations by Palmer's, were virtually complete, and were purchased under the 1908-1909 programme. They were turbine-powered, but coal-fired, and their armament was different from their predecessors'.

Ordered: 8 May 1908, finally purchased 3 May 1909.

	Yard No.	Laid down	Launched	Completed
Albacore	786	1.9.1905	9.10.1906	Mar 1909
Bonetta	787	1.9.1905	14.1.1907	Mar 1909

DIMENSIONS: 215ft 3in bp × 21ft ¼in ext, 20ft 11¾in mld × 12ft 7in.
DISPLACEMENT: 440 tons
MACHINERY: Parsons turbines, 4 Reed boilers, built by Palmer's, 250lbs
COMPLEMENT: 56 (35 nucleus crew)

Sir Charles M'Laren MP, the Chairman of Palmer's, offered the First Lord these two 'stock boats' for £70,000-£80,000 each on 5 December 1907 then later stated that they would not press for immediate payment. On 23 January this was modified to the statement that they 'would be prepared to accept such price as the Admiralty might be pleased to fix'. In their initial offer the firm made it clear that they had worked in 45 tons of material to strengthen the vessels. They claimed that the design was an improvement over the old 30-knotters: '(1). The fore end is about 2ft to 3ft higher than in the older vessels, as the top of the turtle back is carried out horizontal instead of being sloped down at the fore end. The forward upper part of the vessel has also a much greater flare out than is usual. Owing to these alterations the boats have proved to be exceptionally dry in a seaway. The turtle back being longer, the gun and navigating positions are thus further aft, which is a considerable advantage in rough weather. At the after end of the turtle back, instead of a narrow conning tower with a flying platform on top, and low berthing plates at the sides, there is a large, completely closed-in bridge-house the full width of the vessel. The fore end of this is pointed and forms a very efficient breakwater. The bridge deck is ample in area for two 12pdr guns with large arcs of training and the navigating position and the searchlight, the latter being raised sufficiently to show clear over the guns. Below in the bridge there is a large chart house well lighted at the front and the sides, galley, petty officer's accommodation, and water closets. The entrance to the crew spaces on the lower deck are also covered and protected by the bridge deck.

(2) The structural strength of the vessels is much greater than that of the 30kt class, the following being some of the principal additions. The centre keelson is of greater scantling and there is a side keelson extending for nearly half of the vessel's length on each side, which was not in the older vessels. The sheer strake and upper deck stringer are 10 per cent thicker. The deck is framed on the Palmer-Long patent longitudinal system, which very greatly increases the strength of the upper part of the vessel against both tensile and compressive strains . . .

(3) The after end of the vessel differs from the older type in having an overhanging stern which allows the rudder and steering gear to be practically submerged. The vessels have been found to steer very much better when going astern with this form of stern; and the turning circle going ahead is somewhat reduced . . .

(4) . . . Accommodation for the officers equal to that in the 'River' class, there being separate cabins and a large ward-room . . .'

Immediate Admiralty comments[47] were that the load was about 50 tons greater than 30-knotters. As a result the freeboard was about 5ft as opposed to 7ft on all recent boats and 5ft 9in on earlier ones: 'The longitudinal system of deck construction adopted in these vessels has not been accepted in recent designs submitted by Messrs Palmer, and is not as effective as the usual Admiralty system of framing . . . the boilers fitted in these vessels do not meet Admiralty requirements; apart from the fact that they are of the Reed type (boilers of the Yarrow or White Forster type only being fitted in recent destroyers) – the tubes have reduced ends where they enter the water chambers. This form of tube has not been allowed in boilers for HM service since 1900 . . . The boilers are inferior in design to those now being fitted in destroyers, and it is considered their life would be much shorter than in the more recent

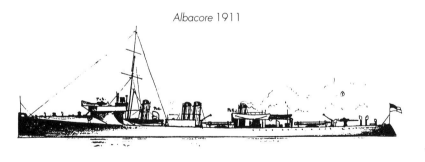

Albacore 1911

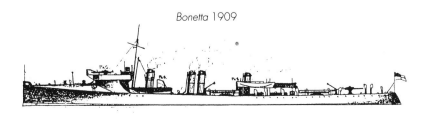

Bonetta 1909

types [eg Yarrow and Thornycroft]. The fire grates are longer than allowed in the later coal burning destroyers and this, coupled with the short stoking space, will reduce the steaming efficiency when required to steam for long periods. The vessels could not be adapted for carrying oil fuel. From the firm's particulars of trial results it is seen that the boilers were very much forced. Also that a light load only was carried.'

On 15 February it was noted that it was not proposed to order: 'The vessels are in this country and in case of emergency could no doubt be purchased.' Seven days later a letter from the Admiralty informed Palmer's that: 'we did not see our way to purchase the vessels at present or in the near future.'[48]

However, both *Tiger* and *Gala* were lost in April and needed to be replaced. So, on 5 May the Board decided to

purchase these boats on condition that the firm ran the trials at its own risk and cost: 'on the distinct understanding that should the vessels not prove satisfactory to the Admiralty [there would be] no obligation on the part of the Admiralty to proceed to the purchase . . . ' Three days later Palmer's accepted an Admiralty offer to buy the vessels at £60,000 each, provided they made the trial speed of 31kts.

On 25 May 1908 a preliminary survey report[49] by G H Bell indicated that both were afloat at Jarrow. The boats were in good condition, though would require considerable cleaning before they were fit for delivery. Their basic data compared closely with *Spiteful* (the bracketed figures with an asterisk [*] in the list below are for *Spiteful*): Dimensions: 215ft bp, 200ft oa × 20ft 9in moulded × 12ft 6in (12ft 10½in*) 6ft 5½in mean draft. (5ft 8¼in*) 408

Bonetta as built, showing the different form of forecastle, the integral bridge and the other improvements from earlier versions of the 30-knotter type. The plan also shows alterations made by 1910, and then by 1915. (National Maritime Museum, London: 125666)

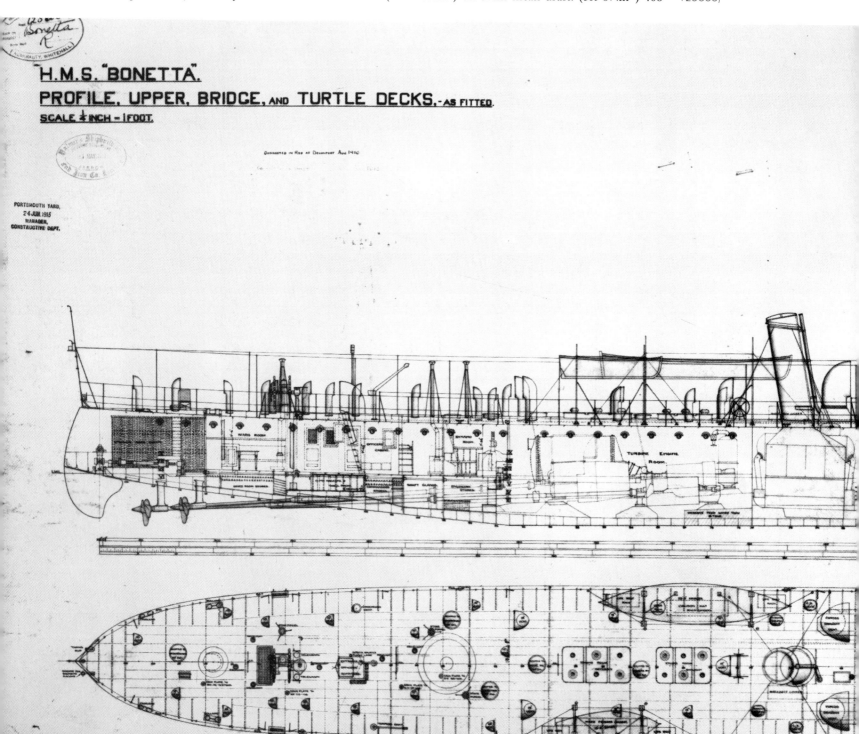

H.M.S. "BONETTA".
PROFILE, UPPER, BRIDGE, AND TURTLE DECKS, - AS FITTED.
SCALE ⅛ INCH = 1 FOOT.

tons displacement with about 46 tons load (330 tons – 35 tons load*): round up of upper deck 9in (6in*). The main armament consists of three 12pdrs, but arrangements to fit two 6pdrs (presumably in addition to the 12pdrs) on the upper deck could be made if necessary. The firm should be able to deliver in two to three months if desired. The builders had already run trials with the vessels and were reducing the rudder area slightly to improve steering.[50]

As it turned out the vessels waited a long time before they were accepted. A series of trials demonstrated that they had no hope of making the specified speed of 31kts. The speed of *Albacore* on trial never rose above 26.75kts – finally, the two vessels being alike, this result was accepted for both. Finally on the 3 March 1909 the First Lord and the Controller met representatives of Palmer's and agreed on the price of £45,000 each for the destroyers. The Admiralty to put armament in. No more trials were needed, Palmer's trying to complete both by 25 March as they were to be purchased within the present Financial Year, which ended on the last day of that month.[51] Wireless telegraphy was not fitted at this time.[52] There were defects in the steering gear of both vessels due to bad workmanship.[53] The dockyard work on *Bonetta* cost £96 less than estimated = £450 whilst the total contract work £46,224 – total (with £1 credit on materials) = £46,673.[54] They had four funnels with the middle pair closely grouped. Both spent their careers in home waters.

Albacore was sold on 1 August 1919 to T R Sales. *Bonetta* was sold on 7 June 1920 to Ward at Hayle, then broken up at Briton Ferry.

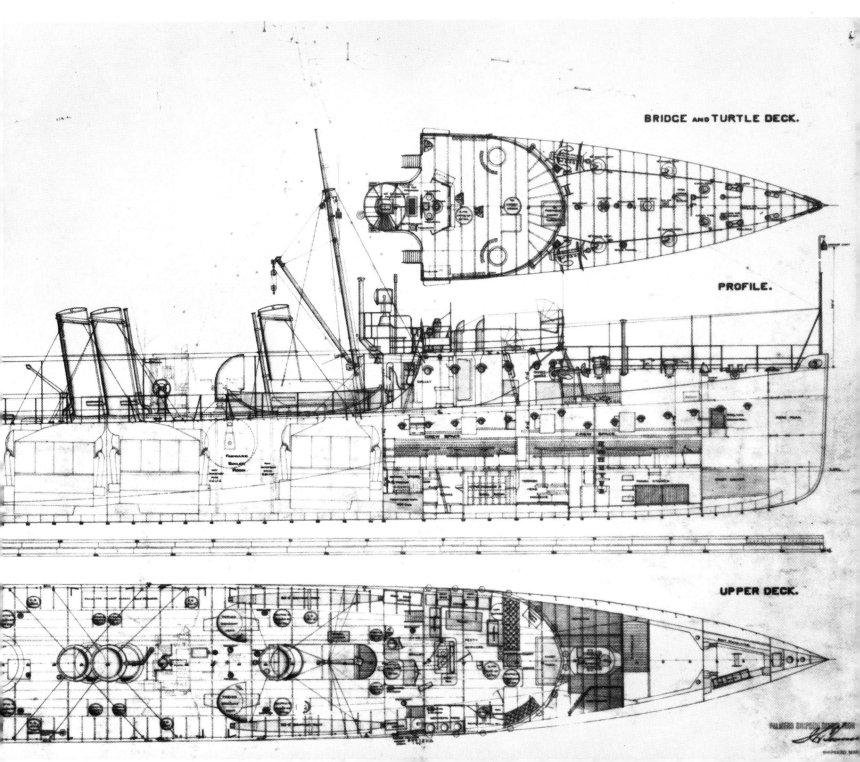

BRIDGE and TURTLE DECK.

PROFILE.

UPPER DECK.

Part II: Builders

Thornycroft

John Isaac Thornycroft began building his first steel steam launch in his father's back garden on the banks of the Thames when a teenager, helped by his younger sister. From this small beginning in the 1860s he rapidly created a firm which grew into one of the two great British torpedo boat specialists, in a curious love-hate relationship with 'our friends lower down the Thames', Thornycroft's being based at Chiswick, at the opposite end of London from Yarrow's yard at Poplar on the Isle of Dogs. At the beginning of the twentieth century, just after building their last 30-knotter, the firm was driven by rising labour costs, and the increasing size of torpedo craft, into moving to Woolston, a suburb of Southampton. Before that they had designed and built very large numbers of light, high-speed craft, including the first British torpedo boat, *TB No 1* – or *Lightning* – which was nearly equipped with a hull designed on hovercraft lines. This was not, however, the first torpedo *craft* for the Royal Navy, as she had been preceded by the very different *Vesuvius* (see the present author's contribution on British torpedo craft in *Conway's All the World's Fighting Ships 1860-1905*). Thornycroft's also played an active part in the evolution of the torpedo boat, with many built for the RN and many foreign navies.

This chapter deals with all the vessels and some of the designs produced by this firm for TBDs and similar vessels for which documentation survives, except for the 32kt *Albatross* – for which see the chapter on the 'Specials'. The inevitable growth in size and power of torpedo craft caused Thornycroft's to evolve a number of designs which foreshadowed the enlargement of the TB into the TBD. Yarrow's were producing similar designs, and so, to a lesser extent, were other firms. Some of these designs were in the small torpedo cruiser style of the torpedo gunboat (TGB) type, but some were enlarged and up-gunned torpedo boats, as, indeed were the TBDs themselves.

Prototypes – 1892-1893 Programme

An undated memorandum[1] by S W Barnaby, Thornycroft's chief naval architect and the son of Nathaniel Barnaby, the ex-DNC, states that ever since the success of the *Ariete*, a record-breaking torpedo boat built for Spain in 1887, Thornycroft's had tried to persuade the Admiralty to buy a 27kt torpedo catcher embodying nearly all the features of the torpedo boat destroyers except the decks forward and aft of the machinery space which were added at the request of the Admiralty. 'It was not until 1892 that we were asked to send in designs to the Admiralty for 27- and 28-knotters which should have a more powerful gun armament than the torpedo boats then building in France. We sent designs of vessels

of 200 tons and 300 tons having speeds of 27 and 28kts respectively, the larger vessel being more heavily armed . . . Subsequently Messrs Yarrow and ourselves were asked to tender for the smaller type of 27kts, but the armament of the larger was to be carried. This necessitated an increase of displacement to about 237 tons and in 1892 we received an order for *Daring* and *Decoy* and at the same time the *Havock* and *Hornet* were ordered from Messrs Yarrow.' This account was probably written in the late 1890s.

ORDERED: 27 June 1892 for delivery 27 July 1893 and 27 August 1893.

	Yard No.	Laid down	Launched	Completed
Daring	287	Jul 1892	25.11.1893	Feb 1895
Decoy	288	Jul 1892	7.2.1894	Jun 1895

DIMENSIONS: 185ft oa/185ft wl × 19ft × 13ft + 7ft

DISPLACEMENT: 287.8 tons full load

MACHINERY: 2 shafts 19in.27in.27in.27in × 16in (triple expansion with two low pressure cylinders), 2 water tube boilers, 200 pounds per square inch working pressure

WEIGHTS: (for *Daring* in hundredweight, quarters, pounds) Hull 1390.3.5½, woodwork 132.0.10½, boilers 907.0.3, engines 1064.3.4, fittings 483.0.4, spare gear, 114.1.8 = 4099.2.8½ = 204.98 tons

COSTS: (from Thornycroft's records – references to particular documents are given in brackets) On 13 June 1892 (A/4) the tender which was to be accepted was completed – the price for two vessels was £66,948. This divided into £28,698 for the hulls, £35,502 for machinery and £2748 for ?. On 10 October 1892 (D/12) there was the following estimate for one ship: £33,474 with revised machinery prices on 18 November 1892. Later, £7/10/- was added to the cost for stiffening for the 6pdrs and £19/15/- for a portable screen and earth closet. On 1 May 1894 a letter to the Austrian Naval Attaché stated that the Admiralty was paying £36,840 for each vessel

---

On 18 March 1892 the Admiralty wrote to John Thornycroft:[2] 'I am desired by Admiral Fisher to inform you with reference to your informal and confidential conversation with him yesterday, that he will be pleased to receive from you any offer or proposals that you may wish to make in reference to the construction of Torpedo Boat Destroyers and give them his careful consideration.' Tweddle, the company secretary, wrote to Donaldson (the partner who ran the commercial side of the firm's activities) three days later: 'Mr Thornycroft had a letter from Admiral Fisher . . . Mr Thornycroft wishes this matter kept quiet as he does not want Yarrow's to know

The 'as fitted' plan of *Decoy* showing her both as built and with such later alterations as raised funnels. Visible on this profile, decks and sections plan is the way that the forward two water tube boilers are trunked into the one funnel whereas only one boiler feeds the after funnel. Also visible is the Thornycroft semi-tunnel stern, a characteristic feature which added slightly to the speed in calm conditions – an advantage, however, which was more than counterbalanced by the way it 'slammed' in anything approaching bad weather. The 'vee' shape with its apex pointing forward by the muzzle of the 12pdr is the chart table. Rails on the deck connect forecastle and after torpedo tubes and spare torpedoes could be moved between the two on a trolley. (National Maritime Museum, London: 64135)

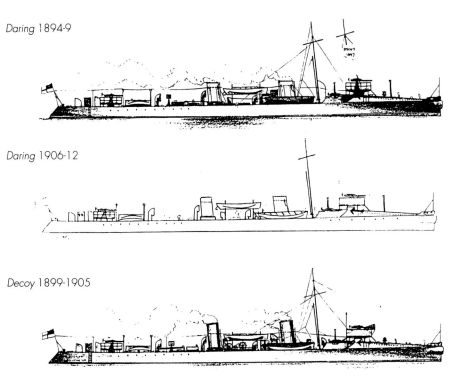

Daring 1894-9

Daring 1906-12

Decoy 1899-1905

fact of Their Lordships' being in negotiation for vessel of the types referred to shall not be communicated to the Agents of any Foreign Government nor allowed to find its way into the Newspapers.' A copy of the letter was sent by Donaldson to John Thornycroft with the note 'This I have firm, so keep it dark, Obadiah, keep it dark . . . P.S. I will register this so as to ensure its reaching your hands – the Admiralty letter was enclosed in two envelopes both sealed the inner one marked "strictly confidential" and the outer one . . . [word illegible].' Three days later a letter (A/4) almost certainly written by Donaldson to 'My dear Partner' (Thornycroft) rejoiced that: '*The* invitation to tender has come from the Admiralty – there are to be two types, one with a considerable load and armament and the other lighter – speed in both cases to be from 26 to 28kts. Tenders have to be sent in on 16th May so there is ample time, and I have handed the letter to Barnaby [the firm's chief naval architect] . . . to get the loads adjusted . . .' The tenders, specifications and designs HO 5398 and HO 5400 for 'a class of vessel specially qualified to act efficiently against Torpedo Boats' were sent to the Admiralty on 14 May 1892. Speeds were to be 27 and 28kts respectively. The armament of the larger vessel was shown 'in accordance with your suggestion' – one torpedo tube in the bow, a 12pdr gun on the conning tower and four 3pdr QF guns one on either side of the conning tower, just abaft it, and the other two en echelon aft. 'As a suggestion we offer the alternative arrangement shown in tracing (HO) 5399 – that is, two 12pdrs, one on each side

what we are likely to offer in the way of speed.' On 13 April a reply was sent to Admiral Fisher: 'We beg to acknowledge receipt of your letter S 4847/4630 of the 12th instant which shall be considered most strictly confidential and we hasten to give you our assurance that the

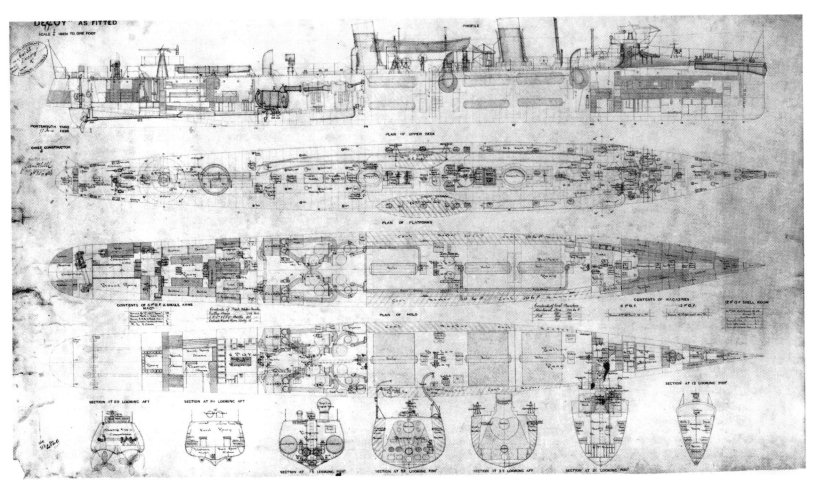

of the conning tower and two 3pdrs just abaft of these giving four guns firing in the line of the keel ahead – a third 3pdr is mounted on the conning tower aft . . . It will be observed that the outline of these vessels will be very similar to existing torpedo boats . . . Care has been taken to limit the draught of water as much as possible . . . By the adaption of three screws in the larger vessel together with the particular form of stern used [Thornycroft's at this time built their torpedo craft with sterns which were so shaped as to fit the screws into a partial tunnel, an effect enhanced by shaping the rudders to increase that tunnel effect. This made for greater propulsive efficiency, but, as we shall see later in this book, produced an unfortunate effect in bad weather], we are able to give exceptionally small draught for the size and power.' Thornycroft's proposed employing a modification of Humphry's four cylinder triple expansion engine, which was lighter but better balanced, anticipating improvements in speed, steadiness in running and reduced maintenance cost; but the ordinary type of triple compound engine could be substituted if the admiralty preferred. Thornycroft's confidently predicted that the specified speeds would be obtained from 4800ihp in the case of the larger vessel and 3200ihp in the case of the small one.

The Admiralty found the Thornycroft and Yarrow designs generally satisfactory and they were asked to quote for one or two boats, although they preferred to avoid the former's suggestion of premiums for higher-than-contracted speeds. The description of the design was of a torpedo boat type fitted with a turtle back, two conning towers, two funnels, one signal mast and a bridge above the conning tower. Thornycroft patent twin rudders were to be fitted. Dimensions: 180ft × 18ft 6in + 5ft 3in draft forward, 6ft 6in aft on 200 tons displacement. 3200ihp to give 27kts. Coal carried sufficient to steam 1000 knots (nautical miles) at 10kts speed. One fixed bow torpedo tube with powder impulse [ie a gunpowder charge was used to blow the torpedo out of the tube]. Five 3pdr QF guns with 100 rounds per gun, and magazines provided to stow the above amount of ammunition. Not less than 2ft metacentric height with all weights on board. Corticine deck covering, hand pumps, galley, capstan and ships bell etc provided for in the specification which also gives a list of outfit including two 12ft dinghies, anchors, cables and sundries. The electric light included a 16in Projector ('n.b. the smallest size in 1st class service boats is 20 inches'). It specified a premium of £50 for each complete tenth of a knot in excess, and a penalty of £50 for each tenth of a knot in defect of the guarantee speed of 27kts.

Tweddle wrote to Donaldson[3] on 27 May 1892 stating that the Admiralty had acknowledged receipt of the proposals, but at the moment did not propose to do anything about the 300-ton design. Thornycroft's were being asked to submit tenders for one, and for two examples of the smaller design, incorporating the additional requirements the Admiralty had produced. Barnaby was looking into this but was not yet sure to what extent the design would have to be modified. The matter was urgent because the tender had to be in by 14 June, but: 'it certainly looks like an order for the 200 tons vessels'. In the tender dated 13 June 1892 the vessels were to be built on a covered slip and would be delivered in twelve and thirteen months if two were built. The tender was actually submitted to the Controller a day later together with the amended design HO 5429 and specification 'for a fast seagoing Torpedo Boat Destroyer', but the Admiralty's modifications meant an increase in displacement of the hull to 215 tons as well as larger engines and boilers. Two alternative drawings of gun positions (HO 5430 with the 12pdr abaft the conning tower and HO 5431 with the 12pdr in front of it) were also sent.

On 27 June the tender of the 13th for 'two fast seagoing torpedo boat destroyers' for £66,948 was accepted,[4] but although they wanted to give the company as free a hand as possible in design, the Admiralty insisted that all details must be vetted by officers of the Controller of the Navy's Department, and that any modifications considered necessary be carried out by Thornycroft's without extra charge. Machinery modifications were asked for; the auxiliary machinery was to be placed in the engine room if possible and the boiler tubes to be galvanised throughout. As electricity generating machinery the 'Parsons turbine is not acceptable . . . electric light machinery should be in accordance with the usual Admiralty specifications except that the rpm might be somewhat increased. The position of the condenser under the cabins was not satisfactory. In view of the probability of a higher power being required, it should be considered whether a margin cannot be given for more power both in the boilers and engines, in the latter probably by increasing the revolutions. Hull: details of scantlings to be submitted for approval. Outside and deck plating to be galvanised, exposed steel surfaces in living and store spaces to be cork cemented or canvas covered. Torpedoes to be stowed forward under the turtle back. Steel water tight flat forward to be fitted and crew accommodation to be revised. Magazines to be lined with teak. Armament fittings to be tested by test firings on receipt: 'Material to be manufactured by approved firms and under Admiralty tests and supervision.' Cabins were not required for each officer. Arrangements to be made for steering from outside the conning tower as well as inside. 'You will be held responsible for the efficiency of the whole of the main and auxiliary machinery . . . [for] . . . a period of twelve months from the date of the vessels first commission . . . fair wear and tear and mismanagement by crew will be covered by the Admiralty.'

On 29 June 1892 Thornycroft's accepted the terms, agreeing that the heating space of the boilers would be increased if this could be done without adding to the displacement. By the beginning of August 1892 Barnaby was pressing Pledge of the DNC's department[5] to send the details of the crews so he could decide the position of the bulkheads. He also hoped to get the DNC's assent to employing the usual practice in torpedo boats in general details of construction, notably in the matter of watertightness of shell and deck plating 'which we do not propose to caulk, and in the matter of coal bunkers which we do not propose to make watertight'. There was also the further question as to the necessity of making watertight the torpedo room flat.

Despite intense rivalry, there was also solidarity on matters of mutual interest. Donaldson wrote to Yarrow's (who were building the other pair of prototype destroyers) on 20 October 1892, to warn them that an attempt would be made to make them pay for 'a whole budget of alterations the Admiralty had made in the catchers such as two extra gun positions – two Downton's pumps and a main drain through the ships with valves at bulkheads, regular WCs in the seamen's heads, water tight decklight covers etc. etc.'

Trials: *Daring* was first tried at the Lower Hope on 17 January 1894, then ran a long series of preliminary trials, all off the Maplins, experiencing such problems as, 'funnels were extremely hot' and 'not much vibration at engines but it was very bad at stern'. Harding, the Admiralty overseer reported[6] on her twelfth preliminary trial that 'means fitted for cooling bulkhead and fore end of engine room and for keeping cool coamings abreast of funnel do not keep these parts cool. Engine room would be unbearable if hatches were closed, and the hot coamings would be a just cause of endless complaints, and would seriously injure naked feet.' Thornycroft were asked to rectify this. She ran a coal consumption trial on 18 September 1894 at 9.908kts for twelve hours, on one boiler only, making 37.73 nautical miles per ton of coal. *Decoy* made her first preliminary trial on 31 July 1894 with sixty people on board. Thornycroft's figures for the official trials of these two are as follows:

No.	Trial		Displacement	Knots	IHP	RPM
287	19.7.1894	(Measured Mile)	237.7	28.213	4644	389
	ditto	(3 hours)	–	27.706	–	378
288	21.8.1894	(Measured Mile)	237.25	27.641	4049	366
	ditto	(3 hours)	–	27.163	4009	368

On 28 September 1894 Donaldson informed the chief engineer of the Austrian Navy, to whom he was trying to sell ships:[7] 'of course you knew that *Hornet* was *hors de combat* through her machinery being broken up. Her crew is to be put into our destroyer *Daring* which is at Portsmouth.' This attempt to discredit the rival firm of Yarrow's does not appear to have been successful; Thornycroft's got no orders for torpedo craft from Austria whilst Yarrow's did.

Both seem to have spent their service lives in home waters. *Daring* was sold on 10 April 1912. *Decoy* was sunk in a collision with the *Arun* on 13 August 1904.

27-knotters, 1893-1894 Programme

ORDERED: 12 October 1893 for delivery in 13, 14, and 15 months.

	Yard No.	Laid down	Launched	Completed
Ardent	297	Dec 1893	16.10.1894	25.3.1895
Boxer	298	Feb 1894	28.11.1894	Jun 1895
Bruiser	299	Apr 1894	27.2.1895	Jun 1895

DIMENSIONS: 201ft 8in oa / 201ft 6in wl × 19in × 13ft + 7ft 3¼in

DISPLACEMENT: 245 tons light, 301 tons full load

MACHINERY: 2 sets 19in.27in.27in.27in × 16in, Thornycroft water tube boilers

WEIGHTS: (*Ardent*, in hundredweight, quarters, pounds.) Hull 1516.0.5½, woodwork 139.1.5, boilers 866.1.0½, engines 1045.1.12½, fittings 515.3.7¼, spare gear 135.2.20¼ = 11503.2.2½ = 57.547 tons

COSTS: Tender price £110,520 for all three. First costs £39,555, £39,505 and £39,406

A letter to the Admiralty of 27 February 1893[8] referred to Donaldson's conversation with Admiral Sir Anthony Hopkins and subsequently with the Controller regarding the possibility of rapidly increasing the 'out-turn' of vessels of the *Daring* class. With the drawings and patterns ready and approved, contracts for materials fixed, and rates of wages settled, the company could build new vessels alongside *Daring* and *Decoy*, and promised delivery of the first boat of a series in from seven to eight months from date of order, and of the others at intervals of one month each. Costs would be about the same price as currently agreed, namely £33,474 per boat. Completion could be expedited if more men were put on them, but the boats, boilers and machinery were so small that such an expedient was limited.

A 'very confidential' letter to the Admiralty dated 18 August 1893[9] acknowledged the Controller's letter of 16 August 1893 which asked the firm to tender for three torpedo boat destroyers and requested that they receive preference in the placing of future orders as recognition of the company's costly pioneering efforts. The tender was being sent off on 5 September 1893[10] – £36,840 for one boat, £110,520 for three. It was noted that the boiler surface area was being increased. The tender being however sent to the Controller a day later[11] with the design HO 6301 on two sheets, together with hull and machinery specifications for the three destroyers; length had been increased to 200ft and displacement to 237 tons. There were also some modifications to the engines and an increase in the power of the boilers to give the required speed. The company claimed it could have achieved 'a length of 195ft if the galley could have been placed abaft the engines but fear the difficulty of carrying the food forward to the crew's quarters in rough weather would render such a proposal inadmissible'.

The Admiralty seem to have preferred Thornycroft's design.[12] The hull arrangements were fine except that placing the galley aft meant that provisions would have to be stowed elsewhere as well as in the provision room. On 12 October 1893 the tender for three vessels at £105,795 was accepted.[13] The bow tube was to be omitted, the separate steam bilge pump should not be less in capacity than those now being fitted, these two being the only provisos, but it was stressed that the date of completion should not be exceeded.

Donaldson of Thornycroft's passed on a 'groan' from Barnaby on 13 November 1893 asking for approvals from the Admiralty in various matters to enable him to go ahead. On 30 October Thornycroft's sent a list of drawings for approval which had not yet been approved: 'Result, apart from rudders, we have not yet been able to send a single drawing to the yard yet, one month after the receipt of the order'.

On 25 April 1894[14] the Admiralty proposed to substitute 18ft 'unsinkable' boats of Wright and Company's reindeer hair type for Berthon boats, which would mean a rebate of £60 per ship. On 1 June 1895 the Chilean Navy, who were interested in buying ships of this type, were informed that *Ardent* steaming at 13kts consumed 1.54lbs of coal per ihp per hour, giving a radius of action of 2750 nautical miles. *Boxer* at the time of writing held the record as the fastest vessel in the world.

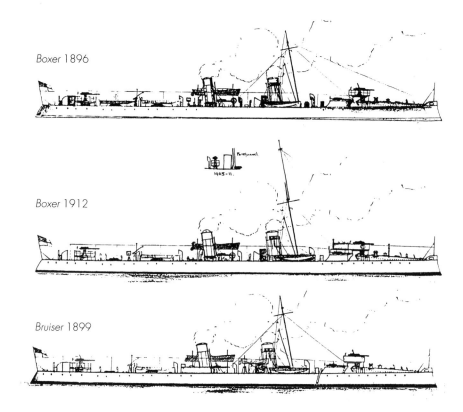

Boxer 1896

Boxer 1912

Bruiser 1899

Ardent as built and as altered a year later in 1896. (National Maritime Museum, London: 58586)

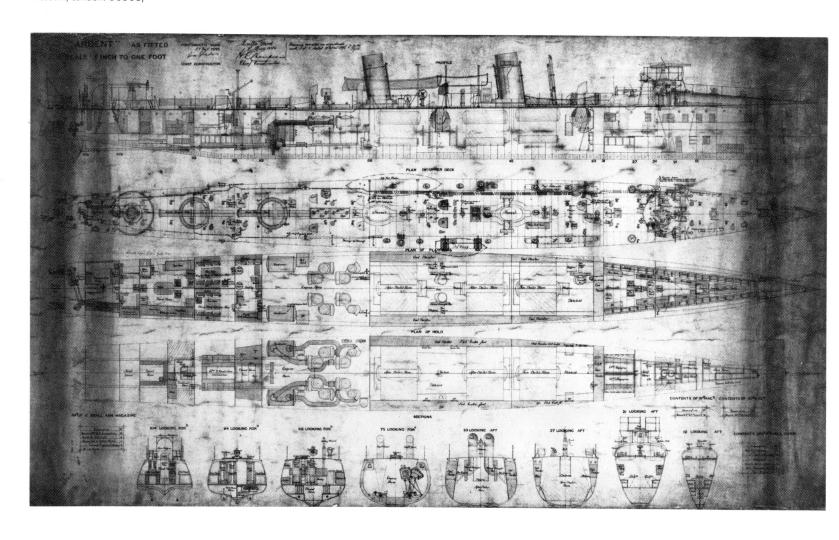

Thornycroft's version of the official trials gives the following results:

No	Trial		Disp	Knots	IHP	RPM
297	15.12.1894	(Measured Mile)	245.4t	27.84	4343	399
		(6 [?] hours)	249t	27.97	4205	398
298	25.1.1895	(Measured Mile)	243½t	29.076	4487	412
		(3 hours)	243t	29.175	4542	410
299	29.3.1895	(Measured Mile)	–	27.809	4681	372
		(3 hours)	–	27.97	4257	370
		– ? –	250.7t	28.14	4252	377

Ardent served in the Mediterranean from April 1895 till she was sold on 10th October 1911. *Boxer* served in the Mediterranean from May 1896 till she returned home by 1911 and was lost on 8 February 1918 in a collision with SS *St Patrick* in the Channel. *Bruiser* also went out to the Mediterranean in May 1896 and was home by 1911. In 1911-1912 she was at Lamlash with a submarine flotilla and was sold on 26 May 1914 to Cashmore, Newport.

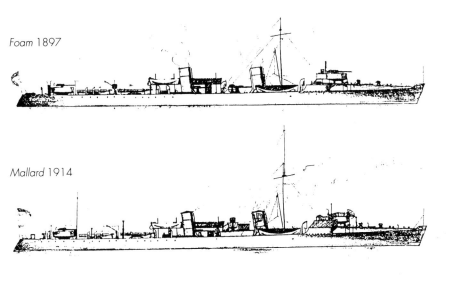

Foam 1897

Mallard 1914

Desperate as built. (National Maritime Museum, London: 94419)

30-knotters, 1894–1895 Programme

ORDERED: 10 May 1895 (first three), 30 May 1895 (*Mallard*), for delivery ?.

	Yard No.	Laid Down	Launched	Completed
Desperate	305	1.7.1895	15.2.1896	Feb 1897
Fame	306	4.7.1895	15.4.1896	Jun 1897
Foam	307	16.7.1895	8.10.1896	Jul 1897
Mallard	308	13.9.1895	19.11.1896	Oct 1897

DIMENSIONS: 210ft oa/208ft wl × 19ft 6in × 13ft 6in + 5ft 8in
DISPLACEMENT: 272 tons light, 352 tons full load
MACHINERY: 2 shafts 20in.29in.30in.30in × 18in, 3 water tube boilers, 220lbs, 5700ihp
WEIGHTS: (305 in hundredweight, quarters, pounds) Hull 1578.3.27½, woodwork 124.2.15, boilers 976.3.2, engines 1259.1.11, fittings 566.3.27, spare gear 134.3.22 = 4641.2.21¼ = 232.084 tons
COSTS: Contract price for 305–307 = £155,000 [?] for all three, contract price for 308 = £51,500.
FIRST COSTS: £54,579, £54,724, £54,432 and £54,715

On 20 December 1893 Thornycroft's[15] wrote to the Secretary of the Admiralty in compliance with his letter (S 15076/143 51) of 29 November 1893 asking the firm to submit design and specifications for two torpedo boat destroyers proposing to berth officers forward and the POs and crew aft, 'owing to the difficulty in trimming the vessel with the powerful machinery we propose to adopt'. An alternative in which the officers were berthed aft and the crew partly forward and partly aft was also submitted. The company cautiously proposed guaranteeing only 28kts, since 27¼kts was about the highest known in foreign vessels, but their proposed machinery of at least 5000ihp gave them no doubt that this speed would be considerably exceeded. With a view to maximum weight-saving, aluminium and aluminium alloys were proposed for some features. If more than two vessels were ordered, savings could be made and additional vessels could be supplied for £49,000 each. The cost for the first two would be £100,500 for both, with delivery in fifteen and seventeen months. Thus both the Admiralty and the firm were proposing to go one better than the original 27-knotters only just after those vessels had been ordered, though the matter would not be taken up fully until half a year later.

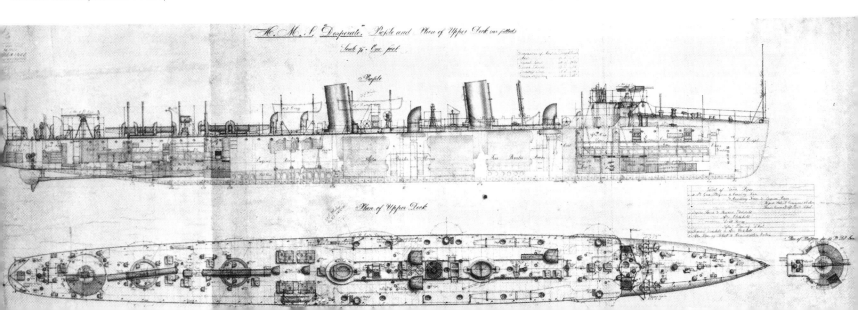

As we have seen in the chapter on ordering the first 30-knotters, the idea of using spare moneys from the sums set aside in this year's Estimates for prototypes was mooted by the DNC on 27 July 1894.[16] At first Yarrow's were favoured, but by 27 July Fisher was proposing 'to write confidentially to Yarrow asking for tenders for one, two or three boats, similarly to Messrs Thornycroft for one or two boats . . . ' This was done and 'Thornycroft was inadvertently asked to tender for one, two or three rather than one or two. No action to be taken as they have already acknowledged.'

An internal Thornycroft memo of 24 October 1894[17] stated that for the new proposed destroyers to carry the specified load and use the present pattern of engine, the smallest displacement possible would be about 316 tons. It would be important to use stronger steel than in *Ardent*. It was proposed that certain parts of the hull not forming the shell should be of aluminium. In reply to the Controller's letter S11872/12043 Thornycroft's sent on 15 November 1894[18] tenders for one (£59,000), two (£116,000) or three (£172,000) 30kt torpedo boat destroyers, for delivery in sixteen, eighteen, and twenty months. It was regretted that the accommodation and speed required could not be obtained with less than 315 tons displacement (300 tons was the stipulated displacement) which could itself only be obtained by using: 'a stronger and more costly steel in some parts of the hull and making a free use of aluminium bronze for certain of the fittings.' A speed of 30kts was guaranteed, but a much higher speed on trial was expected. The concluded by urging a quick decision to avoid the dispersion of their most skilled workmen engaged in the nearly completed *Ardent*, *Boxer* and *Bruiser*.

On the same day (15 November 1894) a letter was also sent to the Secretary of the Admiralty on the same theme, and requesting a repeat order for an *Ardent* for which they could offer rapid delivery. However, the Admiralty was not interested in such repeats, and their comments[19] were reserved for the 30kt designs. Thornycroft's one was a triple screw vessel measuring 215ft × 21ft with 315 tons displacement. There was some use of aluminium alloy (94 per cent aluminium mixed with 6 per cent copper) internally and in fittings whilst HT (high tensile) steel was also used. Thornycroft's design could on the whole be accepted subject to restrictions on use of aluminium and HT steel. The arrangement of boilers made in order to limit funnels to two and get over some difficulties experienced at first in *Daring* involved three stokeholds whilst it was essential for economy of men to limit to two. There was no objection in principle to adoption of triple screws 'and Messrs Thornycroft no doubt have in view the great manufacturing advantages obtained by constructing three sets of engines of *Ardent* type for a new vessel requiring 50 per cent more hp.' It would be interesting to compare the results with other firms' twin screw boats. Thornycroft proposed three accommodation alternatives: (1) Officers forward, all crew aft. (2) Part of crew forward, part aft, officers right aft. (3) Crew right forward and right aft, officers between the engines and the aft crew ((2) was proposed to be adopted). The machinery was on the whole satisfactory. Thornycroft

proposed 210lbs working pressure for the steam but there was no objection to an increase to 250lbs.

'Not one of the designs can be recommended as it stands,' but Thornycroft's proposal could be revised to make it acceptable. Since the invitation to tender was sent there had been some experience with vessels of the *Ardent* class. *Boxer* on preliminary trials with proper trial displacement maintained 29.3kts for over an hour and 29.17kts on the official trial of three hours and seemed to confirm that a 30kt vessel could be obtained on not much more displacement than *Ardent*. Revised tenders should be requested, and Thornycroft's were asked the speed they would be prepared to guarantee for vessel of about the same size and displacement as *Boxer*.

So on 15 March 1895 in reply to a letter of 15 February 1895 drawings HO 6973 A to D showing a 30kt design were handed over to the Admiralty. Thornycroft's requested the astern requirement be altered to ½ full revolutions instead of full revolutions as specified. There was no provision in the hull specification for the use of aluminium: 'but as the problem of getting the speed in view of the conditions as to coal consumption is a very tight one, we may find it necessary to reconsider the question when working out the details.' Slight alterations in the machinery specification were proposed. Also in the same letter, design HO 6977 for an 'improved *Boxer*' type was included – size of machinery increased to comply with conditions on coal consumption, and accommodation also increased – involving an increase in price – but 28kts could be guaranteed. The prices of the 30-knotter design were given as £34,150 for each of two and £33,850 for each of three (hulls for the three = £64,950, boilers and machinery = £96,900, auxiliary machinery £4650 =

Boxer – a photo probably taken about 1898 off Portsmouth early in the ship's career, before weather cloths were standard round the 12pdr platform, which is of its original small dimensions here. (National Maritime Museum, London: G12577)

total of £166,500 – the discrepancy between these and the previous figures is not explained) delivery in eighteen, nineteen and twenty months.

Basic details of the design were: 210ft oa × 19ft + 5ft 6in/6ft 10in draft, 260 tons trial displacement and 5400ihp. The Admiralty commented[20] that there was 'just a doubt' with the beam proposed whether a 2ft metacentric height would be reached; Thornycroft's were to be asked to reconsider this. The displacement was considered to be under-estimated by at least 20 tons. There were no objections seen to using special (HT) steel in portions of hull, but they should not provide for use of aluminium in the specification, though there was a desire to leave this open for further reconsideration. There was no objection to the machinery design but a few modifications should be made to the hull specification. The prices quoted by the London firms were seen as high, but given their pre-eminence a reduction was suggested of only £4000 a boat. Fisher proposed giving Thornycroft's an order for three boats.

An acknowledgement of the Admiralty's letter of 25 April 1895 (which had presumably incorporated the above remarks) was sent on 7 May 1895. Thornycroft's considered their prices fair, but they reluctantly accepted, given the shortage of work in the London area, but they attempted to turn the situation to their advantage by suggesting that six vessels, instead of the three at present proposed, would spread their fixed costs. On 25 May 1895 Thornycroft's wrote in reply to an Admiralty letter of 24 May 1895 that they were prepared to construct an additional one or two destroyers to the same conditions as the ones just ordered for £51,500 each and to deliver in eighteen months, but begged the Admiralty to extend the order to three vessels for the reasons already given. However only one additional order (for 308) resulted from these appeals. The class were designed with more flare to the bow and the stern raking forward rather than aft. The machinery was designed for 5400ihp, and the three boilers arranged front to back to back to fit the two-funnelled arrangement.

Trials. *Desperate* completed nine successive preliminary trials, not surprisingly, as she was the first 30-knotter to complete. *Fame* burnt 1.677 pounds of coal per hour per ihp at 13kts using two boilers, *Mallard* burnt 2.08 pounds per ihp per hour at full speed. During *Mallard*'s official trials her port engines suddenly reversed and commenced moving at full speed astern owing to the locking gear on a small lever controlling the differential valve of the reversing gear becoming loose. Thornycroft's figures on the official trials show the following:

No.	Trial	Disp	Knots	IHP	RPM
305	26.6.1896 (Measured Mile)	–	30.156	–	395
	4.9.1896 (Measured Mile)	276.6t	30.006	5901	396
306	15.4.1897 (Measured Mile)	–	30.021	5819	393
	(3 hours)	273.2t	30.17	5879	393
307	7.5.1897 (Measured Mile)	–	30.35	5854	397
	(3 hours)	270.2t	30.184	5654	393
308	17.9.1897 (Measured Mile)	–	30.096	5870	395
	(3 hours)	247½t	30.115	5905	395

Angler and *Ariel* were built to the same lines. In 1902 S W Barnaby, giving evidence during the destroyer enquiry of that year, stated that *Fame* was the only destroyer built by Thornycroft's where they had found evidence of weakness – a crack developed in the curved coaming over the boilers.

Desperate served in the Mediterranean from about 1900 to 1913. She was sold for breaking up to Ward & Co. of Milford Haven on 20 May 1920. *Fame* was sold on 31 August 1921 at Hong Kong, having gone to China by 1897 and stayed there. *Foam* was sold on 26 May 1914 at Chatham, having been on the Mediterranean Station from 1897 to 1913, and was then broken up in Norway. *Mallard* was another vessel to have served in the Mediterranean, from 1902 until 1913 in her case, then she was sold on 10 February 1920 to the South Alloa Ship Breaking Co.

1895-1896 Programme

ORDERED: 23 January 1895 (313) for delivery ?.

	Yard No.	Laid down	Launched	Completed
Angler	313	21.12.1896	2.2.1897	Jul 1898
Ariel	314	23.4.1896	5.3.1897	Oct 1898

DIMENSIONS: 210ft oa/208ft wl × 19ft 6in × 13ft 6in + 5ft 8in

DISPLACEMENT: 272 tons standard, 352 tons full load

MACHINERY: 2 shafts, as *Desperate*, 3 water tube boilers, 220lbs

WEIGHTS: (313 in tons) Hull 79.84, woodwork 6.25, boilers 48.78, engines 64.4, fittings 29.54, spare gear 6.72 = 235.6

COSTS: Penalties £250 per ¼ kt below 30kts. £500 per ¼kt below 19kts, rejection at 28 kts. £15 per day late delivery. First costs £54,294 and £54,293

The invitation to tender was for vessels 'similar in all respects to the last order.'[21] To be built in accordance with plan HO 6973 A and B. Repeat of *Desperate* with the same lines. *Angler*'s first official trial was a failure. To complete a twelve-hour consumption trial, *Angler* on trial burnt 1.84lbs of coal per ihp per hour using two boilers at 13kts. *Ariel* at full speed burnt 2.11lbs of coal per ihp per hour. The 'special', *Albatross* (see 'Specials' chapter), was also part of this programme.

Angler 1907

No.	Trials	Disp	Knots	IHP	RPM
313	27.5.1898 (Measured Mile)	–	30.558	6002	402
	3.6.1898 (3 hours)	277t	30.372	5835	398
314	7.8.1898 (Measured Mile?)	278.1t	30.82	6090	397
	17.8. 1898 (3 hours)	276.1t	30.194	6143	396.7

Ariel went out to the Mediterranean in 1901 and was lost there on 19 April 1907, wrecked at Malta, whilst testing harbour defences. It was a pitch-dark night and she ran on the rocks by Ricasoli breakwater. Her crew were, appropriately, rescued by *Bruiser*

Angler served with the Mediterranean Fleet from 1903 till 1913 when she came home. She was sold on 20 May 1920 to Ward, Milford Haven.

1896-1897 Programme

ORDERED: 21 April 1896 for delivery ?.

	Yard No.	Laid down	Launched	Completed
Coquette	319	8.6.1896	25.11.1896	Jan 1899
Cygnet	320	25.9.1896	3.9.1898	Feb 1900
Cynthia	321	16.7.1896	8.1.1898	Jun 1899

DIMENSIONS: 210ft oa, 208ft wl × 13ft 6in × ? + 7ft 4in

DISPLACEMENT: 367.3 tons full load

MACHINERY: 2 shafts 20in.29in.30in.30in × 18in, 3 water tube boilers, 220lbs, 5700ihp

WEIGHTS: (319, in hundredweight, quarters, pounds) Hull 1741.2.3., boilers 1004.2.20½, engines 1311.0.20½, fittings 614.0.12¼, woodwork 1281.1.27, spare gear 148.3.10½, plus 240.2.15½ ballast = 5189.1.25 = 259.473 tons

FIRST COSTS: £53,939, £53,746 and £53,884

The invitation to tender for this class was for a vessel:[22] 'from the same specification and design as those now building but embodying all improvements which have been communicated to you to date.' Delay in delivery was due to the effect of the Engineers' strike, also *Cynthia* was further delayed by a hitch in the delivery of her drawings. Lines similar to those of 305 (*Desperate*) etc, but slightly altered. The lines of this class were also used for the Japanese *Murakumo* class, and for Order Number 2143. The firm's figures for the official trials follow:

No.	Trials	Disp	Knots	IHP	RPM
319	26.7.1899 (Measured Mile)	300.6t	30.31	5925	389.5
	20.12.1898 (3 hours)	–	30.371	5805	383.9
320	5.5.1899 (Measured Mile)	295t	30.35	5738	394.5
	(3 hours)	–	30.305	5729	393.7
321	26.10.1899 (Measured Mile)	301.8t	30.21	5542	385.7
	(3 hours)	–	30.205	5494	384½

Coquette was mined on 7 March 1916 off the East Coast. *Cygnet* and *Cynthia* were both sold on 29 April 1920 to Ward, Rainham for breaking up.

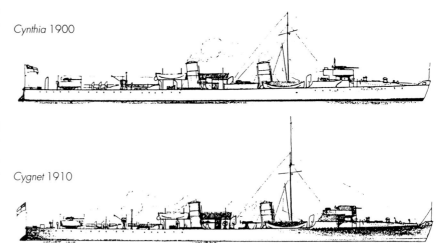

Cynthia 1900

Cygnet 1910

1897-1898 Programme

ORDERED: 7 September 1897 for delivery ?.

	Yard No.	Laid down	Launched	Completed
Stag	334	16.4.1898	18.11.1899	Sept 1900

DIMENSIONS: 210ft or 215ft oa, 208ft bp, 208ft wl × 19ft 9in × ? + 7ft 6in

DISPLACEMENT: 354 tons standard, 286 tons light, 370.6 tons full load

CREW: 63

MACHINERY: 2-shaft triple expansion, as *Coquette* 5800ihp

COAL: 78 tons

WEIGHTS: Hull 89.694 tons, boilers 50.168 tons, engines 69.51 tons, fittings 33.204 tons, woodwork 6.88 tons, spare gear 29.82 tons = 279.276 tons

FIRST COST: £54,795

In response to the Admiralty's request for tenders probably issued before the end of May 1897 Thornycroft:[23] 'proposes a practical repeat of the 30kt vessels of the *Coquette* class now building by them but with somewhat increased HP. The proposals are generally acceptable subject to some modifications in detail . . .' The firm by that stage had already got three 30-knotters through trials successfully. The differences from *Coquette* were 3in more beam and a different superstructure. The keel plate was the only mild steel plate in her bottom all the other plates being of high tensile steel. The Thornycroft data for *Stag*'s official trials are as follows:

Trials	Disp	Knots	IHP	RPM
19.6.1900 (Measured Mile)	299.1t	30.55	5588	386.4
(3 hours)	–	30.345	–	–

Stag was sold to Ward, Grays, on 17 March 1921, she had served in the Mediterranean from 1902 till 1913.

Stag 1902

1899-1900 Programme

It appears that Thornycroft were asked to tender for this programme, though no orders were placed, by a letter sent 5 October 1898 (tenders to be in by 16 November) which had an additional clause for Thornycroft's only; that the torpedo tubes should be spaced some distance apart and not close together at the aft end of the vessel as in the previous design.[24]

Thornycroft's also built the following TBD-type vessels for foreign navies:

Yard number 322 *D 10* 1896-1897

'Division boat', torpedo boat leader for the Imperial German Navy.

ORDERED: 28 May 1896 for delivery 28 May 1897.

DIMENSIONS: 211ft 9in (212ft in specification) oa, 209ft 9in wl × 19ft 6in × 13ft 6in + 7ft 8in

DISPLACEMENT: 300 tons light, 366.3 tons full load

GUNS: 5–50mm QF

TORPEDOES: 1 bow tube, 2 broadside tubes

MACHINERY: 2 shafts, 20in. 29in.30in × 18in, three '*Daring*' type water tube boilers, 215lbs per square inch working pressure.

TRIALS: 388 tons displ/27.73kts/5542ihp/394rpm

WEIGHTS: (in tons) Hull 86.05, boilers 50.704, engines 65.55, fittings 23.8, woodwork 5.1, spare gear 9.75 = 240.954.

On 20 February 1895 a secret and confidential letter[25] was sent to Admiral Bendermann of the torpedo department at Kiel, offering designs HO 6918 A and B and specifications for a division boat as arranged by S W Barnaby on his recent visit to Kiel, and in accordance with the German Admiral's letter of 19 December 1894. The price would be £59,000 with delivery in fifteen months at Kiel. It was regretted that a tender for the construction of a vessel of the *Boxer* type could not be submitted yet as trials with the *Boxer* with the weights needed for a division boat on board, which had been sanctioned by the Admiralty, were delayed by ice in the Thames. On 29 May 1895 Admiral Bendermann was sent the plans (HO 7007 A and B) of the twin screw vessel proposed 212ft × 19ft 3in + 7ft, 27kts with a division boat's load on board

were guaranteed. The price would be £52,500 excluding armament. The detailed schedule of trials in the contract states that these should be done at Kiel with a German crew well trained in torpedo boat work, but the contractors allowed a representative plus one man in each stokehold. 27½kts were to be obtained in four runs in calm water – or a penalty of £250 per ¼kt would be enforced, down to 27kts, £500 per ¼kt between 27 and 26kts, and rejection below 26kts. There should be a deep water trial in wind force 6 to 10 in the open Baltic or North Sea. There was an arbitration clause under German law. A searchlight was to be fitted, but the Germans would supply guns and torpedo tubes after arrival at Kiel. They would also supply a 10ft dinghy, and two gigs would be carried as well. At 12kts on her consumption trial she burnt 2.65lbs of coal per ihp per hour, a higher figure than *Angler* or *Fame* at full speed, probably, it was noted, because Thornycroft's stokers were more skilled than German ones. She was broken up in 1922.

Yard numbers 329–332 *Murakumo, Shinonome, Yugiri, Shiranui* 1897-1899

Torpedo boat destroyers '30-knotter' type for the Imperial Japanese Navy.

ORDERED: 15 January 1897 (329–330), 7 May 1897 (331–332).

	Yard No.	Launched	Completed
Murakumo	329	Nov 1898	1899
Shinonome	330	15.12.1898	1899
Yugiri	331	26.1.1899	1899
Shiranui	332	14.3.1899	1899?

DIMENSIONS: 210ft oa, 208ft wl × 19ft 6in × 13ft 6in + 6ft 10in

DISPLACEMENT: 360½ tons full load

GUNS: 1–12pdr, 5–6pdr

TORPEDOES. 2–18in torpedo tubes

MACHINERY: 3 water tube boilers

TRIALS: (*Shiranui*) 280 tons displ/30.47kts/5770ihp/385.1rpm

WEIGHTS: (in tons for 329) Hull 84.5, boilers 50.4, engines 64.51, fittings 32.606, woodwork 6.971, spare gear 8.043 = 247.005

NOTES: Carried 2–18ft Berthon folding boats, 1–18ft gig and 1–10ft dinghy each. The guns were provided by Armstrong's

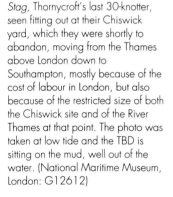

Stag, Thornycroft's last 30-knotter, seen fitting out at their Chiswick yard, which they were shortly to abandon, moving from the Thames above London down to Southampton, mostly because of the cost of labour in London, but also because of the restricted size of both the Chiswick site and of the River Thames at that point. The photo was taken at low tide and the TBD is sitting on the mud, well out of the water. (National Maritime Museum, London: G12612)

On 13 April 1904[26] this design was offered to Austria for £50,737 for one vessel, giving 15 per cent profit to Thornycroft's. 329 was wrecked in a typhoon in 1909, salved and taken out of service in 1921, then used for a short time as a depot ship before scrapping. 330 was also wrecked in a typhoon in 1909, was salved and then sank in another typhoon in 1913. 331 was out of service in 1921 but used as a depot ship for a short time before scrapping. 332 went out of service 1918, and was used as a tender till broken up in 1923.

Yard numbers 337, 338 *Kagerou, Usugumo* 1898-1900

Torpedo boat destroyers '30-knotter' type for the Imperial Japanese Navy.
ORDERED: 6 May 1898.

	Yard No.	Launched	Completed
Kagerou	337	22.8.1899	1900
Usugumo	338	26.1.1900	1900

DIMENSIONS: 210ft oa, 208ft wl × 19ft 6in × 13ft 6in + 6ft 11½in

DISPLACEMENT: 368 tons full load

GUNS: 1–12pdr, 5–6pdr

TORPEDOES: 2–18in torpedo tubes

MACHINERY: 2 shafts, 3 water tube boilers, contract speed 30kts

TRIALS: (*Kagerou*) 285½ tons displ/30.54kts/5690ihp/387.4rpm

WEIGHTS: (337) (in tons) Hull 85.8, boilers 50.027, engines 17.787, fittings 33.085, woodwork 7.345, spare gear 8.211 = 252.255 (not counting the weight of the torpedo tubes)

COSTS: Hull and fittings £20,750, propelling machinery £21,750, boilers etc £9500, auxiliary machinery not connected to propelling machinery £1500, electrics £1000 = £54,500

NOTES: On 16 January 1900 writing to the Swedish Navy,[27] Thornycroft's stated that it had been possible to get 31kts out of these vessels, which were designed for 30kts, by minor adjustments to the engines

337 was out of service in 1918, then was a tender till broken up in 1923. 338 was wrecked in a typhoon in 1911, salved, out of service 1911, broken up 1927. A letter was sent to S W Barnaby, who was in Asia at the time, on 23 March 1900[28] about the Japanese enquiry about the price for additional boats to be built under licence in Japan. The price would be in the region of £29,500 per vessel. Barnaby was asked to do his best to persuade the Japanese to order duplicates of the machinery already provided for 337 etc. They would gladly trade orders for a larger number of sets of machinery, say for four or six vessels, in return for frame sketches and other detailed particulars to enable them more readily to build the hulls in Japan: '. . . We fear if the Government only order one such vessel all the profit on it would be absorbed in the cost of new patterns and trials . . . ' This was leading up to the order for the following pair of destroyers.

Yard numbers 356, 357 *Shirakumo, Asashio* 1900-1902

Torpedo boat destroyers for the Imperial Japanese Navy.
ORDERED: 7 or 16 November 1911.

	Yard No.	Laid down	Launched	Completed
Shirakumo	356	11.12.1901	1.10.1901	1902
Asashio	357	3.4.1901	10.1.1902	14.5.1902

DIMENSIONS: 216ft 9in oa, 215ft 9in wl × 20ft 9in × 13ft 9in + 8ft 3in

DISPLACEMENT: 400 tons light, 432 tons full load

CREW: 59

GUNS: 1–12pdr, 5–6pdr

TORPEDOES: 2–18in torpedo tubes

MACHINERY: 2 shafts 22in.29½in.31in.31in × 19in, 4 Thornycroft-Schultz water tube boilers, contract speed 31 knots with 7500hp

TRIALS: (*Shirakumo* 4.1.1902) 331.3 tons displ/31.82kts/7648ihp/400rpm

COSTS: Jones Burton and Company received £721 net commission for their work as agents (A/7–4 December 1901). There are indications that Thornycroft's, having cut their original tender price to secure the order were later at least in danger of making a loss on the transaction.

As early as December 1899 S W Barnaby was considering the possibility of using four boilers in the new proposed 31kt boats, but initially turned the idea down because it would have meant lengthening the boats. On 20 April 1900[29] Thornycroft's wrote to the Japanese Navy's Inspector General (Admiral Kamimura) offering designs HO 9964 A and B for an improved 31kt destroyer (210ft oa × 20ft 4in + 7ft 7in). Larger engines and boilers than those fitted in the Japanese 30kt vessels were proposed but the arrangement of armament would be the same as in these earlier destroyers. There would be slightly more accommodation for the sixty officers and men proposed. Three boilers of the *Daring* type would discharge their smoke from two funnels: 'This better arrangement forms an important feature of our torpedo boat destroyers as it is difficult to distinguish than from torpedo boats at a distance – a condition which was considered indispensable by the British Admiralty in the earliest boats, which condition, however, had to be relaxed on account of the different types of boiler used by other builders.' The beam was greater than the earlier Japanese destroyers, ensuring sufficient stiffness for stability whilst decreasing the period of rolling. One destroyer to this design would cost £56,000, two £55,500 each and four £55,000 each.

On 25 May 1900 another letter to the same officer referred to the conditions handed to the firm by Captain Takagi and Lieutenant Yamamoto, and this would mean that a larger vessel would be necessary than tendered for in the previous letter, and as new patterns and plans would therefore be needed so it would not be possible to deliver within the time asked for, which was fifteen months, as this time was supposed to be strictly adhered to; they therefore proposed a modified *Albatross,* for which the machinery drawings and patterns were ready, so the delivery date could be met. She would carry a 40- to 50-ton load, could be guaranteed for 31kts and would offer considerable advantages in price over the original *Albatross* and could be built for £64,000. This would offer the great advantages of 'larger capacity and seaworthiness, more powerful machinery and at the same time our guarantee of delivery in the time you specify'.

Another letter to Admiral Kamimura, written on 1 June 1900 stated that in order to meet the Japanese conditions a longer vessel would be required, the price being £57,250 if only one was ordered. Delivery would be in eighteen months but best endeavours would be used to deliver in a shorter time, if possible fifteen months. On 30 June 1900 Thornycroft's had just heard that the Japanese Government were probably going to order more than one destroyer, and as an inducement to order from them Thornycroft's produced new prices of £57,250 for one, £56,750 for each of two and £56,250 for each of three. A letter dated 24 August 1900 was sent to Constructor Commander Takagi stating that the firm 'do not see any way to guarantee more than 31kts speed, although we expect that the vessels will do considerably more . . . We would remind you that in all the boats built for you we have exceeded our speed by at least half a knot more than that guaranteed in our contract and we prefer not to depart from our practise, viz: that of always having a margin of speed in hand . . . we think fears of air pressure are groundless.' The firm was putting in four boilers instead of three and these of an improved type, – and it was to be expected that air pressure would be as low as that in other types of boiler. The firm was prepared to make a further reduction in price of £1000 per vessel if two were ordered.

There were problems during *Asashio*'s trials: she was hit by a barge while mooring; the fans failed, causing the loss of several trials; while a letter of 17 May 1902 notes that the engines of *Asashio* had been damaged in trials and new cylinders, etc were required. Earlier, on 31 January 1902 Thornycroft's had written to the Admiralty offering a place at the trials to an Admiralty observer (the Japanese had given permission) and pointing out the rapid building time of this new design.

These vessels were steamed out to Japan. *Magne* (378) was built to the same lines. Both were taken out of service in 1922 and scrapped in 1923.

Yard Number 378 *Magne?* – 1905

Torpedo boat destroyer for the Royal Swedish Navy, *Shirakumo* (356) type.
DIMENSIONS: 216ft 9in oa, 215ft 9in wl × 20ft 9in × 13ft 9in + 8ft 5in
GUNS: 5–57mm
TORPEDOES: 2–18in torpedo tubes
MACHINERY: 2 shafts, 4 water tube boilers
TRIAL: 375½ tons displ/30.58 kts/7659ihp/396.4rpm

There is a long history of preliminary negotiations to this vessel. On 16 January 1900 Thornycroft's wrote[30] to the Swedish Navy Board asking to be allowed to amend the tender S Barnaby had presented the previous September, offering a speed of 31kts with the smaller of the three designs submitted. Three months later the Swedes were sent details of the *Albatross* in the hope that they would be interested. Nothing came of this. On 30 July 1901[31] a letter to Beardmore (at that time were temporarily linked to Thornycroft's) stated that the firm had been asked to tender for alternative 30, 31 and 32kt destroyer designs. They had been asked to tender two years previously and Barnaby had presented the tender personally, giving him

Here we see *Decoy* as she was after several years of service in 1902. She is anchored with awnings spread amidships and aft, and her boat alongside. (National Maritime Museum, London: N1947)

the chance to find out from some friendly officers at the Admiralty the prices and particulars of tenders of some half-dozen other firms. On 19 August 1901[32] Thornycroft's offered the Swedes the following designs: 10830 – a 30kt vessel similar to those built for the British and Japanese Governments, 10822, a 31kt ship similar to those building for Japan, and 10831, similar to the *Albatross* but with larger boilers. The prices were to be £50,000; £52,000; or £66,000 (an alternative 32kt design costing £56,600 was also offered) respectively. These prices excluded armament, delivery would be in fifteen months except for the *Albatross* type, which would be ready in eighteen months. A telegram of 27 August 1901[33] told John I Thornycroft and the other directors that Barnaby had been unsuccessful, an offer of a £48,000 vessel from 'Poplar' (Yarrow) securing the order. Thornycroft's offer had been £52,250, which they felt unable to reduce. The *Mode* was therefore built by Yarrow.

Unfortunately the correspondence which actually resulted in an order a couple of years later does not seem to have survived, but it is clear that this time the firm offered the same types of design as before, this time successfully. Thornycroft's did not fit the armament, this being done in Sweden, where the destroyer was towed by the tug *Little Briton*. Regarded as a better sea-boat than Yarrow's *Mode*, subsequent Swedish-built destroyers owed much to *Magne*'s design.

Thornycroft's also designed the eight boats of the *Nembo* class built in Italy for that country's navy, and the six boats of the *Harusame* class for Japan.

Thornycroft destroyer designs – not built

Finally let us look at the destroyer designs which Thornycroft's offered to assorted customers, but never built. The listing is carried on to 1902, after which the majority of designs were for destroyers of the 'River' or subsequent types, rather than versions of the TBD:

HO.6237: Twin screw 'improved' torpedo boat destroyer. Appears to be Thornycroft's first destroyer design offered to a foreign customer (on 13 July 1893 to Italy and then on 18 July to the Brazilian Navy together with twin and single screw torpedo boats like those building for the RN). Dimensions: 185ft × 19ft + 6ft 9in, two 4 cylinder compound engines, three water tube boilers, two funnels, 27kts. Five 6pdr guns (four grouped forward, one on the conning tower aft), two torpedo tubes en echelon. Thornycroft's were prepared to alter the armament if requested.[34]

HO.6267: Twin screw 'sea-going torpedo boat', actually a torpedo boat destroyer. As HO 6237 except armed with one 12pdr and two 6pdrs, all forward. Offered to Brazil.[35]

HO.6283: 'High sea torpedo boats', actually torpedo boat destroyers. Tender to Brazil on 23 August 1893 for six for £216,000 (£36,000 each).

HO.6800: Destroyer for Brazil, offered 26 September 1894 via Bywater, Tanqueray & Phayre Ltd. for £70,000 complete (designs HO 6803, HO 6730, HO 6316, HO 4178, HO 3665 also offered at the same time). Dimensions 215ft × 21ft + 7ft. Armed with nine 2pdr (Vickers-Maxim 37mm) pom-poms of which five were supposed to 'fire ahead without mutual interference' (which is unlikely in view of blast effects) and two single 18in torpedo tubes. Three shafts and three triple expansion engines, four water tube boilers, 6600ihp, 30kts, two funnels.

On 12 October 1894 Runeberg was offered HO 6800, HO 6803 and HO 6739A. On 23 November 1894 HO 6800 was offered direct to the Russian Naval Attaché for £59,000. On 26th of the same month a letter to Runeberg pointed out that though Prince Oukhtonsky considered the price high as compared to Yarrow's boat: 'Mr Donaldson pointed out that ours was a larger and heavier vessel, and the machinery was of considerably greater power than the Yarrow vessel.'

On 20 February 1894 HO 6730, HO 6800 and HO 6803 were offered via Jones Burton & Co. to the Japanese Navy.

HO.6803: Destroyer for Brazil (see HO.6800) for £48,000. Dimensions 200ft × 19ft × 7ft. One 12pdr and five 6pdrs given, but crossed out, and replaced by seven 2pdr pom-poms (37mm), two single 18in torpedo tubes. Two triple expansion engines, three water tube boilers, two funnels, 4400ihp, 27kts. Speed to be made on three-hour trial carrying 40 ton load.

HO.6959: Engine and boiler arrangements for a torpedo cruiser. On 5 March 1895 offered to Captain Horn, Royal Norwegian Navy, in answer to his advertisement, for £32,500. The ship was to be of 275 tons displacement, and to carry 22 tons of armament, 50 tons of coal, and 13 tons of crew, provisions and effects.

HO.7007: Destroyer for Spain. Dimensions 212ft × 19ft 6in + 7ft, 28 kts. Two 350mm torpedo tubes, Five 50mm or four 75mm guns.

HO.7108: Destroyer. On 29 May 1895 four offered to the Chilean Naval Commission, then in Paris, for £58,150 each (= £51,500 + £5150 for the guns + £1150 for the torpedoes) delivery could be in 18,19, 20 and 21 months, owing to present Admiralty contracts this could not be faster. Penalty of £200 per month for late delivery. Displacement about 270 tons, eleven watertight compartments, 30kts. In a second letter on these (1 June 1895), an alternative 28kt design was offered for £39,000 each excluding armament.

HO.7292: Destroyer. For Argentina. Dimensions 217ft × 22ft + 8ft, 26kts. One 12(?)pdr, four 6pdr, one bow torpedo tube, two deck tubes. Twin shafts.

HO.7344; Destroyer for Spain. Dimensions 200ft × 19ft + 6ft 8in, 28kts.

Yarrow

Alfred Fernandez Yarrow began building light, fast steam launches of steel at Poplar on the Thames in the 1860s at much the same time as his great rival, John Isaac Thornycroft, did at Chiswick, further up the Thames. These two young men between them developed the torpedo launch into the torpedo boat. The firms they founded as small boat-building operations still both exist in much altered form, and between them were the main British builders of first torpedo boats and then of destroyers. With the French firms of Le Normand and the German Schichau Company (both of later origin) they built, or at least originated the designs for, the vast majority of the world's torpedo craft up to the early twentieth century. Even after that their role in the development of the destroyer worldwide was greater than that of any other firm. Above all, both firms played the major role in developing the first TBDs. The prototypes were their responsibility, and their suggestions and influence provided much of the impetus for the Admiralty's first venture in this field. Of the two, Yarrow's seem to have been the more successful commercially, building and designing more torpedo craft for export than their rivals. Their TBDs were built faster than the Chiswick firm's. However, it is probably true to say that Thornycroft's vessels were built to higher and more costly standards. It is probably true that (only in a relative sense) Yarrow's were more concerned with building down to a price, and Thornycroft's more with sheer quality and ingenuity, and that Yarrow's put an emphasis on speed, both in construction and on trial, whilst Thornycroft's emphasised strength and durability. Both firms were world-leaders in the business of building very fast, very light and very strong vessels. Both were the major players in developing another aspect of light, strong construction; the building of river gunboats. Both were marine engineers as well as boatbuilders. Both moved at much the same time from the Thames, Yarrow to the Clyde, Thornycroft to the Solent, both just after the beginning of the new century – the rising cost of labour in the London area bore the main responsibility for both moves. One is reminded more, in both cases, of the early history of aircraft manufacturers rather than that of other shipbuilders.

When the question of enlarging torpedo boats into torpedo boat destroyers became an issue because of the growing size and apparent effectiveness of the French torpedo flotilla, Thornycroft's and Yarrow's were both called into discussions by the Controller (then the redoubtable John Fisher) but they were both clearly much more than passive agents of that powerful personality's will. Both had been suggesting enlarged versions of their torpedo boat designs as 'catchers' for some time, both appear to have made major contributions to the 1892 discussions, and the general concept of the TBD was clearly an enlargement of the torpedo boat designs that both had been building for some time. It was also their hard-won experience in building vessels of this kind which was transmitted to the other builders who became involved in TBD construction, causing a quarrel which, together with success in the export field (the relative importance of these two influences on Yarrow's policy is difficult to make out), helped keep Yarrow from building more destroyers for the Royal Navy for most of a decade.

26-knotters, 1892-1893 Programme

Locomotive boiler version – prototype.
ORDERED: 2 July 1892 for delivery 2 December 1892.

	Yard No.	Laid down	Launched	Completed
Havock	?	1.7.1892	12.8.1893	Jan 1894

Water tube boiler version.
ORDERED: 2 July 1892 for delivery 2 December 1892.

	Yard No.	Laid down	Launched	Completed
Hornet	?	1.7.1892	3.12.1893	July 1894

DIMENSIONS: 185ft oa, 180ft bp × 18ft 6in × 11ft + 7ft 6in
DISPLACEMENT: 240 tons light, 275 tons full load
MACHINERY: 2 shafts 18in.26in.39½in × 18in, 2 locomotive boilers, 180lbs (*Havock*), 8 Yarrow water tube boilers, 175lbs (*Hornet*)
COAL: 47 tons
FIRST COSTS: £36,526 and £36,112

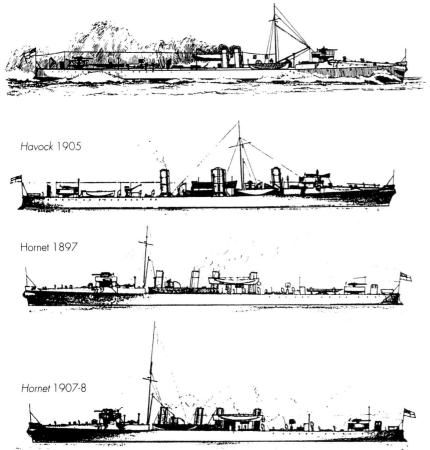

Havock 1894

Havock 1905

Hornet 1897

Hornet 1907-8

Yarrow's initial 1892 design[36] was of the torpedo boat type, fitted with conning tower forward and deck houses, with a breakwater in the place of the usual turtle back. It had three funnels and a signal mast. Accommodation was provided for thirty-three or thirty-four officers and men. Dimensions were 175ft × 18ft and displacement was 200 tons. With 3200ihp Yarrow's guaranteed to beat the best results attained by the latest French Normand boats, which were expected to attain 27kts. Many details were not included: scantlings, for example, were not listed but only said to be proportional to those for last six TBs built for the Royal Navy. Yarrow's asked to have a free hand in the design especially as regarded machinery and pointed out that the price for the earlier example of such a boat must of necessity be high owing to the need of superior workmanship and the necessity for making experiments; fifteen to sixteen months would be required for completion. The tender also provided for alternatives with two locomotive or eight [misreading for three?] 'tubulous' [water-tube] boilers, but the company would not build a boat with loco boilers unless others were ordered with tubulous boilers. This original design would alter somewhat before an order was placed.

In May 1892 the Admiralty decided that both Thornycroft and Yarrow were to be informed that their designs were in the main considered satisfactory, and that they should be asked to quote for one or two boats. Yarrow were also be asked to tender for a 'tubulous' boiler for second boat and to state speed.

There were six points raised in the initial comments on Yarrow's design.[37] These included the fact that a specification in detail should be submitted, that the lower deck forward should be made watertight (and plated over). Galvanised wire netting panels were to be fitted to the guard rails. All bottom and deck plating was to be galvanised. The after steering wheel should be in the conning tower, with both wheels arranged to work from outside the tower: 'It seems an open question as to whether Yarrow's patent system of reducing vibration is included in tender or not.'

A separate description[38] of the Yarrow tender runs as follows: '. . . Freeboard not shown. Estimates speed of 27kts to require 3200ihp and states with tubular boilers that they expect 3600ihp. They consider that with loco boilers there is a reasonable prospect of obtaining 27kts but suggest that the penalty should only come in force if the speed falls below 26kts. Dimensions: 180ft × 18ft 6in with 220 tons deadweight . . . Stability not given but presumably complies with conditions . . . Scantlings: require careful consideration, proposes making drawings proportional to the last TBs built for the Royal Navy, detail specification being forwarded. Outfit: not mentioned but presumably conforms. Remarks: ask to have a free hand in the design as they did in the *Herald* and *Mosquito* [small prefabricated lake gunboats for Lake Malawi]. They do not offer to build one boat only with loco boilers. Submit to try two sister vessels, one with tubulous [water tube] and one with loco boilers. They believe the former will come out best on trial but that the latter will be preferred in actual service. Funnels may be arranged with a bend aft to avoid access to water. Suggest

The 'as built' plan of the first TBD, *Havock*. Her subsequent re-boilering altered her so much that a new 'as fitted' plan was drawn up to show her altered form, rather than having the alterations shown on the drawing shown here. The railway track connecting the forecastle with the rotating torpedo tubes aft was to enable torpedoes to be transported on a small trolley. The reindeer hair boat is stowed upside down on the centre line, whilst the larger gig is on davits to port of it. (National Maritime Museum, London: 60932)

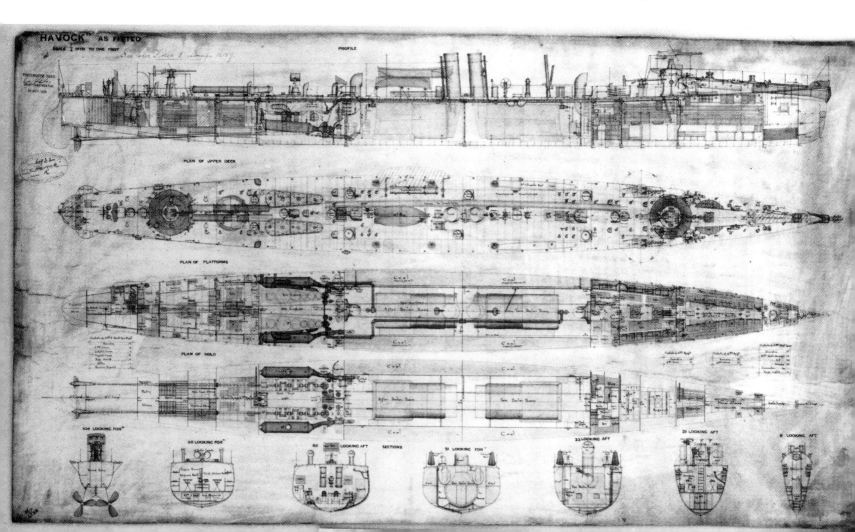

that the engines should be balanced on Yarrow patent plan to prevent vibration. Propose to confine galvanising of the hull to portion below load water line.'

On 27 June 1892 the Admiralty wrote to the firm[39] that: ' . . . they are disposed to place the construction of two of these vessels with you provided you agree to accept the sum of £66,948 for which another firm will construct, two similar vessels . . . ' The conditions to be as for Thornycroft (the 'other firm'), except one vessel was to have locomotive and the other one tubulous boilers. Delivery to be in four to five months for both. 'No objection to your proposal to use your patented system of counterbalancing engines to reduce vibration, or to use copper for boiler tubes and loco boiler firebox providing this is covered by price.'

Yarrow's then, characteristically, tried to 'push their luck' as is indicated by an Admiralty letter of 1 July indicating that the ' . . . Admiralty cannot enter into an undertaking to a preference being given to your firm in placing further orders for this type of vessel . . . should the vessels built by your firm prove relatively successful when compared with those built by other firms, that fact will of course be given due weight by their Lordships whenever further orders of the kind are being placed. Yarrow's letter of the 2nd accepted the order for 'fast seagoing torpedo boat catchers'.

Final modifications to the design were still to come, for on 14 September[40] Yarrow's submitted their revised specification: 'The hull to be specially designed with a view to secure a good combination of speed with manouevring

power, and the design of the vessels and their machinery to be generally similar to the 1st class TBs Nos. 82–87 . . . plating whenever possible to be hammered into shape cold. Plating of sheer strake amidship 8½lbs, tapering to 6 ½ under machinery and 4½ at ends. Frames 20in apart, plates vertical seams double riveted, lapped, horizontal single riveted. Floor plates 7lbs under machinery 5lbs fore-and aft. 10lbs bulkheads. Conning towers 20lbs.'

Though not built to the over-optimistic timetable hoped for when they were ordered, the two Yarrow prototype TBDs were completed well before their Thornycroft rivals, with the conventionally locomotive-boilered *Havock* in service well before her half-sister. Both were successful in proving the concept of evolving a destroyer from an enlarged version of a standard torpedo boat. On her full power trial *Havock* 'behaved well'[41] whilst *Hornet*'s preliminary trial produced the following note: 'Vibration slight at all speeds . . . steers readily and well and heels but very little in turning.'[42] However her consumption trial was not a very satisfactory one[43] 'as regards management and the results compare unfavourably with . . . *Havock*'. It was suggested that the firm should be asked to run another, but this was not approved because it would have caused delay in delivery.

There was little difference between the two TBDs except for the obvious fact that the *Havock*'s two locomotive boilers were placed end-to-end giving her two closely-spaced funnels, whilst *Hornet* with water tube boilers had four funnels with the middle pair closer to each other than to the fore and aft funnels. In 1899-1900 *Havock* was

Profile deck and sections plan of the first water tube-boilered TBD, Yarrow's *Hornet*, with her four funnels. The plan shows her as built and as altered in 1905 and then again in 1906. (National Maritime Museum, London: 92674)

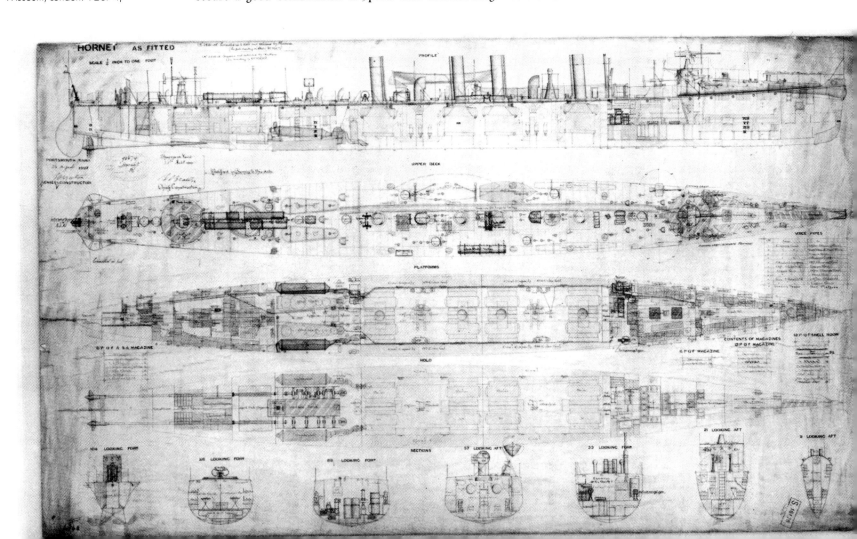

HORNET AS FITTED

reboilered by Hawthorn Leslie with water tube boilers, which left her with what by then was a standard three-funnelled layout for TBDs, with the middle funnel thicker than the other two, and leaving the mast between number one and number two funnels.

Havock served entirely around the British Isles. She was sold on 14 May 1912. *Hornet* was briefly in the Mediterranean, in 1900, but before and after served in home waters. She was sold on 12 October 1909 to the London Ship Breaking Co.

27-knotters, 1893-1894 Programme

ORDERED: 12 October 1893 for delivery 12 August 1894, 12 October 1894 and 12 December 1894.

	Yard No.	Laid down	Launched	Completed
Charger	991	Nov 1893	15.9.1894	Jan 1896
Dasher	992	Dec 1893	28.11.1894	Mar 1896
Hasty	993	Dec 1893	16.6.1894	May 1896

DIMENSIONS: 195ft oa, 190ft 8in bp × 18ft 6in × 11ft 3in + 7ft 3in
DISPLACEMENT: 255 tons light, 295 tons full load
MACHINERY: 2 shafts 18in.26in.39½in × 18in, 2 locomotive boilers, 180lbs
FIRST COSTS: £41,133, £40,890 and £41,141

The success of the prototypes meant that Yarrow's were rapidly given an order for three of the first 27-knotters. A significant addition was made to the letter inviting a tender, however, which would cause a great deal of trouble between the firm and the Admiralty.[44] 'Their Lordships, while recognising the good work done by your firm in the construction of torpedo vessels, consider it desirable to encourage other firms in undertaking work of this class. It must be understood, therefore, that [the Admiralty] consider themselves entitled to make use of information in their possession respecting the TBD type as may appear necessary.' In their design for this tender 24 tons extra load reduced the top speed by a knot (the comparable figure for the Thornycroft design was 27kts).[45] The price for three would be £108,600.[46] Hollow shafting as specified to be fitted, heating surface per ihp to be not less than in *Havock*, whether feed heaters fitted or not. Power of engines to be indicated by the Admiralty on the trials. Boats to be fitted with loco boilers with copper fireboxes and tubes. Delivery ten months approximately, twelve months and fourteen months. On 25 October 1893 they were asked to reconsider their prices for auxiliary machinery, and the steering engines were changed to ones of Yarrow's own design.

These vessels were basically a revision of the *Havock* design with twin deck torpedo tubes instead of the bow tube of their predecessor, but with the same closely-spaced twin-funnel arrangement. However the rapid improvement of water-tube boilers made the locomotive boiler arrangement an undesirably obsolete feature by the time these ships were completing and they were very

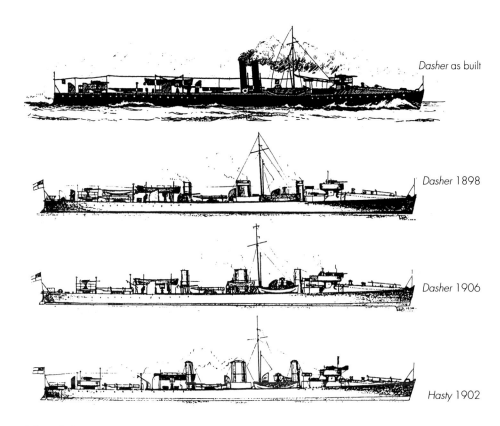

Dasher as built

Dasher 1898

Dasher 1906

Hasty 1902

rapidly reboilered, adopting the three-funnelled arrangement of the majority of the other 27-knotters. Earle's refitted and reboilered all three in 1899-1900.

All three served throughout in home waters and were sold at much the same time, *Charger* to Ward on 14 May 1912 and broken up at Silvertown. *Dasher* was sold the same day but to King and Sons, whilst *Hasty* was sold on 9 July 1912 to Cox, Falmouth.

30-knotter designs, 1894-1895 Programme

Yarrow's were asked to tender on 14 August 1894 for one, two or three TBDs 'generally similar in type to those now building by you for the Admiralty, but shall have a speed of 30 knots per hour.'[47] However:[48] 'It will be seen from the papers that Mr Yarrow considers he has a grievance against the Admiralty in regard to the adoption of portions of his designs by rival shipbuilders, but as will be seen by the papers referred to he has no real ground of complaint except that of the monopolist.' The firm was apparently particularly annoyed that details of their anti-vibration system had been passed on (information from D K Brown). However, because 'Yarrow showed the most progressive spirit' it was felt that they should be invited to tender for the construction of two or three TBDs of 30kts speed.

On 14 November 1894 Yarrow submitted their designs numbers 1, 2, 3 and 3*.[49] Although probably a speed of 30kts might be obtained on 280–300 tons, 'we are of opinion, to be safe in guaranteeing the speed a greater displacement will be necessary' and so they submitted proposals for 350–400 ton vessels. Aluminium had only just been produced in commercial, albeit still very expensive, quantities, but Yarrow's could point to experience with aluminium in a torpedo boat built for France. In fact, the boat had been moored after delivery near a sewer outfall in conditions which caused very rapid electrolytic decay of her plating, and she became unfit for service in a very short time. However, they suggested the metal could be used for some parts of the hull and numerous fittings, and offered to make many of the internal fittings usually supplied by the Admiralty which they found unnecessarily heavy for this class of vessel. The company also pointed out that the speeds guaranteed included an ample margin, although the penalty for reduction of speed made it clearly advantageous to a contractor to promise speeds without such a margin and risk the comparatively small penalty for the sake of securing an order. They proposed to balance the machinery in accordance with their most recent practice. As regards speeds, they pointed out that the highest possible speed meant lighter and more costly materials and also a price which allowed for the introduction of every improvement available at the time. 'Should the vessels prove sufficiently successful and it be desired by the Authorities that the machinery designs be distributed as a guide to others, we would respectively [sic] submit that, prior to such being done, an equitable arrangement be made between the Admiralty and ourselves. The prices named are based on the estimated cost of *Havock* and *Hornet* and not on the price paid for those vessels which left us no profit, although we were the first to prove to the Admiralty that those speeds

could be obtained, involving large amount of study and costly experiments.'

The speeds given in the listing of designs which follow are for, respectively: hull built of ordinary steel/of higher class steel/of ordinary steel and aluminium/of higher class steel and aluminium:

Design (1). Twin screw, dimensions 200ft to 205ft × 19ft 6ft × 5ft 6in. Displacement 300 tons on trial speeds: 29/29¼/29½/29¾kts.
(2) Twin screw, dimensions 210ft to 215ft × 20ft 6in × 5ft 9in. Displacement 350 tons. 29¾/30/30¼/30½knots.
(3) Triple screw, dimensions 220ft to 225ft × 21ft 6in × 6ft. Displacement 400 tons. 30¼/30½/30¾/31kts.
(4) (Is this the original design 3*?) Twin screw as design (3).

Design (2) was the one for which weights were given. The high quality steel mentioned was 'Yolla metal'.[50] The DNC's view of these proposals was unfavourable: aluminium is subject to rapid corrosion under the action of sea water and could not be 'recommended for incorporation into any part of the hull structure exposed to the continued action of sea water or high temperatures combined with stress', and the ½kt advantage could not justify the risk. As regards the use 'Yolla Metal', its strength and

Hasty as built. As with the *Havock*, the subsequent reboilering of this ship and her two sisters was too major an alteration to be shown on the same 'as fitted' plan, so a new one had to be produced. (National Maritime Museum, London: 64328)

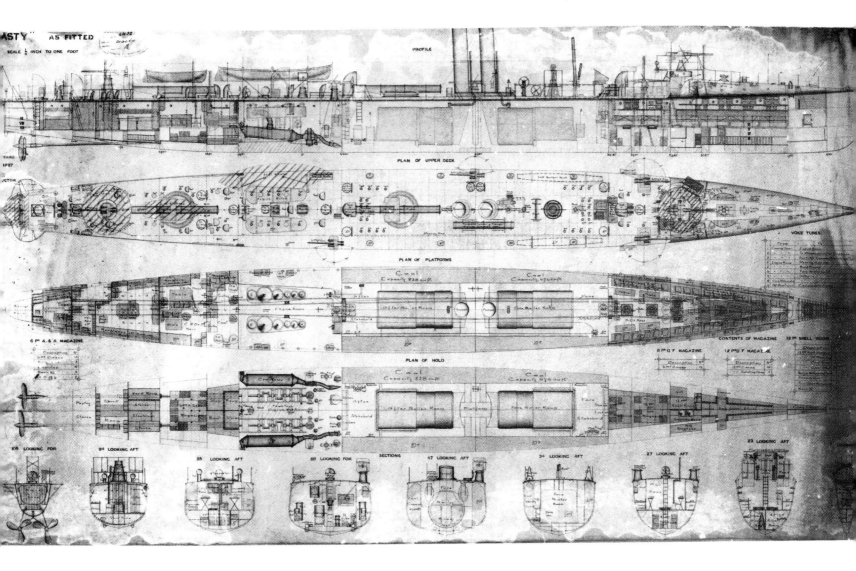

rigidity was an unknown factor and there were doubts about whether it could be worked while hot without great risk of the material cracking. It could be limited to such parts of the hull as require no 'working' either hot or cold, such as deck plating, stringers, bulkheads, sheer strakes, bottom plating above water etc, but the reduction of scantlings by from 10 to 15 per cent proposed by Yarrow could not be accepted.[51]

All firms had exceeded the maximum displacement laid down. Yarrow design (1) was 300 tons but only 29kts and designs (2) and (3) were too large. Their design of machinery amounted to that for an enlarged *Hornet* and neither engines nor boilers were satisfactory in their present form. Whilst, as to Yarrow's remark on possible use of his drawings: 'as the Admiralty have no intention of repeating this firm's designs, no arrangement with them is necessary.' It was considered rpm should not exceed 400. The desirability of having two low pressure cylinders should be pointed out to Yarrow. Their proposed boiler power considered small. 1.8 sq ft of heating surface per ihp should be allowed and the ease of replacement of boiler tubes was 'considered . . . of primary importance'. 'Not one of the designs can be recommended as it stands', and revised tenders should be submitted.

Yarrow's new design was for a vessel measuring 200ft × 19ft 6in with 5800ihp and displacement estimated at about 285 tons. They proposed using 'Yolla metal' but not to galvanise it as zinc did not adhere to it, which drew the comment that this was unacceptable if this was really so; therefore Yarrow would have to adopt mild steel of similar tensile strength. A few detail modifications in hull and machinery specifications were required. The after 6pdr position was too far aft and should exchange its position with that of the wheel.

The DNC reported to the Controller that while the new designs could be accepted as satisfactory with some minor detail modifications, the prices quoted by Laird were very reasonable but those quoted by the London firms were high. He suggested £4000 a boat reduction. Laird was offering £140,250 for three boats with delivery in fifteen months – but Yarrow's price was 7.5 per cent more, and the Admiralty wanted them to reduce the delivery time to the same as Laird's as well as cutting the price.

However, this did not result in an order because 'Yarrow declined the price offered by the Admiralty'.[52] The next invitation to tender, in October 1895, was declined by the firm on the ground that foreign contracts would keep them fully occupied for the next twelve months. In July 1898 the DNC, listing the firms that had built successful 30-knotters noted[53] that: 'Yarrow's have also built successful vessels of about this speed for foreign navies and may therefore be added to the list'. They were sent an invitation to tender on 5 October 1898 which included the following: 'Your particular attention is called to the very

Dasher early in her career, at Portsmouth in 1895, when still fitted with locomotive boilers. The lack of a bow tube and the higher funnels distinguish her from *Havock*. The funnels of a couple of cruisers can be seen over her bow. An awning is rigged over the sided 6pdrs and the space between them. (National Maritime Museum, London: B6691)

considerable changes which have been made in this class of vessel since the building by you of HMS *Charger*, *Dasher* and *Hasty* . . . if desired, every facility will be granted you before tendering to examine TBDs of 30kts speed.' In fact the firm would not to fulfil another order for a British warship until they built three 'River' class destroyers (*Ribble*, *Teviot* and *Usk*) as part of the 1901-1902 Programme.

Yarrow destroyers for abroad

This firm was the most consistently successful builder and designer of destroyers and torpedo boats for other navies, both at this time and in the inter-war period. In 1894 they laid down the *Sokol* (or *Pruitki*) for Russia. Completed the next year she was then used as the basis of a large class of Russian-built near-copies. Some years later the twenty-two vessels of the *Boiki* class were also built in Russia to a Yarrow design. Japan had the six vessels of the *Ikazuki* class and the two of the *Akatsuki* class built by Yarrow (thereby ordering the same number of vessels in the same pattern as they did from Thornycroft's). Like their great rivals higher up the Thames Yarrow also built one destroyer for Sweden (*Mode*). They designed one destroyer for Portugal, and built a class of four boats (*Corrientes* class) for Argentina.

Laird

The Birkenhead firm of Laird – soon to be taken over by the steel firm of Cammell's and to be called Cammell-Laird – was one of the pioneers of iron shipbuilding. It remained one of the largest and best-known firms, building liners and large warships, but also smaller, faster vessels. These included torpedo vessels such as the pioneer torpedo gunboat *Rattlesnake* for the Royal Navy, and others for Chile and Argentina. In 1892 the firm was commencing its first torpedo boat (*TB 97*) for the Royal Navy. Laird's were to build numbers of all three main types of TBD, plus one high-speed 'Special'.

26-knotter design, 1892-1893 Programme

Early in 1892 Laird's submitted an unsuccessful design for a TBD.[54] This was of the torpedo boat type with a turtle back, two conning towers, and two funnels (unlike the TBDs which followed from Laird's, all of which were four-funnelled). Dimensions were 175ft × 17¼ft + 6ft mean draft with 185 tons displacement. 2700ihp was to give 26½kts whilst the 30-ton load would include 12 tons of coal which was expected to give a 700-nautical mile range of action. Armament was to consist of two 6pdr guns with 100 rounds per gun, plus one fixed bow torpedo tube and two revolving deck tubes with two 18in torpedoes per tube (making a lighter gun armament and a heavier torpedo one than for most of the other designs submitted at this time). No specification was furnished for

this design and neither premium nor penalty were asked for. It rather sounds as if Laird's had put rather more effort into their larger design – for which details do not survive.

26-knotters, 1892-1893 Programme

ORDERED: 6 January 1893 for delivery 21 February 1894 and 6 April 1894 respectively.

	Yard No.	Laid down	Launched	Completed
Ferret	596	1.7.1893	9.12.1893	Mar 1895
Lynx	597	1.7.1893	24.1.1894	Aug 1895

DIMENSIONS: 199ft oa, 195ft bp × 19ft 8in × 11ft 6in + 9ft
DISPLACEMENT: 280 tons (Navy List)
MACHINERY: 2 shafts, 19in.29in.43in × 18in, 4 Normand boilers, 175lbs, 4475ihp
FIRST COSTS: £36,168 and £36,463

Initially only the Thornycroft and Yarrow designs were accepted, but of the remainder Laird's seemed to be one of the most promising, and was to be developed into a form which finally won Admiralty approval and an order. It is not clear at what stages along the process of modifying the firms design that the following comments were made by the Admiralty: thirteen points in all were raised initially including the fact that the coal boxes alongside the engines were too narrow for use, the galley should be placed below (presumably it had been sited on deck), the conning tower should be of ½in-thick plating and the sills of watertight doors should be well above the waterline.[55]

Later the DNC's department commented:[56] 'The design is generally satisfactory but if an order is placed the firm should be informed: (1) Steam ejectors [pumps] should be 30 tons capacity instead of 20 tons. (2) Auxiliary machinery should be placed in the engine room if possible. Arrangements should be provided for steering from outside as well as inside the conning towers. (4) Upholstery should be provided. (5) The question of stability should be further considered as it is questionable whether the metacentric height asked for would be obtained, judging from the figures forwarded.' The last comment proved prophetic: the Laird 26-knotters would be amongst the least stable of all the TBDs. It was probably at this stage, or not much later, that the following information was given. The dimensions were now 185ft × 18ft 6in + 5ft draft forward and 6ft aft, with 8ft over the screws and a displacement of 210 tons. Generally similar to the first class torpedo boats but with three pole masts. 3000ihp should give 27kts with a load of 30 tons: 'This trial is considered by them to be a very high performance with the load named.' Armament was 'as on sketch' (the Admiralty guidance sketch?), with spare torpedoes stowed under the turtle back forward. The metacentric height

Ferret in 1906, steaming past three battleships at Portland. By this time she has been fitted with a topmast. (National Maritime Museum, London: N2033)

Lynx 1897

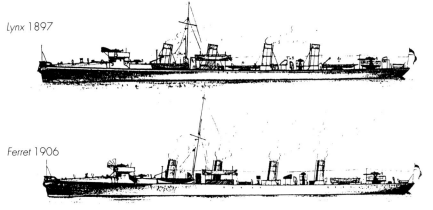

Ferret 1906

was to be 2ft. Steering was by a single balanced rudder. The engines were placed between the boilers: fore and aft sails were provided – these had been fitted to a good many torpedo boats and were useful both for steadying these craft in a seaway and providing extra propulsion when making passage or in an emergency.

By July 1892:[57] 'Messrs Laird's design for hull is generally satisfactory except so far as regards a few details which would not affect the question of cost &c, . . . The question of stability will require further investigation by the firm, but no difficulty is anticipated.' For machinery three designs were submitted: one with water tube boilers of Normand design to be manufactured by themselves; the second design with a Thornycroft boiler, and the third with two loco dry bottom boilers similar to that accepted from Yarrow. The second looked most promising, but since they already had boats boilered on this plan by Thornycroft, the first was proposed for any Laird order, as it would provide experience with another type of tubulous boiler, but it should only be accepted on the conditions that the heating surface should not be less than 2¼ sq ft per ihp.

The letter (dated 29 July 1892)[58] which probably resulted from the above comments asked them for further details of the alternative boiler arrangements. The foremost 6pdrs were to be carried in the alternative positions shown on the sketch. The question of stability should be further gone into as the metacentric height was unlikely, judging from the specification figures. On 17 August the amended design was generally approved, but the tender was considered high and the firm was asked to accept a price for two vessels of £66,948 'as has been accepted by two other firms of high standing and large experience in this class of work.'

It was not until January of the next year that the order for two TBDs with Normand-type boilers was placed[59] – at the figure mentioned above. There was a £250 penalty for every ¼kt or fraction thereof between 27 and 26kts, £500 for each ¼kt below 26kts, and rejection below 25kts. Delivery was to be in thirteen and a half and fifteen months, with a penalty of £15 per day late. There was no objection to the use of galvanised steel tubes instead of copper ones in the boilers; and there was a twelve months' guarantee for the main and auxiliary machinery. Modifications to the tender included separate magazines for the 12pdr and 6pdr ammunition forward, the 12pdr to be mounted on a pedestal and not a holding-down ring. The 6pdrs were to be moved further forward and a breakwater to be run along the sides to cover them. Alternative positions for the 6pdr guns were to be reserved amidships. The conning tower aft was to be of ½in side plates. Lockers and hanging berths were required for the men. A seamen's 'head' and urinal with flushing arrangements was to be provided on deck abaft the forward conning tower and a small signal yard fitted. A separate cabin was not required for the commanding officer, and the space freed should be fitted up for bread and provisions. It was desirable to increase the size of the rudder whilst watertight doors and openings in bulkheads were to be avoided

as much as possible, Frame spacing should not exceed 20ft.

At the end of August 1894 *Lynx* ran her full power trial, making over 27kts, but:[60] 'Steering astern, as with *Ferret*, very unsatisfactory (considered as of great importance in this class of vessel) . . .', the question being raised with Laird's resulted in the reply that they were trying a new rudder to give better control.

Ferret spent her life in home waters. In 1908 she was laid up and selected for experiments with shrapnel shells. In 1910 she was dismantled at Chatham, then her hulk was sunk the next year as a target. *Lynx* also served throughout in home waters. In 1902 she was refitting with her original builders. She was sold on 10 April 1912 to Ward, Preston.

27-knotters, 1893-1894 Programme

ORDERED: 7 February 1894 all for delivery by 31 March 1895.

	Yard No.	Laid down	Launched	Completed
Banshee	598	1.3.1894	17.11.1894	Jul 1895
Contest	599	1.3.1894	1.12.1894	Jul 1895
Dragon	600	1.3.1894	15.12.1894	Jun 1895

DIMENSIONS: 213ft oa, 208ft bp × 19ft 3in ext/19ft 3in mld × 12ft 3in + 9ft 6in

DISPLACEMENT: 290 tons light, 345 tons full load

MACHINERY: 2 shafts, 19in.29in.43in × 18in, 4 Normand boilers, 200lbs, 4400ihp

FIRST COSTS: £38,069, £38,058 and £38,093

Contest shown at sea in 1898. Note the as yet unraised funnels, the light colour of the turtleback and the lack of extension to the 12pdr platform, both indicating a date in the first decade of her service, whilst the mast between the first and second funnels combined with the straight bow, uncluttered by a bow tube, make it clear she is a 27-knotter. (National Maritime Museum, London: N2030)

Contest 1899

Banshee 1906

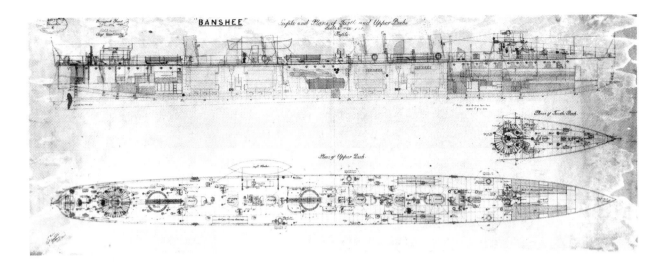

Banshee as built – notice how Laird's place the engines between the two sets of boilers. (National Maritime Museum, London: 60677)

On 2 July 1893,[61] when the question of ordering 27-knotters was first being mooted there was reluctance to entrust more to that builder: 'Pending trial of vessels now building by Laird, we submit not to place further orders with that firm, the class of work being novel to them . . .' However, by early the next year the Admiralty was clearly happier about the firm's capabilities and ordered three vessels to a modified design. There were only a few alterations needed:[62] the searchlight would foul the forward torpedo tube at one part of the latter's training and one or the other should be moved slightly. The torpedo davits shown forward were not required. The arrangements for the accommodation of the officers aft would be subject to later modifications. The scantlings were generally the same as *Ferret*'s but, in view of the increased length, might be increased amidships. A girder was to be worked under the upper deck on each side throughout the length of the engine and boiler rooms. The 12pdr was to be mounted on a pedestal, not a holding-down ring. The amount of heating surface was to be 2¼ sq ft in the boilers pending the completion of the trials of *Ferret* when it would be decided whether a reduction could be permitted.

These vessels all 'behaved well in all respects on trial'. On *Dragon*'s trial there was: 'Very little flame from funnel tops, and only on opening hatches for men to and froing from stokehold.'[63] The funnels of this group had all been

raised by 1903. *Banshee* went out to the Mediterranean in 1896 and remained there until returning home in 1911 to be sold on 10 April 1912 to Ward, Briton Ferry. *Contest* remained at home for all her service life. On 11 July 1911 she was sold to Ward, Preston. *Dragon*, like *Banshee*, went to the Mediterranean until returning home in 1911, and then was sold on 9 July 1912 to the West of Scotland Ship Breaking Co.

30-knotters, 1894-1895 Programme

ORDERED: ? for delivery ?.

	Yard No.	Laid down	Launched	Completed
Quail	606	28.5.1895	24.9.1895	Jun 1897
Sparrowhawk	607	30.5.1895	8.10.1895	Jun 1897
Thrasher	608	30.5.1895	5.11.1895	Jun 1897
Virago	609	13.6.1895	19.11.1895	Jun 1897

DIMENSIONS: 218ft oa, 213ft bp × 21ft 6in × 12ft 9in + 9ft 6in
DISPLACEMENT: 355 tons light, 415 tons full load
MACHINERY: 2 shafts, 21in.32½in.48in × 18in, 4 Normand boilers, 220lbs, 6300ihp
FIRST COSTS: £49,847, £49,909, £49,782 and £49,884

The original proposal was to ask Laird to tender for only one of the pioneer 30-knotters, but presumably the speed and efficiency with which their first TBDs were built influenced the Admiralty to modify their request to tender to a maximum of three TBDs when the letter was prepared in August 1894.[64] However when Birkenhead Iron Works (Laird) wrote[65] on 14 November 1894 to the Admiralty to tender for one vessel they found it necessary to exceed the specified displacement by 9 tons = 309 tons plus 8 tons margin: ' . . . to get a vessel sufficiently strong and with the machinery sufficiently accessible in all its parts to ensure good seagoing and seakeeping qualities which we hold to be of essential importance . . . [we] adhere to Normand type boilers which have given such excellent results' – the engines were to be similar to those of *Ferret* and *Lynx* except with two low pressure cylinders instead of one. The firm was in a position to commence work at once.

This was unsatisfactory, the firm having submitted

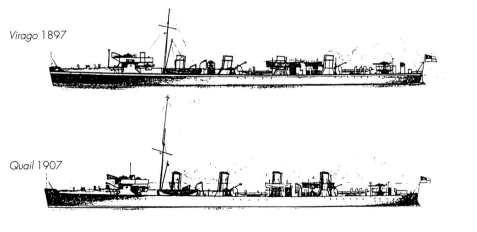

Virago 1897

Quail 1907

proposals for vessels which were practically repeats of *Banshee* with a speed of 28½kts when, in view of developments in other nations, especially France, it was not desirable to build less than 30-knotters. Dimensions of this design[66] were 214ft × 22ft with 309 tons displacement (this was considered an under-estimate). The sheer strake and upper deck stringer were to be of steel known as 'Yolla metal' (a very high tensile steel), but the Admiralty took a very wary (and sensible) approach to this metal. The design exceeded the maximum displacement laid down. The weights given 'appear based on the design and not the actual weights of *Ferret* - the latter would indicate a trial displacement of 330 tons . . . [the ihp appears] sufficient to reach 30kts even with this design . . . ' which was basically an enlarged *Banshee*. The accommodation looked inadequate. 'Not one of the designs can be recommended as it stands' though the Laird proposals could be revised to make them acceptable. The firm should be informed and asked to submit a revised tender. 'In view of the satisfactory completion by Laird of *Ferret* and *Lynx* submitted they should be put on same footing as other firms and asked to tender for two or three vessels.'

In April 1895[67] the DNC had looked at the new designs for 30-knotters which could be accepted as satisfactory with some minor detail modifications. The prices quoted by Laird were 'very reasonable', which, no doubt, taken with their good record of efficient building helped persuade the Admiralty to place the large order listed above. Originally Fisher proposed to give an order for three boats to the firm at their offer of £140,250 for the three, and with delivery in fifteen months. The design measured 207ft × 21ft 6in with 300 tons displacement and 6000ihp. The beam was considerably increased from that of similar vessels built by Laird previously, so there would be no doubt about the metacentric height being adequate. This time no proposals were made for the use of HT steel. The only objection to the hull was that accommodation aft was too restricted. Accommodation should not be worse than *Banshee*. If necessary the vessel should be lengthened by 6 to 7ft. Minor alterations to the engines were also needed.

Thrasher was involved in an accident soon after completion and was never quite as fast as her sisters after the necessary repairs. All had their funnels raised by 1903.

Quail went to the North American and West Indies Station soon after completion. She returned home in 1903, to go out to the Mediterranean in October 1904. She returned again in 1906. In 1908 her bows were damaged in a collision. *Sparrowhawk* went in 1897 to Esquimault (British Columbia) to join the local British squadron. She then went to China shortly before being lost in the mouth of the Yangtze on 17 June 1904. *Thrasher* was on the Mediterranean station from October 1902 to 1906, when she returned home. She was sold on 4 November 1919 to Fryer. *Virago* went to the Pacific soon after completion. Then, in 1903, she went to China, and stayed there till sold on 10 October 1919 for breaking up in China.

1895-1896 Programme

ORDERED: 23 December 1895 (first three), 9 January 1896 (last three).

	Yard No.	Laid down	Launched	Completed
Earnest	621	2.3.1896	7.11.1896	Nov 1897
Griffon	622	7.3.1896	21.11.1896	Nov 1897
Locust	623	20.4.1896	5.12.1896	Jul 1898
Panther	624	19.5.1896	21.1.1897	Jan 1898
Seal	625	17.6.1896	6.3.1897	May 1898
*Wolf**	626	12.11.1896	2.6.1897	Jul 1898

* = originally *Squirrel*, but name changed well before completion

DIMENSIONS ETC.: As *Quail* except + 9ft 9in

FIRST COSTS: £54,211, £52,300, £51,786, £51,88, £51,632 and £51,724

These seem to have been straightforward repeats of *Quail*. Launched with lower funnels, these were all raised by the early years of the new century.

Earnest sailed for the Mediterranean in September 1898 and returned home in 1906. She was sold on 7 January 1920 to Castle, Plymouth. *Griffon* also sailed for the Mediterranean in September 1898 and returned home in 1906 and was sold to Castle on the same date as her sister. *Locust* also went to the Mediterranean, but not till 1902, though she also returned in 1906. She was sold on 6 October 1919 to J Jackson. *Panther* similarly went to the

Lynx on trials, before being fitted with mast, boats and armament (though the cap for the fixed bow torpedo tube can be seen). The four funnels, standard on Laird-built TBDs, emphasise the length of the vessel given up to boilers. Besides the smoke from all four funnels, steam is being blown off from the second boiler, via the steam pipe in front of the second funnel. (National Maritime Museum, London: N2037)

Seal 1911

Wolf 1914

Mediterranean in 1902 and returned in 1906. She was sold on 7 June 1920 to J Kelly. *Seal* also was based in the Mediterranean from 1902 to 1906. She was sold on 17 March 1921 to Ward, Rainham. *Wolf* was used for the experiments on destroyer structure carried out by the Destroyer Committee investigating the strength of these craft after the loss of *Cobra*. Unlike her sisters she stayed at home throughout her career, and was sold on 1 July 1921 to S Castle, Plymouth.

1897-1898 Programme

ORDERED: ? 1897 for delivery ?.

	Yard No.	Laid down	Launched	Completed
Orwell	633	9.11.1897	29.9.1898	Jan 1900

DIMENSIONS ETC.: As *Quail* except 216ft 9in oa and 9ft 7in draft
FIRST COST: £55,533

In May 1897 discussions on the firms to order from for that year's programme had begun.[68] Laird's were definitely to be included. Their tender, when it arrived later in the year, was for a 'practical repeat of the [?successful?] class building by them with all improvements to date and with the introduction of HT steel in some portions of the structure.' No objections were seen to placing the order for one vessel with only some detail modifications.

Orwell had her funnels lengthened soon after comple-

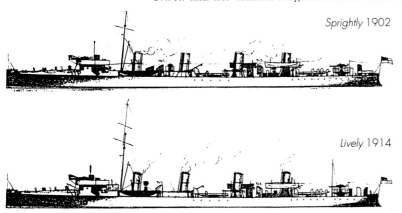

Sprightly 1902

Lively 1914

tion. She served in the Mediterranean from April 1900 to 1906, after which she was in home waters until sold on 1 July 1920 to Castle, Plymouth.

1899-1900 Programme

ORDERED: 30 March 1899 for delivery in 15 and 16 months.

	Yard No.	Laid down	Launched	Completed
Lively	639	20.6.1899	14.7.1900	Apr 1902
Sprightly	640	20.6.1899	25.8.1900	Mar 1902

DIMENSIONS: 219ft oa, 215ft bp × 21ft 9in × 12ft 3in + 8ft 7in
DISPLACEMENT: 385 tons light, 435 tons full load
MACHINERY: As *Quail* [?] except 6250ihp [?]
FIRST COSTS: £63,327 and £63,430

Laird's were one of the firms considered suitable for building more destroyers when the matter was discussed in October 1898, and the firm's 'mixed tender' of 25 January 1899 was accepted on 30 March. They had offered two TBDs for £59,053 each (hull £21,750, machinery £37,303). Some sources suggest (and the author followed them in his contribution on British torpedo vessels to *Conway's All the World's Fighting Ships 1860-1905*) that these vessels had already been ordered by the builders as private ventures, but there is no suggestion that this was so in the order documents, and it seems unlikely. Both were completed with lengthened funnels, unlike their predecessors.

Both *Lively* and *Sprightly* went out to the Mediterranean in November 1904 and returned in 1906 and both were sold on 1 July 1921 to S Castle, Plymouth.

TBDs built for foreign navies

Of all the larger shipbuilders who built TBDs Laird's were the firm who came closest to making a speciality of building the type, the nearest to Thornycroft's and Yarrow's in being considered a builder of torpedo craft. This was as true for foreign orders as it was for domestic ones. They built one TBD (*Som* or *Boevoi*) for Russia and two classes, one of four boats (*Capitan Orella* class) and one of two (*Capitan Merino Jarpa* class) for Chile.

Seal in 1914 with enlarged conning platform, with a searchlight platform above it, and what appears to be a semaphore mounted on it. This shot offers a clear view of the Berthon boat between the first two funnels, and the propeller guard aft also stands out. As it is after the 1913 redesignation her class letter (B) is painted up. (National Maritime Museum, London: N2054)

White

John Samuel White ('Sammy White's' as they were widely known) was the only shipbuilding firm building for the Admiralty which had successfully made the transition from wooden sailing warships to steel steam-powered ones. They had moved into building torpedo boats by way of turning their excellent sturdy medium-speed steam ships' boats into wooden Second Class torpedo boats. They had gone on to build a number of larger steam TBs including the *Swift – TB 81* – which was the largest TB of her day and an important step towards the TBD.

26-knotter design, 1892-1893 Programme

They were one of the firms to offer a design for the original 1892 invitation to tender for the 26-knotters. The features of their design were summarised as follows: '(1) TB type with Conning Tower and rudders on the turnabout system. [White's patented system with a keel sloping down for about two-thirds the length of the vessel and then abruptly 'cut up', with a rudder in front of the screw(s) as well as behind. This made for a very manoeuvrable craft which could spin round very quickly.] One signal mast. 200ft × 20ft, displacement not stated. (2) IHP not stated, speed not less 26kts. (3) 12 tons load and 15–20 tons coal, *ie* coal sufficient to steam 1000 knots [*ie* nautical miles] at 10kts speed. (4) Provided for fitting four torpedo tubes and four quick-firing 3 or 6pdrs. (5) Not stated. (6) 54 tons. (7) Frame, 2in × 1½in × ³⁄₁₆in . . . apart fore and aft 1½in × 1¼in × ³⁄₁₆in reverse bars 1-in × 1¼in × ³⁄₁₆in in the engine room floors, 10lb in engine room, 7½lbs elsewhere, plating ³⁄₁₆in amidships tapering at ends. Sheer strake and deck stringer ⁵⁄₁₆in amidships tapering at ends. deck (?) plating ³⁄₁₆in amidships tapering at ends. (8) List of sundries supplied, galley, stove, capstans, and three boats provided, anchor and fittings are shown on drawing but not mentioned on list. Armament and. fittings to be supplied by Admiralty. (9) No premium or penalty clauses.'

The DNC departmental view was that the 'design [was] generally satisfactory but accommodation will require revision, deck plating should be galvanised and steering wheels should work from outside as well as inside Conning Towers.'[69] Twelve points in all were raised of which the other most important one was that White's must submit distinct proposals from the firm of engineers they proposed to use,[70] who were Maudslay, Son & Field.

In July 1892 the firm submitted a revised and lengthened design: '(1) 200ft × 20ft, 260 tons; 20 tons carried on trial, freeboard about 5ft 3in. Generally similar to First Class torpedo boats. (2) 4500ihp, 27kts. (3) 30 tons. (4) As sketch. (5) Guaranteed metacentric height not less than 2ft with all weights on board. (6) Full scantlings given. (7) In agreement with conditions, candle lamps provided for. (8) Turnabout system of rudders.' White's design was generally satisfactory, but the revised, more powerful,

Maudslay machinery involved an extremely experimental form of boiler, so only an order for a single ship was recommended. White's had now increased length and proposed that speed for absolute rejection should be 24kts instead of 25kts.[71]

27-knotters, 1893-1894 Programme

ORDERED: 7 November 1893 for delivery by 31 March 1895.

	Yard No.	Laid down	Launched	Completed
Conflict	945	3.1.1894	13.12.1894	Jul 1899
Teazer	946	3.2.1894	9.2.1895	Mar 1899
Wizard	947	3.4.1894	27.2.1895	Jul 1899

DIMENSIONS: 205ft 6in oa, 200ft bp × 20ft 0 ¹¹⁄₁₆in ext/20ft mld × 11ft 4in + 8ft 3in
DISPLACEMENT: 320 tons light, 360 tons full load
MACHINERY: 2 shafts by Maudslay, 4 White boilers, 4500ihp
FIRST COSTS: £42,748, £42,932 and £42,722

However, nothing further happened until the next year, when White's were asked to tender for 27kt TBDs. They tendered for up to three TBDs with water tube boilers. An Admiralty letter was sent on 3 November 1893 and accepted by the builder on the 7th of that month, accepting the tender for three TBDs with Maudslay machinery for a total of £115,839, with the following provisos: it was considered that the deck and bottom plating could be reduced in scantling, but the lower plates of bulkheads were too light, as was also the watertight plating of the

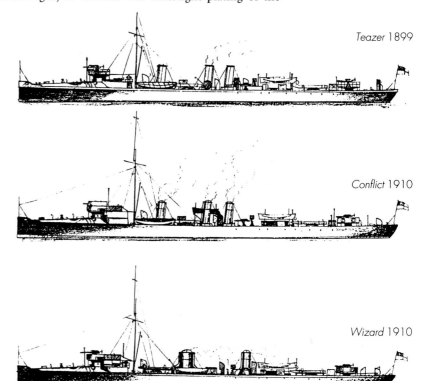

Teazer 1899

Conflict 1910

Wizard 1910

lower deck forward and over the magazine aft; double rivetting should be used for the lands of the sheer and keel plates and the bottom plating under the machinery. The boiler arrangement should be modified so that two single revolving torpedo tubes could be fitted. Modifications should be made to the machinery. The four cylinder type of triple expansion engine was preferred. 'Experience having shown that the ends of copper tubes when above water burn through quickly, those tubes in the tubulous boilers proposed having their ends above water level should be made of steel galvanised, further the arrangement of tubes must be considered with a view to the removal of deposit. of soot.' A two-year guarantee was required for the boiler. The third and last vessel was to be delivered before 31 March 1895.

White's boats, however, had difficulty making their contract speed, were delivered late, and were not well-regarded in service. A particularly unsatisfactory feature, at least of *Wizard*, was that the machinery, and therefore the propellers, turned in the opposite direction to the norm, making for erratic steering and alarm amongst flotilla mates and other vessels forced to keep close company. Lionel Dawson's *Flotillas* has an entertaining account of the preparation of fenders and booming-off spars whenever *Wizard* was seen to be getting under way. Inevitably White's were amongst the DNC's black list of firms not to be invited to tender for 30-knotters under the 1897-1898 programme.[72]

All three served in home waters throughout, except *Conflict* which was briefly in the Mediterranean between 1900 and 1901. *Conflict*'s funnels were raised in 1902. *Teazer* was refitted by White's in 1902, and *Wizard* in 1903-1904. In 1910 *Wizard* was rebuilt with only two funnels, the front pair being trunked into one another, which left a large gap between the mast and the funnel, in between which was the forward torpedo tube.

Conflict was sold on 20 May 1920 to Ward, Milford. *Teazer* was sold on 9 July 1912 to Cox of Falmouth, who later sold her to Cashmore of Newport. *Wizard* was sold on 20 May 1920 to Ward of Milford Haven.

In this photograph taken in 1905, at Dover, the three-funnelled TBD nearest the camera on the right is *Wizard*, with what looks like washing on her forestay (probably either canvas covers or hammocks), with a 30-knotter beyond. Behind her is the cruiser *Sapphire*. A 27-knotter lies astern and behind *Wizard*, and beyond her a 'River' class destroyer. (National Maritime Museum, London: N8714)

Conflict as built and as altered in 1905 and 1917 – notice the lowering of the after 6pdr and the removal of its platform done at the latter date to save weight so depth charges could be carried. (National Maritime Museum, London: 5715)

Thomson

The Clydebank yard of J & G Thomson was one of the more important Glasgow shipbuilders in the last quarter of the nineteenth century, though not yet in the prime place it was to achieve after changing its name when it was acquired by the Sheffield steel firm of John Brown. It was already, when asked to tender for TBDs for the Royal Navy, building transatlantic liners and cruisers for the navy, and had built an interesting torpedo vessel under the prophetic name of *Destructor* ('Destroyer') for Spain. Its first design was clearly a successor of the *Destructor*.

26-knotter design, 1892-1893 Programme

This had a sunken forecastle, one large funnel, two conning towers, one signal mast and was fitted with Thomson's own patent rudder. Dimensions were 175ft × 18ft 6in. It was to have a displacement of 225 tons at 5ft mean draft with a 30-ton load. The ihp was not stated, the speed was to be not less than 24kts. With a load of 20 tons it would also carry 10 tons of coal, the amount estimated for steaming 1000 'knots' (nautical miles) at a speed of 10kts. The armament was to consist of one fixed bow torpedo tube with two 14in torpedoes, the tube to be supplied by the Admiralty, plus two 6pdrs and two 3pdrs with 200 rounds per gun. The machinery height was guaranteed at not less than 2ft. The specification included 'complete accommodation including upholstery for officers and men' plus one 16ft lifeboat and one 16ft Berthon boat.[73] 'On trial the mast shall be unshipped.' It was arranged for one anchor and hawse pipe only. 'The specification is very complete' but did not include a search light. No premiums or penalties were asked for. The DNC's comment was that Thomson's should be told that the speed they quoted was not sufficient. Also the armament was not as powerful as that featured in the designs adopted.

27-knotters, 1893-1894 Programme

ORDERED: 3 November 1893 for delivery in 12, 14 and 16 months.

	Yard No.	Laid down	Launched	Completed
Rocket	269	14.2.1894	14.8.1894	Jul 1895
Shark	270	14.2.1894	22.9.1894	Jul 1895
Surly	271	14.2.1894	10.11.1894	Jul 1895

DIMENSIONS: 203ft 9in oa, 200ft bp × 19ft 6in × 13ft + 6ft 9in
DISPLACEMENT: 280 tons light, 325 tons full load
MACHINERY: 2 shafts 18½in. 26in. 40in. × 18in, 4 Normand boilers, 200lbs, 4100ihp
FIRST COSTS: £39,633, £39,502 and £39,656

The 27kt design produced the next year was totally different from the design described above, as it had three funnels and Normand boilers. Though the order date was given as 3 November 1893 the tender was not finally

accepted until the 7th.[74] As with all of the TBDs these were delivered some time after the Admiralty's somewhat optimistic target date. However, the Clydebank firm was well up amongst the fastest builders, the Admiralty considered their boat satisfactory and they were therefore invited to tender for 30-knotters.

Rocket is shown here flying what appears to be a large black (or possibly red) flag. This fine seagoing shot was taken about 1910. (National Maritime Museum, London: N20848)

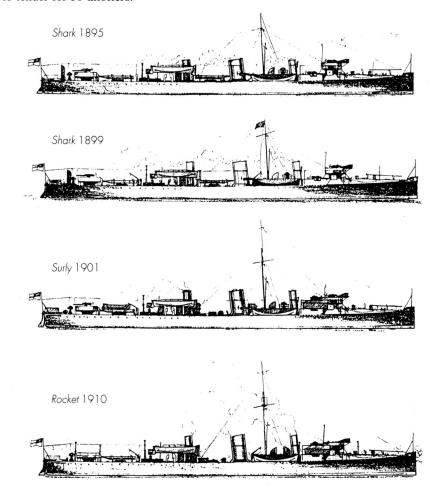

Shark 1895

Shark 1899

Surly 1901

Rocket 1910

Rocket went to Bermuda in 1897 and served on the North American and West Indies station until 1902 when she returned home. In 1910 she had her guns removed and was fitted for wireless experiments. *Shark* and *Surly* spent their service careers in home waters, the former having her funnels raised in 1895, the latter in either 1901 or 1902.

Rocket was sold on 10 April 1912. *Shark* was sold on 11 July 1911 to Ward, Preston. *Surly* was used for many of the early experiments with oil fuel, served during the 1914-1918 war and was not sold until 23 March 1920 to Ward, Milford Haven.

30-knotters, 1895-1896 Programme

ORDERED: ? for delivery ?.

	Yard No.	Laid down	Launched	Completed
Brazen	288	18.10.1895	3.7.1896	Jul 1900
Electra	289	18.10.1895	14.7.1896	Jul 1900
Recruit	290	18.10.1895	22.8.1896	Oct 1900
Vulture	291	26.11.1895	22.3.1898	May 1900

DIMENSIONS: 214ft oa, 210ft bp × 20ft × ? + 8ft 6in (*Electra* lengthened by 4ft after launching, *Recruit* altered during building to 218ft oa, 214ft bp and *Vulture* altered during building to 222ft 3in oa, 218ft bp)

DISPLACEMENT: 345 tons light, 385 tons full load [?] (*Recruit* and[?] *Vulture* 380 tons light, 425 tons full load [?])

MACHINERY: 2 shafts, 4 Normand boilers, 230lbs, 5800ihp

FIRST COSTS: £49,901, £50,008, £50,045 and £50,343

Vulture 1899

Recruit 1908

Kestrel 1918

These four vessels were amongst the first batch of TBDs ordered under the 1895-1896 programme. Thomson's took the same route as the other shipbuilders from whom 30-knotters were ordered and simply produced a somewhat enlarged version of their 27-knotter design with more power. However, in Thomson's case something went wrong as they 'have experienced difficulties of an unexpected character in obtaining the contract speed'. This explains why the lengths (and therefore both lines and tonnage) of the later members of the group were altered during building. In this context it is interesting that the last vessel of the group to be laid down and launched was the first to be completed, presumably because it was possible to make some alterations to *Vulture* before she had her acceptance trials.

All four spent their time in home waters. *Brazen* was sold on 4 January 1919 to J H Lee. *Electra* was sold on 29 April 1920 to the Barking Ship Breaking Co. *Recruit* was sunk on 1 May 1915 by a U-boat off the Galloper Lightship in the North Sea. *Vulture* was sold on 27 May 1919 to Hayes, Porthcawl.

1896-1897 Programme

ORDERED: ? for delivery ?.

	Yard No.	Laid down	Launched	Completed
Kestrel	298	2.9.1896	25.3.1898	Apr 1900

DIMENSIONS: 218ft bp × 20ft 8in ext/20ft 8in mld × 13ft 3in + 8ft 11in

DISPLACEMENT: 350 tons light, 395 tons full load

MACHINERY: 2 shafts, 4 Normand boilers, 230lbs, 5800ihp

COAL: 80 tons

FIRST COST: £56,208

Clearly, the comparative failure of the previous vessels had already become apparent by the time the *Kestrel* began building, which will explain why she was completed to a considerably modified design. Equally clearly the Admiralty continued to believe in Thomson's ability to build TBDs, as they were prepared to let Thomson's tender for both this programme and the next year's one.[75] The design offered in 1897 was described as follows, and was probably similar to that offered for *Kestrel*: '[It] is as far as regards hull a departure from *Brazen* class now building – and with which difficulties have been experienced in obtaining the contract speed which has not yet been realised – machinery essentially a repeat of the *Brazens*' – Dimensions considerably increased – some objectionable features re-appear . . . [particularly the excessive crowding of crews quarters forward] . . . ' *Kestrel*'s new design enabled her to pass her acceptance trials with comparative ease, and she was in service before any of the *Brazens*.

Kestrel served in home waters and was sold on 17 March 1901 to Ward, Rainham.

1897-1898 Programme design

The comments given in the preceding paragraph refer to this design, The tender was not accepted.

Purchased vessels building 'on spec' 1900

ORDERED (purchased) 31 May 1900 for delivery 16 May 1901,
    14 July 1901 and 31 August 1901.

	Yard No.	Laid down	Launched	Completed
Thorn	334	?	17.3.1900	Jun 1901
Tiger	335	?	19.5.1900	Jun 1901
Vigilant	336	?	16.8.1900	Jun 1901

DIMENSIONS: 222ft oa, 218ft oa × 20ft 6in × 13ft 3in + 8ft 11in
DISPLACEMENT: 380 tons light, 425 tons full load
MACHINERY: 2 shafts, 4 Normand boilers, 230lbs, 6400ihp
COAL: 86 tons
FIRST COSTS: £59,722, £60,008 and £59,703

These three vessels, already well forward on the stocks having been laid down 'on spec' by their builders were purchased by the Admiralty for: hull £19,500, machinery £36,228, auxiliaries £1272 = £57,000 each – guaranteed delivery as above. The purchase money was found under the 1899-1900 programme. They were very similar to *Kestrel*.

All three served entirely in home waters except for a brief visit by *Vigilant* to Gibraltar in 1913. *Tiger* sank in collision with the cruiser *Berwick* off St Catherines on 2 April 1908. *Thorn* was broken up in Portsmouth Dockyard in 1919. *Vigilant* was sold on 10 February 1920 to the South Alloa Ship Breaking Co.

TBDs built for foreign navies

Thomson's maintained their relationship with the Spanish navy in this period, building them the two boats of the *Furor* class and the four of the *Audaz* class – that navy's only destroyers at this stage.

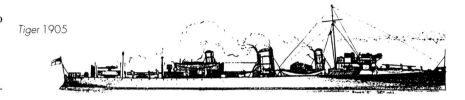

Tiger 1905

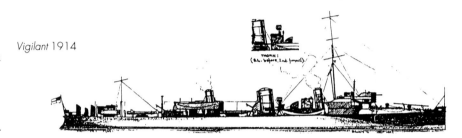

Vigilant 1914

Profile and upper deck plans of the Thomson 'stock' boat *Thorn*, showing her as built and as altered up to 1914. Note the small mast added aft, the enlarged bridge with searchlight platform added, etc. (National Maritime Museum, London: 14956)

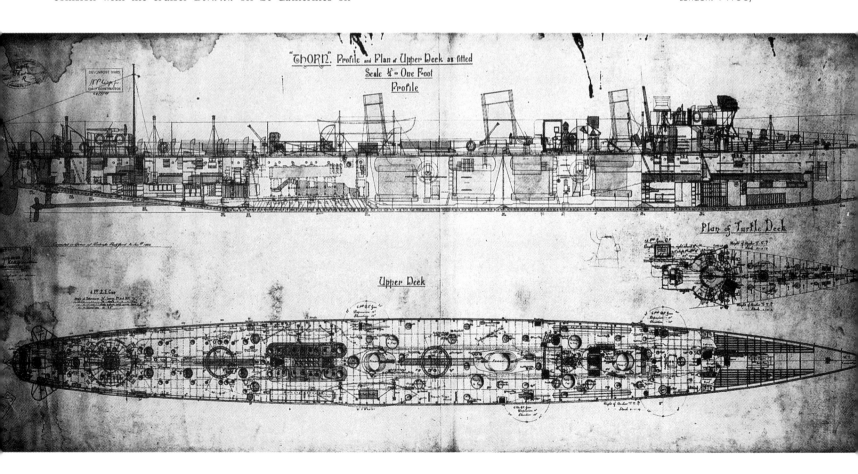

"Thorn". Profile and Plan of Upper Deck as fitted
Scale ¼" = One Foot
Profile

Plan of Turtle Deck

Upper Deck

Naval Construction and Armament Company (later Vickers), Barrow

The Barrow company was a fairly new, but ambitious, one. It had already built liners, cross-channel steamers and major warships by the time it was invited to tender for 27kt TBDs, and it was completing three torpedo gunboats for the Royal Navy. It was to go from strength to strength after being taken over as part of the conglomerate owned by the steel firm of Vickers.

27-knotters, 1893-1894 Programme

All ordered 8 December 1893 for delivery within 14 months.

	Yard No.	Laid down	Launched	Completed
Sturgeon.	233	1.3.1894	21.7.1894	Jan 1896
Starfish	234	22.3.1894	26.1.1895	Jan 1896
Skate	235	20.3.1894	13.3.1895	Jan 1896

DIMENSIONS: 194ft 6in oa, 190ft bp × 19ft × 12ft 5in + 7ft 7in
DISPLACEMENT: 300 tons light, 340 tons full load
MACHINERY: 2 shafts, 18in.27in.42in × 18in, 4 Blechnynden boilers, 4000ihp
FIRST COSTS: £39,075, £38,288 and £35,811

The Barrow company, shortly to be taken over as the shipbuilding part of the armament firm Vickers, was proposed on 2 July 1893 as one of the firms to tender for one or more 27-knotters.[76] Its original design was turned down on 7 November, but they were given fourteen days from that date to submit amendments.[77] Points to consider were: 'many of the details given in the specification are too elaborate. The specification should be revised on the lines of Torpedo Boat practice.' From experience it was doubtful if the ihp estimated was sufficient for 27kts with the machinery dimensions given and 100lbs steam pressure. More detailed information was needed on the water tube boiler proposed, especially the method of removing and renewing tubes. Airlocks for the boiler rooms were not required. Condenser tubes would have to be arranged to enable them to be withdrawn without removing parts of the machinery. The circulating inlet should be arranged so as to enable advantage to be taken of speed of vessel in assisting circulation. There was no objection under these conditions to reducing the diameter of the circulating pumps to 22in.

On 8 December the revised design was accepted for a price of £99,300 for three boats, but extra details were mentioned; the strengthening of the hull except of the plating to the turtle deck could be reduced somewhat, the arrangement of magazines, heads, bulkheads etc given in the guidance design should be adhered to. The fan cowl between the aftermost funnels should be clear of the sweep of the torpedo tubes, or at least made portable. Wire netting outer panels were to be fitted between the lower guard rail and the deck. A two-year guarantee of the boiler was required.

These were not amongst the best of their type. In 1898 a report[78] made it clear that they were the only ones to have a clearly identified structural weakness: 'The only part of the hull of which the weakness has been accountable for breakdowns in these vessels after delivery is the propeller bracket, and that only in the early 27kt vessels built at Barrow. The brackets in these vessels were of forged scrap iron.' It is not surprising that Skate was the first, and her sisters amongst the first, of this type of vessel to be sold off.

These destroyers had three funnels, the midships one being thicker than the other two. Unlike most of the other 27-knotters the mast was situated in front of the forefunnel. The forward boiler was of slightly smaller diameter than the others.

Skate served briefly (1900-1901) in the Mediterranean, at which stage her funnels were raised, otherwise, like her two sisters, she served entirely in home waters. In 1902 Starfish was experimentally fitted with a spar torpedo to investigate its potentialities as an anti-submarine weapon against the 'Holland' submarines which had just come

In this picture of *Skate* taken in June 1897 her Berthon boat has been hoisted out by the derrick, which is still rigged outboard, and is towing astern, whilst the whaler is only partially visible behind the stern. The 12pdr gun is trained to starboard, in front of it is the rectangular shape of the chart table. She is carrying her anchor berth number for the Diamond Jubilee Review. An awning is rigged aft. (National Maritime Museum, London: N1951)

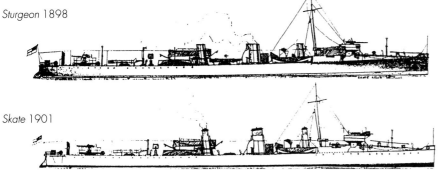

Sturgeon 1898

Skate 1901

into service with the Royal Navy. *Skate* was sold on 9 April 1907 to Cox, Falmouth. *Starfish* was sold on 15 May 1912 to Ward, Preston. *Sturgeon* was sold on 14 May 1912 to the Thames Ship Breaking Co.

30-knotters, 1895-1896 Programme

ORDERED: 23 December 1895 (first pair) for delivery ?. The second pair were ordered somewhat later.

	Yard No.	Laid down	Launched	Completed
Avon	249	17.2.1896	10.10.1896	Feb 1899
Bittern	250	18.2.1896	1.2.1897	Apr 1899
Otter	251	9.6.1896	23.11.1897	Mar 1900
Leopard	254	10.6.1896	20.3.1897	Jul 1899

DIMENSIONS: 214ft 3in oa, 210ft bp × 20ft × 12ft + 8ft 3in
DISPLACEMENT: 355 tons light, 405 tons full load (*Leopard* 350 tons light, 400 tons full load)
MACHINERY: 2 shafts, 20½in.31in.34in.34in × 18in, Thornycroft boilers, 220lbs, 6300ihp
COAL: 86 tons
FIRST COSTS: £52,905, £52,773, £54,501 and £54,276

In October 1895 the Barrow firm was noted as one which had completed at least one TBD satisfactorily and so was put forward to tender for 30-knotters.[79] As usual the design merely was a larger and more powerful version of the 27-knotter, and as with several other builders it proved to be difficult to coax it up to the required speed.

It is not clear from the surviving papers precisely how and why the second pair of Vickers vessels were ordered, and there is some suggestion that the *Leopard* was part of the next year's programme. However, this seems unlikely in view of her date of ordering, despite the fact that her tonnage was slightly less than the others and her yard number is not directly in sequence with them. It is likely that as the last one in line she was enough behind the others to benefit from the experience of the first to go on trial, and be modified accordingly. If this was so it would explain why she was then hurried through to completion ahead of *Otter*.

Avon served in home waters throughout her career as did *Bittern* and *Leopard*. *Otter* went out to China in 1900 and spent the rest of her time there. *Avon* was sold on 1 July 1920 to Castle, Plymouth. *Bittern* sank in the Channel on 4 April 1918 after colliding with SS *Kenilworth*. *Otter* was sold on 25 October 1916 at Hong Kong. *Leopard* was sold on 10 June 1919 to J Jackson.

1897-1898 Programme design

The DNC advised against asking the firm for a tender for this programme, presumably because their first 30-knotters had not yet attained this speed 'as they have had considerable difficulties in connection with the machinery which have prevented the advancement of the vessels . . . ' Vickers did propose a repeat of the *Avon* class with slight increase in dimensions and horsepower. By July 1898, however, Vickers' vessels had attained a 'satisfactory' speed and therefore were asked to tender for the next Programme.

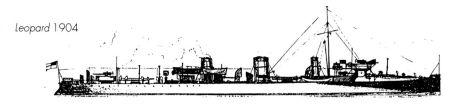

Leopard 1904

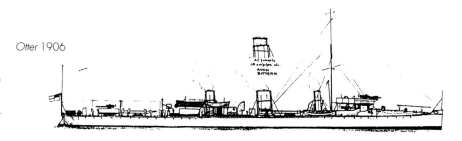

Otter 1906

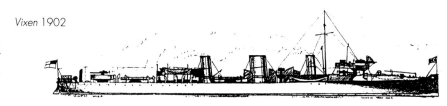

Vixen 1902

1899-1900 Programme

ORDERED: 30 March 1899 for delivery in 15 months.

	Yard No.	Laid down	Launched	Completed
Vixen	278	7.9.1899	29.3.1900	Mar 1902

DIMENSIONS, ETC.: As *Leopard*
DISPLACEMENT: As *Leopard*
MACHINERY: As *Leopard*
FIRST COST: £64,238

The original offer for this contract appears to have been turned down because it was Vickers' revised tender of 25 January 1899 which was accepted.[80] It was for £60,000 (£19,000 hull, £41,000 machinery) with modified Normand boilers instead of Thornycroft ones. The drawings were modified to move the forward torpedo tube from between numbers one and two funnels (where it had been in all her earlier sisters) to between number two and number three.

Vixen served in home waters throughout her career and was sold on 17 March 1921 to Ward, Grays.

Opposite above, Vixen as built and as modified to 1914. One of the more obvious modifications is the hood fitted over the chart table alongside the muzzle of the 12pdr gun. The shields of the guns are crossed out, indicating that they have been removed, though documentary evidence seems to show that they were merely stowed below rather than landed. (National Maritime Museum, London: 24436)

Opposite below, Avon photographed in 1906. She had already been fitted with a topmast and with the extended bridge. The odd platform mounted in front of the mast above that platform is the chart table moved from the front of the bridge. The Berthon boat (between the fore and middle funnels) has a weather cloth over it. (National Maritime Museum, London: N2086)

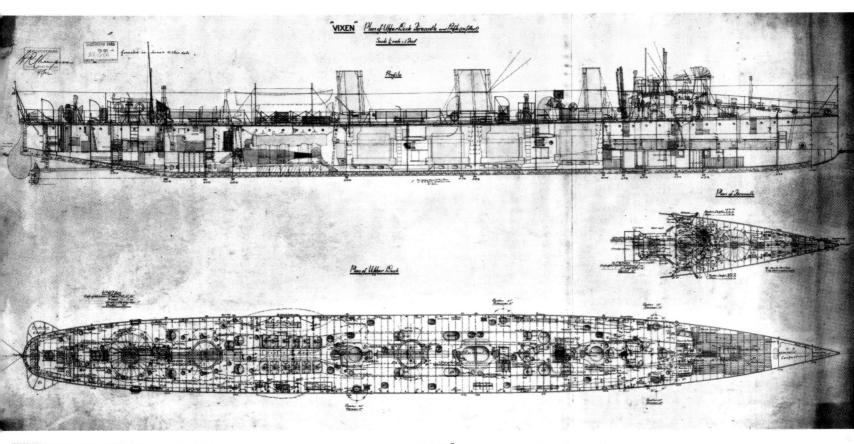

Earle

Earle's of Kingston upon Hull had been a yard of some importance, building ironclads, but by the 1890s the firm seems to have been in decline. Certainly its attempts at building TBDs, in particular to nurse them through their acceptance trials, appear to have played a major part in its decent into bankruptcy. It did, however, re-boiler Yarrow's 27-knotters.

27-knotters, 1893-1894 Programme

ORDERED: 8 December 1893 for delivery on 8 September 1894 and 8 October 1894 respectively.

	Yard No.	Laid down	Launched	Completed
Salmon	384	12.3.1894	15.1.1895	Jan 1896
Snapper	385	2.4.1894	30.1.1895	Jan 1896

DIMENSIONS: 204ft 9in oa, 200ft bp × 19ft 6in × 12ft 3in + 7ft 9in
DISPLACEMENT: 305 tons light, 340 tons full load
MACHINERY: 2 shafts, 19¼in. 28½in.43in × 18in, 8 Yarrow water tube boilers, 185lbs, 3700ihp

The firm's name was added to those to be asked to submit tenders for 27-knotters on 2 June 1893.[81] The initial design was not accepted, and had to be modified before two vessels were ordered. By October 1895 'the vibration in these boats is not yet satisfactory but this will be overcome'. Otherwise they were acceptable – but well behind schedule. These were four-funnelled vessels with the mast just in front of the closely-grouped pair of middle funnels. The main recognition difference was that about 1900 *Salmon* was fitted with a boat in davits to starboard of the middle pair of funnels.

Salmon was home based throughout her career until paid off in 1911. She was sold 14 May 1912 to Cashmore, Newport for breaking up. *Snapper* was also home based throughout her career until paid off in 1911 and was sold 14 May 1912 to King, Gateshead for breaking up.

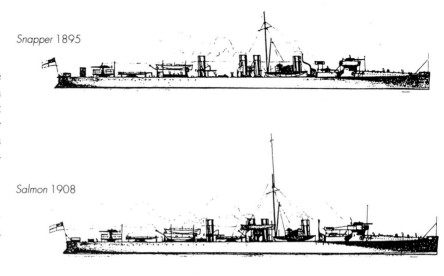

Snapper 1895

Salmon 1908

Bullfinch 1902

30-knotters, 1896-1897 Programme

	Yard No.	Laid down	Launched	Completed
Bullfinch	413	17.9.1896	10.2.1898	Jun 1901
Dove	414	17.9.1896	21.3.1898	Jul 1901

DIMENSIONS: 214ft 6in oa, 210ft bp × 20ft 6in ext/20ft 5¼in mld × 12ft 1½in + 7ft 10in
DISPLACEMENT: 345 tons light, 390 tons full load
MACHINERY: Thornycroft boilers, 220lbs, 5800ihp
FIRST COSTS: £55,196 and £54,948

Most lines plans are drawn as part of the design process before the first plates are laid for the hull. However, here we have a lines plan 'taken off' Earle's *Salmon* in 1902. (National Maritime Museum, London: 32027)

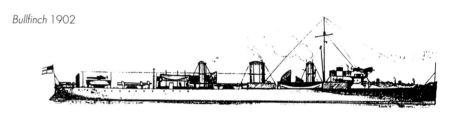

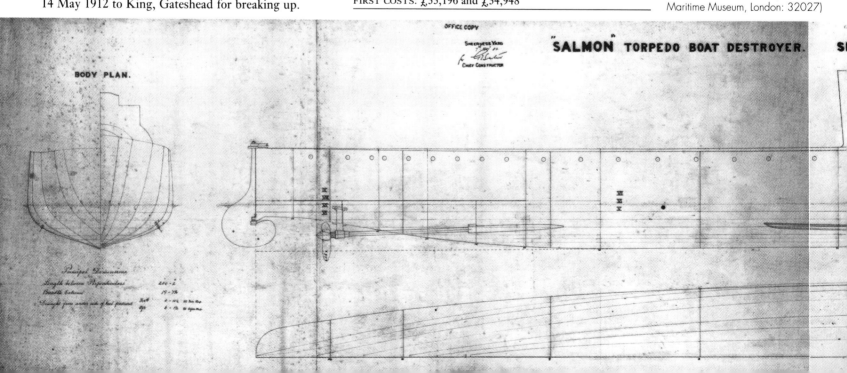

The relative success of the first Earle pair was enough to get their builder an invitation to tender (on 5 October 1895) for two 30-knotters.

Bullfinch was 'received as a 29kt ship'[82] and at low speed (13kts) coal consumption was 2.0lbs per ihp per hour, which meant more bunkerage was needed if it was to be adequate for the guarantee conditions. Like her sister, *Dove* made well under 30kts on trials (just over 29¼kts in fact). Altogether these vessels were a bad bargain for both their builders (who were bankrupt before they were completed) and the Admiralty.

Bullfinch and *Dove* were three-funnelled – the two midships funnels of the Earle 27-knotter design having been trunked together in this development. The mast was also re-positioned in front of the forefunnel. The forefoot was straight. From about 1906 both were fitted with a topmast. Both spent their career in home waters. *Bullfinch* was sold on 10 June 1919 for breaking up to Young, Sunderland and *Dove* was sold on 27 October 1920 for breaking up to Maden & McKee.

1897-1898 Programme

In 1897 Earle's tendered again, offering a repeat of the *Bullfinch* with slightly increased length and some small alterations to internal arrangements.[83] The Admiralty comment of 'no speed trials yet' helps to explain why no order was placed.

Earle's 27-knotter *Snapper* portrayed in 1907. The short, thin funnels make her, for this viewer anyway, one of the least appealing of all the TBDs. (National Maritime Museum, London: N2000)

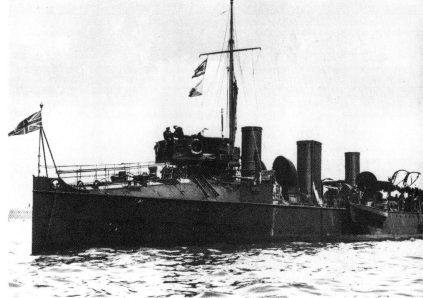

Bullfinch photographed in 1902 off Portsmouth when moored and hoisting out her Berthon boat. Her whaler has already been lowered from its davits. (National Maritime Museum, London: N2091)

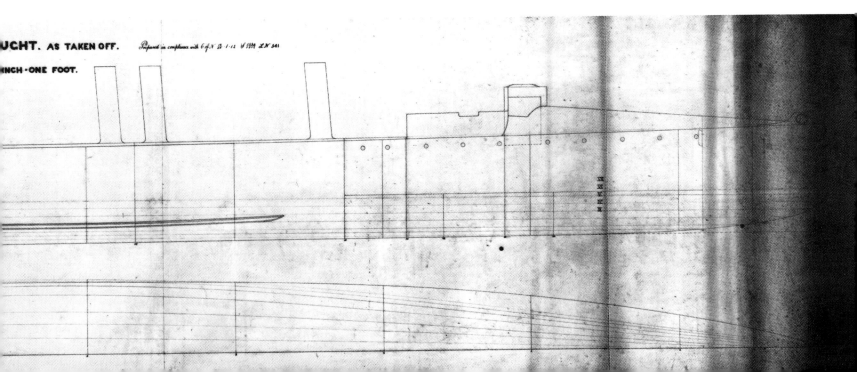

UCHT. AS TAKEN OFF.   *Prepared in compliance with ...*

NCH - ONE FOOT.

Hanna, Donald & Wilson

This firm was rather an 'odd man out' amongst the builders in the TBD programmes. It was neither a successful torpedo boat specialist like Thornycroft or Yarrow, nor was it a large shipbuilder moving into the field like most of the rest. It was probably closest to J S White in the matter of size and in having ventured a couple of times into building TBs (First Class TB No.15 in 1879 and the Indian Navy's *Gurkha* in 1888). However White's were a firm with a long history in shipbuilding, whilst the Paisley company was a general engineering firm which had built some vessels as well as boiler installations and the like, but their attempt to build TBDs was over-ambitious and (unlike White's which, despite the comparative failure of their 27-knotters, went on to build many destroyers for the Navy) was the firm's last naval shipbuilding venture.[84]

26-knotter design, 1892-1893 programme

This design[85] was of the torpedo boat type with two conning towers, one funnel and one signal mast. No dimensions were given (but see the plan). No ihp was

Fervent after reboilering with water tube boilers and as altered in 1905. (National Maritime Museum, London: 5285)

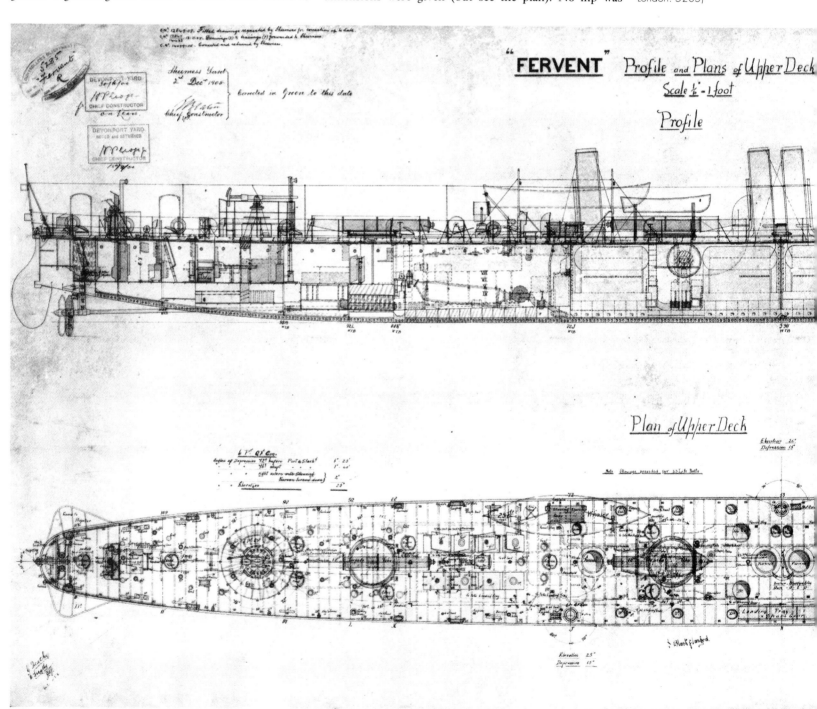

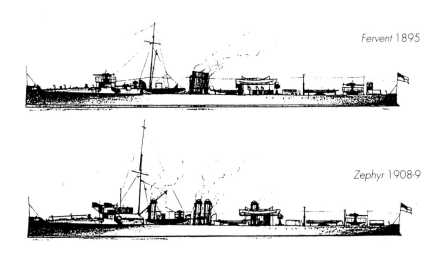

Fervent 1895

Zephyr 1908-9

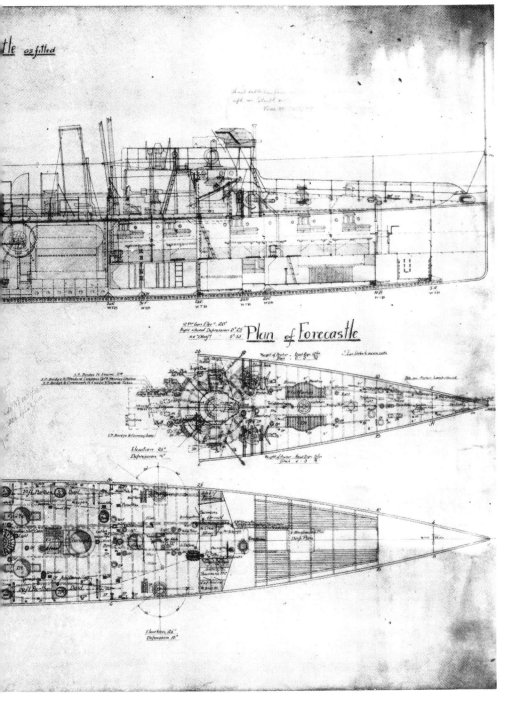

tle as fitted

Plan of Forecastle

stated for this 26kt design, nor was any tonnage definitely stated but presumably it was intended to have a 30-ton load and 20 tons of coal. The armament was to be one fixed 14in bow torpedo tube, one 12pdr QF plus four 3pdrs QF. Thirty tons of coal would give 1000 nautical miles at 10kts. 'Penalty for defect of speed' £50 per tenth of knot and premium £100 per tenth of knot with trials to take place on the Clyde. Storage space was very limited. 'It is questionable whether with the beam stated, viz 15¼ft, the metacentric height can be obtained.'

The DNC's comment (possibly on a modified version of the design) was: '. . . Messrs Hanna Donald & Wilson have submitted a design which cannot be recommended for acceptance . . . the 12pdr and the after 6pdr should be carried with complete torpedo armament, the two 6pdrs forward would be carried as alternatives to the pair of revolving tubes aft. A greater number of 3pdrs could of course be carried, but the limits of complement practically fix the number of guns that can be fought.'

27-knotters, 1893-1894 Programme

ORDERED: 7 November 1893 for delivery by 31 May 1895.

	Yard No.	Laid down	Launched	Completed
Fervent	?	27.3.1894	20.3.1895	Jun 1900
Zephyr	?	23.4.1894	10.5.1895	Jul 1901

DIMENSIONS: 204ft 6in oa, 200ft bp × 19ft mld
DISPLACEMENT: 275 tons trial, 320 tons full load
MACHINERY: 4000ihp
FIRST COSTS: £45,534 and £46,363

The tender for two TBDs was actually accepted by the Admiralty by a letter dated 3 November 1893 but conditionally on a number of alterations being made. The thickness of the floor plates was to be increased, the upper deck strengthened with girders and framing in the engine space also increased in scantling. Modifications were also to be made to the machinery.

As completed these vessels were the only vessels of their kind to have single funnels until the Italian destroyers of the 1930s. The firm had originally offered to fit water tube boilers of their own design, but the Admiralty, presumably wary of an untried type of boiler, had offered for locomotive boilers instead. However, the boilers they were fitted with proved quite inadequate to provide the power to enable them to reach acceptance speed on trials in the late summer and autumn of 1895. The problem chiefly appears to have been with the copper fireboxes of the boilers, most probably because of the poor quality of the copper itself. Whatever the reason, the vessels as built did not fulfil their acceptance conditions. Rather than reject the vessels or make the builders pay heavy penalties, the Admiralty very reasonably offered (August 1897) to pay for reboilering with water tube boilers. The builders offered their own design but the Admiralty preferred to order Reed boilers from Palmer's. Costs were estimated in March 1899[86] as shown in the table on page 76.

On 23 May 1900 Hanna Donald & Wilson wrote to the Admiralty differing from the Admiralty case. When water tube boilers were decided upon the firm, at the Admiralty's request, obtained a tender from Palmer's for boilers, who gave the estimated weight as 57 tons. Subsequently Reed, the patentee, had consultations with Admiralty advisors and agreed with them to increase pressure to 210lbs and grate and heating area were also very considerably increased: 'We sent this specification to the Admiralty on 29 January 1898 to be forwarded to Palmer's who returned it to us on 2 March . . . [The firm protested against] . . . extra weights caused by altered conditions and especially referred to and protested against [on 26 March 1898] the increased grate and heating surface because these obviously increased the weight, but we did not then realise that the extra pressure would also increase the weight. We personally had nothing to do with the adjustment of the boiler specification, nor was our opinion asked, but we thought that the Admiralty with their greater experience were satisfied that 210lbs pressure on the boilers was necessary to obtain 185lbs at the engines . . . we had already protested that we would not be responsible for any trouble that might be caused by extra weight. When the boilers were delivered we found the actual increase was nearly 7 tons. The tender weight [was] 57 tons, [but the weight] as received was $63^{19}/_{20}$ tons. We were not asked to agree, nor was our attention called to the fact that we must allow for 2 extra tons with their air trunks, height of funnels, feed pumps etc. We are prepared to run *Zephyr*'s trials without prejudice with 200lbs pressure, provided that at least 11 tons are deducted from the load to be carried to cover the extra weight of boilers, separators, pumps fans, funnels etc. or to run the trials at 195lbs boiler pressure free of penalties for shortness of

	Original cost each	*Additional reboilering each*
Hull	£9740 & £202 for extras	£200 estimated
Machinery: engines	£19,683 & boilers £3936	£7100 (4 Reed boilers)
Auxiliaries	£1239 & £110 for extras	£400 & £360 & estimated £2500 = £10,560

Rebate for old boilers allowed by contractors £3936 = total £6,624
Total original cost = £34,910 + £6624
Total with reboilering = £41,534 each, or £83,068 for both

speed. We would respectfully remind their Lordships that the *Zephyr* is ready for trials; an early reply will oblige as we do not wish to pay our men off as it would be difficult to get suitable hands when required.'

The answer sent does not survive in the Covers but since the reboilering and the Admiralty's subsequent uprating of the boilers were both due to the original failure of the firm to produce a design which met the requirements for speed laid down in the contract, and, in the second instance, a (justified) fear that the vessels would still not make 27kts, their case does not seem to be a good one. The firm seems to have been somewhat out of its depth from the start, and to have been treated with a certain degree of leniency by the Admiralty, who could have been justified in refusing to accept the TBDs at all. In fact these vessels achieved the unenviable distinction of taking longer to deliver than any other TBDs. They had the general reputation of being amongst the worst 27-knotters, and, despite the reboilering, never reached 27kts on trial. They served throughout in home waters and were both sold for breaking up in 1920.

This fairly well-known shot showing *Fervent* on her unsuccessful original trials is probably the only one showing her in her single-funnelled configuration. Her sister *Zephyr* did not even get so far as running trials. The background, so familiar from many trials photographs, are the hills of the Firth of Clyde. As was usual on trials weights were carried to represent the armament, mast and boats which were not yet fitted. (National Maritime Museum, London: G5305)

Zephyr in 1909, with four funnels, quite unlike her original single-funnelled appearance. The bar protruding from the stern is the propeller guard. (National Maritime Museum, London: N8721)

Palmer's

Palmer's of Jarrow were pioneers of iron construction for cargo steamers with their steam colliers, beginning with the *John Bowes*, and a very major shipbuilder at this time. They had already built torpedo cruisers for the Austro-Hungarian Navy when they tendered in 1892 for a 26-knotter. This was not accepted, but eventually Palmer's boats would, by common consent, be considered the best all-rounders of all the TBDs. The firm also built the last vessels of the 30-knotter type, but these were so much modified, and were purchased so much later that they have their own chapter.

26-knotter design – not built

This design was described[87] as being of the torpedo boat type with two conning towers, three funnels, one signal mast, a balanced rudder, a turtleback forward, and a 'considerable round-up to the upper deck'. Accommodation was provided for thirty officers and men. Dimensions were 190ft × 18ft 6in × 4ft 10in mean draft, 215 tons displacement. The engines were to give 4200ihp and 26kts. Du Temple water tube boilers were to be fitted.[88] The total load was stated as 20 tons excluding coal. The armament, interestingly, was to consist of one 4.7in quick-firing howitzer with 75 rounds (presumably to give a comparatively light weapon with a high rate of fire in comparison to its very heavy shell) and one 12pdr QF with 100 rounds, but no lighter guns at all. Torpedo armament was restricted to a fixed bow tube with two 14in torpedoes. The metacentric height was estimated to be 2.13ft. Only 19 tons of coal was carried giving a range of 1100 nautical miles at 10kts. Two boats would be provided. 'This boat is very fine forward and has not much space for stores, accommodation, etc . . . The method of connecting the frames, beams, sheer strakes etc, is not considered satisfactory . . . Palmer's should be told that a coal bunker capacity of at least 40–50 tons is considered essential, also their attention must be drawn to the lack of longitudinal bulkheads, [and the resulting] very serious loss of structural strength in a vessel of this type.'

A slightly later note[89] added that the boiler room was to be subdivided, the guns to be the standard single 12pdr and three or five 6pdrs, the side bunkers to be made water tight. Further thoughts[90] were that the accommodation was only for thirty instead of the forty asked for and the coaling arrangements for the forward boilers were very unsatisfactory, as was the general subdivision. 'All details asked for have not been conformed to.'

In the DNC's July 1892 report[91] on the modified designs, Palmer's 'is not satisfactory; it provides only for thirty men and the arrangements for working the coals in the foremost stokehold are most inefficient. The size of the boilers proposed is still less than that asked for and the design of the engine makes it very inaccessible and not likely to give satisfaction. In view of the above we cannot recommend the placing of an order for a vessel of such a character with this firm.'

27-knotters, 1893-1894 Programme

ORDERED: 7 November 1893 to be delivered 3 December 1894, 18 February 1895 and on 1 March 1895 (or before 31 March 1895?).

	Yard No.	Laid down	Launched	Completed
Janus	681	28.3.1894	12.3.1895	Nov 1895
Lightning	682	28.3.1894	10.4.1895	Jan 1896
Porcupine	683	28.3.1894	19.9.1895	Mar 1896

DIMENSIONS: 204ft 6in oa, 200ft bp × 19ft 9in ext/19ft 8-in mld × 12ft 2in + 8ft

DISPLACEMENT: 275 tons light, 320 tons full load

MACHINERY: 2 shaft, 18in.27½in.42in × 18in, 4 Reed boilers, 250lbs, 3900ihp

FIRST COSTS: £40,303, £40,911 and £40,360

Next year, however, Palmer's tender for three destroyers was accepted (on 3 November though the order seems not to have been confirmed till the 7th) though with the following remarks:[92] 'Scantlings generally approved but lower plates of bulkheads should be at least amidships, web frames (double or strong) should be worked as required in machinery space and reverse bars from frame to gunwale on every frame, plating of forward and aft water tight flats forward and aft could be decreased to 3½lbs. [It is] preferred to carry fresh water in separate tanks which do not form part of the hull. Accommodation is needed for forty-five men, not forty as in the tender. Modifications to the engines include slight additional length in engine room, which space can be taken from the stokeholds. A two-year boiler guarantee [is required].'

Janus departed for China in 1900, having had her funnels raised and given caps. Sold in 1914, still at Hong Kong, for breaking up. *Lightning* remained in home waters for her working life. On 30 June 1915 she blew up

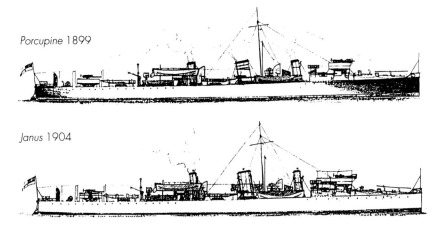

Porcupine 1899

Janus 1904

and sank, probably on a submarine-laid mine, near the Kentish Knock lightship. *Porcupine* also was in home waters throughout until sold on 29 April 1920 to Ward, Rainham.

30-knotters 1895-1896 Programme

ORDERED: (first pair) 23 December 1895 for delivery ?.

	Yard No.	Laid down	Launched	Completed
Star	710	23.3.1896	11.8.1896	Sept 1898 [????]
Whiting	711	13.4.1896	26.8.1896	Jun 1897

ORDERED: 9 January 1896 for delivery in 10, 11, 12 and 13 months respectively.

	Yard No.	Laid down	Launched	Completed
Bat	712	28.5.1896	7.10.1896	Aug 1897
Chamois	713	28.5.1896	9.11.1896	Nov 1897
Crane	714	2.8.1896	17.12.1896	Apr 1898
Flying Fish	715	9.8.1896	4.3.1897	Jun 1898

DIMENSIONS: 220ft oa, 215ft bp × 20ft 9in × 12ft 5½in + 9ft 9in
DISPLACEMENT: 390 tons light, 440 tons full load
MACHINERY: 2 shaft 19in.29½in. 46in × 18in, 4 Reed boilers, 250lbs, 6200ihp
FIRST COSTS: £52,820, £52,236, £52,366, £52,410, £52,376 and £52,410

As Palmer's were completing their order for 27-knotters satisfactorily they were included amongst the second batch

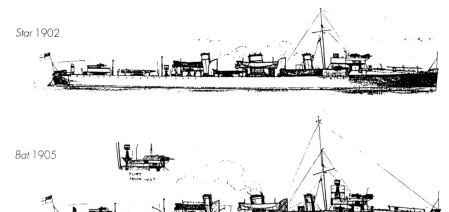

Star 1902

Bat 1905

of firms to be asked to tender in 1895.[93] An order for two was placed initially, followed by one for four boats.

In August 1906 a report[94] was made on the evaluation of stresses of *Crane* in sagging condition, a move made because of reports that several of Palmer's destroyers had cracked their decks.

Star visited Gibraltar in 1905, but otherwise was based in home waters and was sold on 10 June 1919 to Ward, New Holland. *Whiting* went to China in 1897 and remained there till sold on 27 November 1919 at Hong Kong and then broken up in China. *Bat* served in the Mediterranean between 1902 and 1905, and was otherwise in home waters. She was sold on 30 August 1919 to

Opposite below, Star *with* Kangaroo *astern coming into Portsmouth Harbour off Southsea in 1912. (National Maritime Museum, London: N8786)*

Below, showing Crane *as built and as altered to 1914. The most visually significant of the alterations is the fitting of a searchlight tower immediately abaft the 12pdr. (National Maritime Museum, London: 6122)*

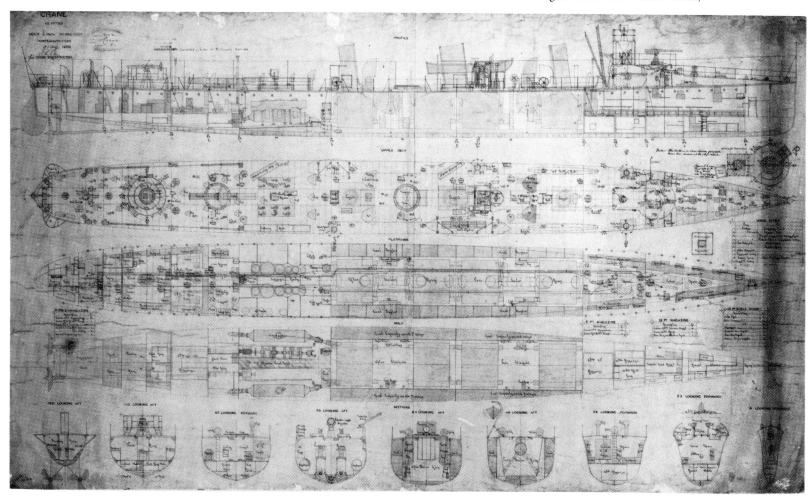

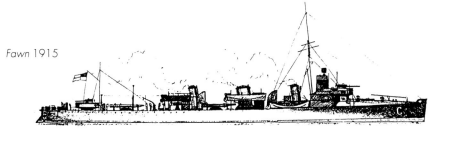

Fawn 1915

Spiteful 1912

Syren 1902

Hayes, Porthcawl. *Chamois* went out to the Mediterranean in 1901, and remained there until she foundered in the Gulf of Patras on 26 September 1904 after a blade broke off the propeller and the unbalanced, still-rotating shaft tore a hole in the hull. *Crane* served in the Mediterranean from 1902 till 1904, and visited Gibraltar in 1912, but otherwise served in home waters. Sold on 10 June 1919 to Ward, New Holland. *Flying Fish* served in the Mediterranean between 1902 and 1905, otherwise in home waters. She was sold on 30 August 1919 to T R Sales.

1896-1897 Programme

ORDERED: ? for delivery ?.

	Yard No.	Laid down	Launched	Completed
Fawn	721	5.9.1896	13.4.1897	Dec 1898
Flirt	722	5.9.1896	15.5.1897	Apr 1899

DIMENSIONS ETC.: As *Star*

By the time these two vessels were ordered from Palmer's that firm's 27-knotters were already entering service and beginning to establish the enviable reputation for seaworthiness and reliability which made them the best-liked of all the different TBD types. This may well have influenced the Admiralty in placing another order with this firm, though, as the papers are missing, we cannot be sure.

Fawn served between 1902 and 1906 in the Mediterranean, otherwise in home waters. She was sold on 23 July 1919 to Ward, New Holland. *Flirt* served throughout in home waters, and was reboiled by Palmer's in 1903. On 27 October 1916 she was sunk by German destroyers in the Straits of Dover.

1897-1898 Programme

ORDERED: ? for delivery ?.

	Yard No.	Laid down	Launched	Completed
Spiteful	734	12.1.1898	11.1.1899	Feb 1900

DIMENSIONS ETC.: As *Star* except 9ft 1in draft
DISPLACEMENT: 400 tons light, 450 tons full load
FIRST COST: £50,977

When considering the possibility of ordering more 'Specials' Palmer's were noted as one of the few firms which 'are as yet in such a position in regard to speeds obtained as to justify their being asked to submit designs and tenders for vessels of 32 or 33kts . . . ' However, it was decided to order more 30-knotters instead and Palmer's design, which was practically a repeat of the *Star* class, was chosen.

The main visual difference from her predecessors was that instead of having three funnels, with a thicker middle funnel, she was four-funnelled with two closely grouped thinner funnels in the middle.

Spiteful served at home throughout her career. She was sold on 14 September 1920 to Hayes, Porthcawl.

1899-1900 Estimates

ORDERED: April 1899 for delivery in 15, 16 and 17 months.

	Yard No.	Laid down	Launched	Completed
Peterel	745	29.7.1898	30.3.1899	Jul 1900 – speculation, purchased
Myrmidon	751	23.10.1899	26.5.1900	May 1901
Syren	752	24.11.1899	20.12.1900	Feb 1902

DIMENSIONS ETC.: As *Spiteful* except 219ft 6in oa and 8ft 11in draft
DISPLACEMENT: 370 tons light, 420 tons full load
FIRST COSTS: £61,577, £61,445 and £61,999

One vessel (*Peterel*) was begun 'on spec' and was purchased on the stocks as one of the three TBDs ordered in April 1899. Contract price £57,149 (£19,286 hull, £37,863 machinery) each.

Opposite below, photographs of destroyers approaching the camera make very dramatic pictures, which is presumably why stern quarter views like this one of *Lightning* are not seen as often. However, they make an interesting change. She is steaming in about 1906 through Portland anchorage, past the battleship *Duncan*, maybe heading for the coaling cranes seen in front of her bow. (National Maritime Museum, London: N20846)

Below, the nearest TBD in this 'trot' from the Portsmouth-based 6th Flotilla moored at Dover in 1908 is *Flying Fish*, recognisable by the figure of a flying fish at her masthead, with *Mermaid* next to her. The larger ship whose funnel can be seen in the background is a cross-channel packet (Denny's *Victoria* of 1907), and the funnels of a large salvage tug (*Triton* of 1882 belonging to the Dover Harbour Board) show between her and the line of destroyers. (National Maritime Museum, London: N8799)

It would appear that this barely-begun vessel, reported to be a duplicate of HMS *Spitfire*, was included in what was referred to as a 'mixed tender' by Palmer's submitted on 15 January 1899 and accepted in April 1899[95] for three vessels. They were to be fitted with closed-in engines with forced lubrication for £700 extra and with Yarrow boilers fitted instead of Thornycroft ones. The name *Dotterel* is given, but it looks as if this was simply a clerical error for *Peterel* rather than a properly allocated name which was later changed. Like the *Spiteful* these were four funnelled vessels.

Peterel served in home waters throughout her career.

Kangaroo 1917

She was sold on 30 August 1919 to T R Sales. *Myrmidon* served in the Mediterranean from 1901 to 1905, then for a year with the Atlantic Fleet before spending the rest of her service life in home waters. She sank on 26 March 1917 in a collision with the SS *Hambourn* in the Channel. *Syren* served in home waters throughout her career and was sold on 14 September 1920 to Hayes, Porthcawl.

1900–1901 Programme

ORDERED: (purchased whilst building?) ? for delivery ?.

Yard No.	Laid down	Launched	Completed
Kangaroo	787	29.12.1899	8.9.1900	Jul 1901

DIMENSIONS ETC.: As *Myrmidon* except 219ft 9in oa
DISPLACEMENT: 390 tons light, 420 tons full load
FIRST COST: £61,597

Basically a repeat of the *Myrmidon* building as a private venture by Palmer's, purchased for the Royal Navy under the supplementary programme for 1900–1901.

Kangaroo went out to the Mediterranean on completion and served there till being attached to the Atlantic Fleet in 1905, and then returning home in the next year. She was sold on 23 March 1920 to M Yates.

Doxford

Doxford's were a firm that mostly concentrated on building cargo ships of various kinds, the 'turret-decked' bulk carriers being invented by the firm. It is a little surprising to see a firm of this kind building TBDs, but they did so with considerable success.

27-knotters, 1893-1894 Programme

ORDERED: 3 November 1893 for delivery 18 December 1894 and 18 September 1895

	Yard No.	Laid down	Launched	Completed
Hardy	226	4.6.1894	16.12.1895	Aug 1896
Haughty	227	28.5.1894	18.9.1895	Aug 1896

DIMENSIONS: 200ft 3in oa, 196ft bp × 19ft ext/18ft 11in × 11ft 5in + 7ft 9in
DISPLACEMENT: 260 tons light, 325 tons full load
MACHINERY: 2 shafts, 8 Yarrow boilers, 185lbs, 4200ihp
FIRST COSTS: £42,055 and £42,007

On 2 June 1893 the Sunderland firm of Doxford was put forward[96] as one of those to be sent tendering details for the 27-knotters. Their tender was accepted by a letter sent on 3 November 1893.[97] Two TBDs with locomotive boilers were to be supplied for £74,260 (£32,460 for the hulls, £41,800 for the machinery), with, interestingly, only 26kts guaranteed. It would seem that the Admiralty was prepared to make concessions in speed to encourage another firm to enter the destroyer-building field; a decision which was to be justified in this case. The price did not include auxiliary machinery. Doxford's design was to be modified by omitting the bow torpedo tube, and at

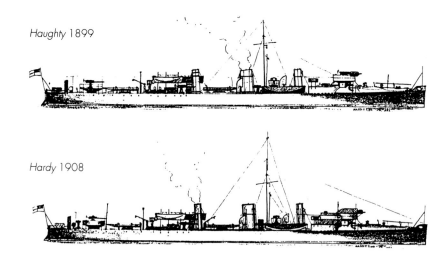

Haughty 1899

Hardy 1908

least 6ft 4in clear head room was to be allowed under the beams and above the water-tight flats which had to be at least 6in above the waterline. It was also considered that the scantlings proposed could be increased, so a revised midships section plan was to be submitted. Many details in the specification would require modification to be carried out to the satisfaction of the overseer. The boilers were to be arranged smokebox to smokebox which would give extra space for the engine room. Delivery was to be in twelve and thirteen months respectively.

On 14 December 1893 the tender for distilling machinery by Caird & Rayner for £295 per ship was accepted, but the price for steering engines, compressing machinery and electric light machinery was considered high. New tenders were asked for. A £340 tender for Caldwell's steering gear for each vessel was accepted on 7 February, but just over a month earlier (on 5 January) the major decision had been made to accept the builders' proposal to fit 'tubulous' (water tube) boilers in place of locomotive ones, though despite this the guarantee speed remained 26kts. There would be a £500 penalty per ¼kt if the

Haughty as built and as modified 1905. The thicker midships funnel has two boilers trunked into it whilst the foremost and aftermost boilers each have a funnel to themselves. The plan views show the original unadorned 12pdr platform crossed out and replaced by a redrawn bridge platform. On the original, multi-coloured, plan, the alterations are shown in a different colour (in this case burnt sienna). (National Maritime Museum, London: 625611

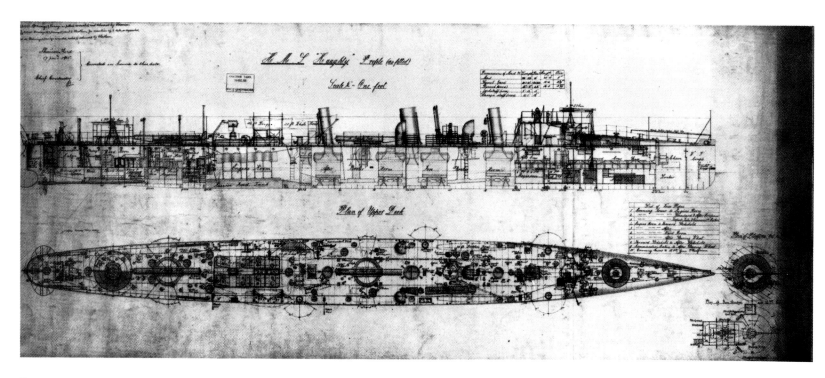

Hardy at anchor in berth F6 at Spithead for the Diamond Jubilee Review in June 1897 with her Berthon boat towing behind. This was before weather cloths were fitted round the 12pdr platform. (National Maritime Museum, London: G5303)

speed was less than this, with rejection if it fell below 25kts. In fact these boats proved satisfactory, so Doxford's were asked to tender for 30-knotters, though not until the third lot of orders for these vessels was to be placed.

Hardy was briefly in the Mediterranean in 1900, otherwise in home waters, sold on 11 July 1911 to Garnham. *Haughty* served at home throughout until sold on 10 April 1912.

30-knotters, 1896-1897 Programme

ORDERED: ? to be delivered ?.

	Yard No.	Laid down	Launched	Completed
Violet	. . .	13.7.1896	3.5.1897	Jun 1898
Sylvia	. . .	13.7.1896	3.7.1897	Jan 1899

DIMENSIONS: 214ft (215ft for *Sylvia*) oa, 210ft bp × 21ft × 13ft 7in + 9ft 7in
DISPLACEMENT: 350 tons light, 400 tons full load
MACHINERY: 2 shafts 19in.29½in.32in.32in × 18in, 4 Thornycroft boilers, 220lbs, 6300ihp
COAL: 90 tons
FIRST COSTS: £54,117 and £55,778

These were essentially an enlarged and more powerful version of the 27-knotters, and they seem to have been reasonably successful and popular vessels.

Both vessels served in home waters throughout their careers. *Violet* was sold on 7 June 1920 to J Houston of Montrose. *Sylvia* was sold on 23 July 1919 to Ward, New Holland.

Sylvia 1899

1897-1898 Programme

ORDERED: ? for delivery ?.

	Yard No.	Laid down	Launched	Completed
Lee	263	4.1.1898	27.1.1899	Mar 1901

DIMENSIONS: As *Sylvia*
DISPLACEMENT: 365 tons light, 420 tons full load
MACHINERY: As *Sylvia*
COAL: 86 tons
FIRST COST: £55,183

Violet and *Sylvia* being considered a success, the firm was asked to tender again in 1897, the resulting vessel being a 'practical repeat of *Violet*'. On 19 February 1901 Doxford's wrote to the Admiralty giving their reasons for why they felt the latter should not enforce the penalty for late delivery of *Lee*, since the circumstances were largely beyond their control.[98]

This provoked a most interesting debate which throws considerable light on the Admiralty's policy towards its contractors. H O Arnold-Forster, then the Secretary to the Admiralty, wrote, 'I shall find it very difficult to defend this perpetual waiving of penalties unless I am furnished with some clear statement as to what is the principle adopted. If on consideration, it be decided that penalties are undesirable, or useless, I can, doubtless defend that conclusion. But in that case, why put in the penalty clause?'

W H White, the DNC, outlined the official policy which had always been followed for torpedo boat destroyers: 'These form a special class and the Admiralty policy has been to extend the sources of supply. Consequently, firms have had to embark on work largely of an experimental character, as each type of destroyer has been ordered. In regard to trials of machinery and the attainment of contract speeds this experimental work has been in many cases long continued and very costly to the Contractors.' After careful examination of the causes of delays in delivery, there was no instance in which it had been thought desirable to inflict penalties. 'No objection would have been felt to inflicting penalties if there had been evidence that the Contractors had not done their best. In the case of the *Lee* Messrs. Doxford are believed to have done what was in their power . . . On the general question of penalties a statement has already been made to the effect that under existing contracts if extra works have been ordered, penalties for late delivery cannot be enforced. Such extra works are almost always necessary in building ships. As a matter of fact remission of penalties has been the rule and the reasons for remission have been given in each case.' The existing system did not make provision for penalties for late delivery, but the new form did, even if extra works were ordered. The policy to be followed in future needed resolving and the question of premiums for early delivery was also likely to be raised if penalties were enforced. 'All these matters are understood to be under the consideration of the Special Committee now sitting.'

Arnold-Forster noted on 15 March: 'In view of the strongly expressed opinions of the DNC, concur in payment being made in the case of the *Lee*.'

Lee served in home waters until wrecked on 5 October 1909 near Blacksod Bay.

1899-1900 Programme

ORDERED: 30 March 1899 for delivery in 15 months.

	Yard No.	Laid down	Launched	Completed
Success	282	18.9.1899	21.3.1901	May 1902

DIMENSIONS: As *Sylvia* except draft 8ft 10in
MACHINERY: As *Sylvia*?
FIRST COST: £63,273

Doxford's 'mixed' tender for one TBD of 25 January 1899 for £51,191 was accepted just over two months later. The vessel (*Success*) was to be delivered in fifteen months. The only slight modification to the design asked for by the Admiralty was that the 'large immersion of the upper tip of the propeller' should be reduced if possible.[99] The main difference from her predecessors was that instead of the thicker central funnel of three, this vessel had two small closely-grouped funnels, making her a four-funnel ship.

Success served at home throughout her career, and was wrecked near Fifeness on 27 December 1914.

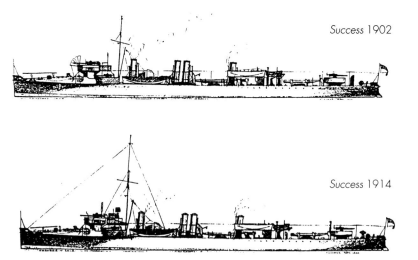

Success 1902

Success 1914

Right, Violet under way, with, apparently, only her after boilers fired up. Taken in 1907 and showing the topmast and enlarged gun platform. (National Maritime Museum, London: N2147)

Below, Lee as built. This plan has the unusual (but not unknown) feature of not showing the guns themselves, though their mountings are drawn in. (National Maritime Museum, London: 17358)

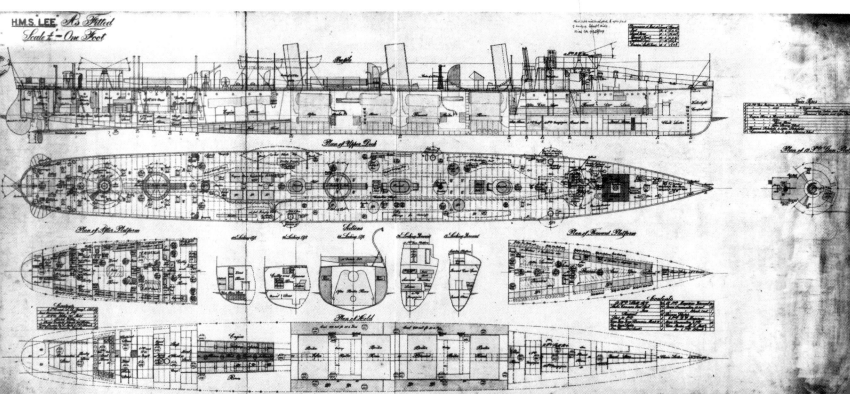

Armstrong

Armstrong's were the greatest armaments firm of the day in Britain, perhaps in the world, but not specialists in torpedo craft. They had began as manufacturers of hydraulic machinery, moved from that to making artillery and then had acquired a shipyard at Elswick from the firm of Mitchell, whose name was temporarily added to Armstrong's to designate the firm. From the late 1880s this yard had been establishing a reputation for building cruisers, and had just built four of those diminutives of cruisers, the torpedo gunboats, two for the Royal Indian Marine and two for Australia.

27-knotters, 1893-4 Programme

ORDERED: 8 December 1893 for delivery in 14 months and before 31 March 1895 respectively.

	Yard No.	Laid down	Launched	Completed
Swordfish	616.	4.6.1894	7.6.1895	Dec 1896
Spitfire	618	4.6.1894	27.2.1895	Nov 1896

DIMENSIONS: 204ft 3in oa, 200ft bp × 19ft mld × 12ft + 7ft 9in
DISPLACEMENT: 320 tons light, 355 tons full load
MACHINERY: By Bellis, 8 Yarrow boilers, 185lbs, 4500ihp
FIRST COSTS: £42,080 and £40,947

Armstrong Mitchell & Co.'s design for a 27-knotter TBD produced in answer to the 1893 request for tenders was not particularly impressive: 'The specification is very meagre, consisting chiefly of framing and a copy of the appendix to the conditions of tendering. The scantlings are rather slight and would require increasing especially in the matter of deck plating and reverse bars. The midships section gives a curved form to the outer part of the deck, thus restricting the deck area which I consider is inadmissible. The space allotted to the stokehold appears largely in excess of requirements, the coaling arrangements are also bad and would require considerable modification. It is considered that this could be done by a rearrangement of boilers and condensers. The deck arrangements will also require to be rearranged especially in the matter of hatches, boat stowage and gun positions. The power and heating surface of boilers proposed appear to be sufficient. A ram bow is proposed. This should be replaced by a straight stem. The design as it stands is not satisfactory, but it could be made satisfactory on the dimensions given.'[100]

The Admiralty's letter of 7 November 1893 to Armstrong stated that they were not able to accept the

Spitfire 1899

The TBD in this picture has a mast between the first and second funnels, and has not yet had a topmast fitted, whilst there is no bow torpedo tube. Therefore she is clearly a 27-knotter early in her career. In fact she is *Spitfire* photographed in 1898 passing Southsea Castle on her way into Portsmouth. (National Maritime Museum, London: N1990)

tender, but gave fourteen days for amended proposals to be submitted. On 8 December Armstrong's revised tender was accepted for a price of £36,500. More detailed provisos were made on the scantlings. It was stated that, in order to carry the foremost torpedo tube, the arrangement of boilers should be transposed, with two boilers being placed in the after stokehold. Other provisos were made, but these were general to all the builders concerned. The machinery was to be provided by G E Bellis and Co. The tender was only accepted, however, on condition that delivery was made within fourteen months.

On 7 February 1894 the Admiralty replied to Armstrong's offer of the 24th of the previous month by placing an order for a second TBD with machinery by Bellis & Co. The price would be £35,850 excluding auxiliary machinery, and she should be fitted with boilers of Yarrow (water tube design as fitted to *Hornet*) or D'Allest type, preferably former. Delivery was to be before 31 March 1895.[101]

When inclined on completion *Spitfire* had a metacentric height of only 1.4ft. This lack of stability meant that 15 tons of lead ballast had to be carried, and it was necessary to run trials with the ballast on board.[102] The trials themselves were not particularly successful and delivery of the two Armstrong boats consequently delayed till November

and December 1896, with the *Spitfire*, the vessel which was ordered later, both launched and delivered before her sister, though both were months after they were supposed to be delivered. The inevitable result was that the DNC made the following comment to the Admiralty Board when invitations to tender for the 1897–1898 Estimates were being discussed: 'We submit that these invitations be *not* sent to the Thames Iron Works, Armstrong & Company, Hanna Donald & Wilson and J S White of Cowes.'[103] It would be some time before Armstrong's built another destroyer to the Admiralty's order, and instead they concentrated on what was their forte, building cruisers and battleships for the navies of the world.

These two destroyers were not particularly well thought of in service, and both were sold for breaking up before 1914. They had three funnels, with the middle one thicker than the other two, whilst the mast was between the first two funnels. *Swordfish* was sold on 11 October 1910 to Cashmore, Newport and *Spitfire* was sold on 10 April 1912 to Ward, Preston

Armstrong's built one more TBD in conjunction with Parson's, the private venture *Cobra*, which was purchased for the Royal Navy, but never completed her delivery voyage (see the Turbine Destroyers chapter).

Swordfish is shown in this 'as built' plan. The reason for the thin-fat-thin sequence of funnels becomes clear when you see that the middle one has the uptakes from two boilers trunked into it. (National Maritime Museum, London: 89066)

Opposite, Hart seen at anchor off Haslar Wall in 1900, in a stern quarter view. From this angle you can see the detail of the stern steering position, used in emergencies, behind its armoured shield. The guns are shrouded by their canvas covers. The whaler has been lowered from its davits and is towing astern. (National Maritime Museum, London: G5304)

Fairfield

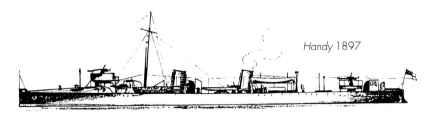

Handy 1897

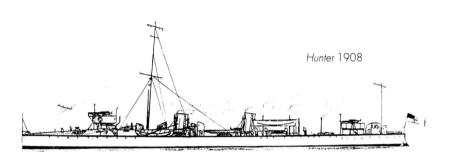

Hunter 1908

Hart 1910

This firm, whose name had recently been changed from Elder's, was probably at this stage the leading Clydeside yard for liners and major warships, occupying the place earlier belonging to Napier's and later to be taken over by John Brown's. Up to the date when it was asked to tender for 27kt TBDs it had not built any torpedo craft, except a rather odd paddle steamer built as a torpedo and mining school and depot ship for the Argentine Navy. However its lightweight construction had included Yarrow-designed sternwheel gunboats and supply ships for the Gordon Relief Expedition to Khartoum.

27-knotters, 1893-1894 Programme

ORDERED: 7 February 1894 for delivery 7 December 1894, 7 January 1895 and 7 February 1895 respectively.

	Yard No.	Laid down	Launched	Completed
Handy	378	7.6.1894	9.3.1895	Oct 1895
Hart	379	7.6.1894	27.3.1895	Jan 1896
Hunter	380	7.6.1894	28.12.1895	May 1896

DIMENSIONS: 197ft 3in oa, 194ft bp × 19ft 5in ext/19ft 4½in mld × 12ft 10in + 7ft 6in
DISPLACEMENT: 275 tons light, 310 tons full load
MACHINERY: 2 shaft 18¼in.27½in.42in × 18in, 3 Thornycroft boilers, 215lbs, 4000ihp
FIRST COSTS: £38,485, £38,472 and £38,602

The tender for three vessels for delivery in ten, eleven and twelve months with Thornycroft's latest type boiler was accepted for £104,400, not including auxiliaries. But the design required numerous modifications.[104] For example, the ihp estimated for 27kts was too small, and the fore and aft slope of the turtleback was considered excessive. Also the lower deck was to be at least 6in above the trial water line. The steering engine was placed on the upper deck just aft of the conning tower: 'this is objectionable'. The forward torpedo tube fouled the forced draught cowls, which should be moved if possible. The searchlight projector was masked on one side by the 25ft whaler: one or other should be moved. The conning tower shown aft in the design was not required. It was felt preferable to hang the rudder over the stern, and that the original accommodation arrangements should be adhered to. The fore end of the forward bunkers were very restricted and this was to be corrected: 'Doors in Water Tight bulkheads are not permissible.' Some modifications to scantlings were needed and corticene was to be fitted on the turtle, upper and lower decks (in the first case only between guard rails). The boilers were to have a two-year guarantee. 'Arrangement of machinery appears capable of improvement. Little or no margin in size of boilers with steam pressure stated.'

These vessels seem to have been reasonably satisfactory though in October 1895 it was noted that:[105] 'The

Fairy shown in 1911, in the Solent, with the enlarged conning platform fitted by this time. Her chart table has been moved to the after end of this platform, and a semaphore can be seen just behind the 12pdr gun. (National Maritime Museum, London: G5283)

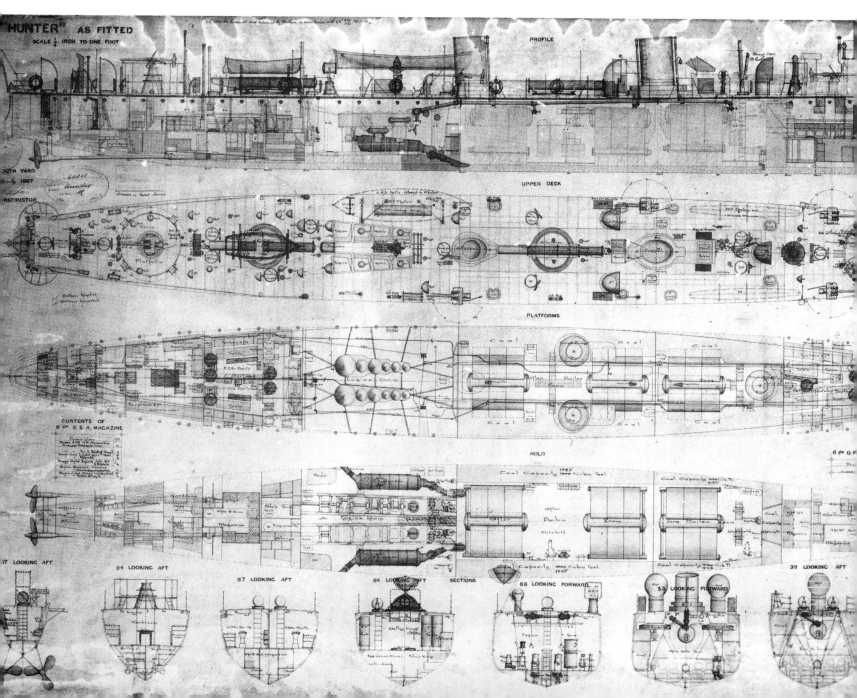

Leven 1902

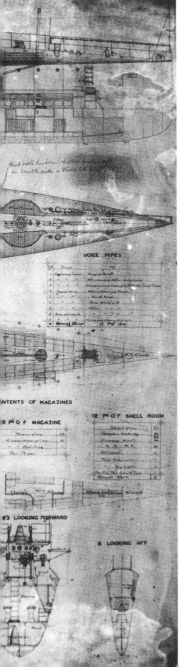

Below, Hunter 'as fitted' profile, decks and sections plan showing modifications to 1906. (National Maritime Museum, London: 64301)

vibration in these boats is not yet satisfactory but this will be overcome.'

Handy went out to China in 1897–1898, was on the sale list in 1914, and sold at Hong Kong in 1916. *Hart* was sent to China in 1896–1897 and was sold at Hong Kong in 1912. *Hunter* in contrast, served entirely in home waters until sold on 10 April 1912 to Ward, Briton Ferry.

30-knotters, 1896-1897 Programme

ORDERED: ? for delivery ?.

	Yard No.	Laid down	Launched	Completed
Gipsy	395	1.10.1896	9.3.1897	Jul 1898
Fairy	396	19.10.1896	25.9.1897	Aug 1898
Osprey	397	14.11.1896	7.4.1897	Jul 1898

DIMENSIONS: 215ft 6in oa, 209ft 9in bp × 21ft × 12ft 2in + 8ft 2in
DISPLACEMENT: 355 tons light, 400 tons full load
MACHINERY: 20in.31in.34in.34in × 18in, 4 Thornycroft boilers, 220lbs, 6300ihp
COAL: 85 tons
FIRST COSTS: £54,363, £54,368 and £54,303

The invitation to tender was sent out on 5 October 1895. The vessels built were a straightforward development of Fairfield's 27-knotter design.

All three served at home throughout their careers. *Fairy* was apparently refitting at Fairfield's in 1902. *Gipsy* was sold on 17 March 1921 to Beard, Teignmouth, and her hulk was in use as a floating pontoon at Dartmouth for many years thereafter. *Fairy* went out in a blaze of glory on 31 May 1918, ramming and sinking the German submarine *UC 75*, one and a half times her size and considerably more strongly built and, inevitably, sinking herself. *Osprey* was sold to J H Lee on 4 November 1919.

1897-1898 Programme

ORDERED: ? for delivery ?.

	Yard No.	Laid down	Launched	Completed
Leven	405	24.1.1898	28.6.1898	Jul 1899

DIMENSIONS: 215ft 6in oa, 209ft 9in bp × 21ft 0¼in ext, 21ft mld × 12ft 2in
DISPLACEMENT: 370 tons light, 420 tons full load
MACHINERY: As *Gipsy*
COAL: 92 tons
FIRST COST: £52,407

In September 1897 Fairfield's were noted as one of the few firms 'as yet in such a position in regard to speeds obtained as to justify their being asked to submit designs and tenders for vessels of 32 or 33kts'[106] though what was actually ordered from them was 'practically a repeat of the *Gipsy* class', which had not yet reached a speed of 30kts 'but will probably do so'.

Leven served in home waters until sold on 14 September 1920 to Hayes, Porthcawl.

1898-1899 Programme

ORDERED: 30 March 1899 for delivery in 14 and 15 months respectively.

	Yard No.	Laid down	Launched	Completed
Falcon	412	26.6.1899	29.12.1899	Dec 1901
Ostrich	413	28.6.1899	22.3.1900	Dec 1901

DIMENSIONS: 214ft 6in oa, 209in bp × 21ft × 12ft 2in + 8ft 9in (*Falcon* 215ft 6in oa, 207ft 9in bp)
DISPLACEMENT: 375 tons light, 420 tons full load
MACHINERY: As *Gipsy*
COAL: 85 tons
FIRST COSTS: £65,119 and £65,557

Fairfield's revised tender, with boilers of the modified Thornycroft type, of 25 January 1899 was accepted on 30 March[107] (though another entry says 'April 1899', this is presumably a clerical error).

Both spent their service lives in home waters. *Falcon* was sunk on 1 April 1918 in a collision with the trawler *John Fitzgerald* in the North Sea. *Ostrich* was sold on 29 April 1920 to the Barking Ship Breaking Co.

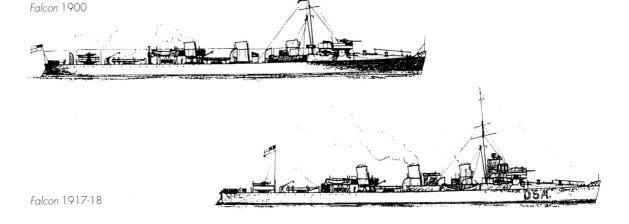

Falcon 1900

Falcon 1917-18

Thames Iron Works

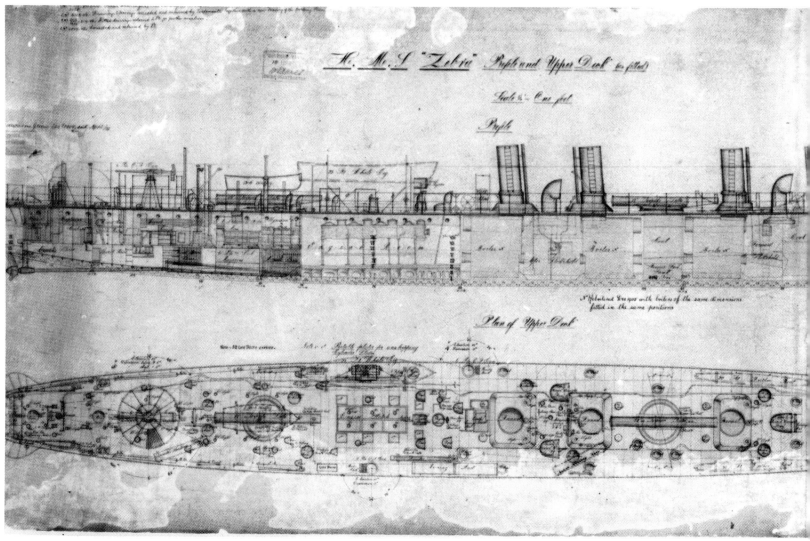

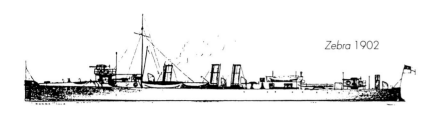

Zebra 1902

Zebra 1905

Zebra as built and as altered in
1905 and again in 1906.
(National Maritime Museum,
London: 103307)

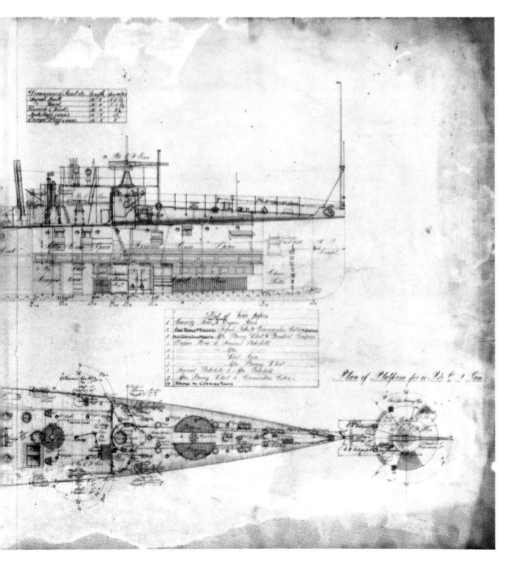

The Orchard Yard at Blackwall had been the largest and best-equipped private shipbuilding yard anywhere during the late eighteenth century, when it monopolised the construction of East Indiamen. In the early nineteenth century it had given its name to a type of ship – the Blackwall Frigate. Since then the yard had been through a number of changes, and had been transformed into an important builder in iron. It had built major warships and liners, and even sub-contracted the hull of a torpedo boat for Maudslay's, the engine builder. At this stage it was known both as 'The Thames Ship Building Co.' and the 'Thames Iron Works', and had just under two decades of life left before the increase of wages in the London area and other economic factors caused it to go into bankruptcy.

27-knotter, 1893-1894 Programme

ORDERED: 7 February 1894 for delivery 7 June 1895.

	Yard No.	Laid down	Launched	Completed
Zebra	. . .	1.7.1894	13.12.1895	Jan 1900

DIMENSIONS: 204ft 6in oa, 200ft bp × 20ft × 11ft 10in + 7ft 6in
DISPLACEMENT: 310 tons light, 365 tons full load
MACHINERY: 2 shafts, 19½in. 28¾in.30¾in.30¾in × 18in, 3 White boilers, 4800ihp
FIRST COST: £44,200

In June 1893 it was proposed[108] to add this firm, in association with Penn & Co of Greenwich, or another approved engine manufacturer, to the list of firms to which invitations to tender for 27-knotters would be sent.

The tender for delivering one TBD within sixteen months, with machinery by Maudslay Sons & Field for £38,598 was accepted, the price not including auxiliaries. However, the six funnels shown in the design (presumably in three pairs, each pair on either side of the centre line) could not be accepted, three on the centre line were preferred. The width of the side bunkers was too small. The arrangement of forced draught fans was also unsatisfactory because of the considerable recessing of the coal bunker bulkhead entailed. The watertight deck should be at least 6in above the load water line and have head room to the upper deck of at least 6ft 4in. Many of the scantlings were too heavy and the rudder was 'unnecessarily heavy'. The arrangements for riveting of the edges of the shell plating were considered insufficient. The ends of vessel were not to be pumped out with a hose, but to have permanent pipes to the 4½in service pump instead. In all the Admiralty pointed out forty-five points for alterations to the hull in its acceptance letter, a particularly high number, and not particularly a good omen for the success the design.

In the event, completion and acceptance lasted into the new century, the Zebra was never particularly highly thought of in service, and Thames Iron Works were not to receive another order from the Royal Navy for a destroyer until another decade had passed.

Zebra spent her career in home waters. Her funnels were raised after 1903. She was sold on 30 July 1914.

Hawthorn Leslie

This Newcastle firm, whose origins lay in engine-building had mostly so far built cargo liners and smaller passenger liners, ships of higher than average quality, but not of outstanding lightness or speed. It had no experience of building torpedo craft, and does not appear to have been invited to tender in 1892. However, the need to involve the maximum possible number of firms in the TBD programme caused Hawthorn Leslie's name to be added on 2 July 1893 to the list of those invited to tender.[109]

27-knotters 1893-1894 Programme

ORDERED: 7 February 1894 for delivery by 31 March 1895.

	Yard No.	Laid down	Launched	Completed
Sunfish	325	17.9.1894	9.8.1895	Mar 1896
Opossum	326	17.9.1894	4.10.1895	Jun 1896
Ranger	327	29.8.1894	28.5.1895	Feb 1896

DIMENSIONS: 204ft oa, 200ft bp × 19ft × 12ft 6in + 8ft 7in
DISPLACEMENT: 310 tons light, 340 tons full load
MACHINERY: 2 shafts, 18½in.28in.42in × 18in, 8 Yarrow boilers, 185lbs
FIRST COSTS: £42,358, £38,193 and £37,913.

The firm's tender, offering either locomotive or water tube boilers, was not accepted at first. The Admiralty wrote to say so on 7 November 1893,[110] but stated that they would consider an amended design if it was submitted within fourteen days. It was considered that the ihp was too low for the estimated displacement and that the use of High Tensile steel was not considered desirable. The lengths of the crew spaces should be at least equal to those in the guidance sketch for tendering. The scantlings of beams, reverse bars and bulkheads were all considered too slight. Reverse bars were to be fitted on every frame on opposite sides alternately. The bow tube was to be omitted. The machinery space being inadequate, the length of the engine room should be increased. Advantage should be taken of the speed of the boat for promoting water circulation in the condensers. A wing-gangway should be provided in the engine room, and there was no objection to moving the engines nearer the centre line. Two ladder-ways should be provided for each compartment, whilst the boilers should be in two stokeholds.

The firm presumably made the appropriate alterations, as a letter of 8 December 1893 stated that an order for one boat for £38,200 would be placed, provided twelve months delivery was promised and the forward torpedo tube moved to the position shown in the guidance sketch. The scantlings of the skin plating could be reduced somewhat. Watertight doors were not to be fitted and starting platforms should be arranged between the engines to enable both to be manipulated by one man if necessary. Air locks were not required for the stokeholds, etc.

In 1917-1918 the forefunnel of Opossum was raised.

Sunfish had been given taller funnels in 1900. All three vessels served in home waters throughout their careers. Sunfish was sold on 7 June 1920 to J Kelly, Opossum on 29 July 1920 to Ward, Preston and Ranger on 20 May 1920 to Riddle & Co.

Sunfish 1902

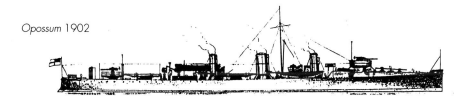
Opossum 1902

Opossum 1919

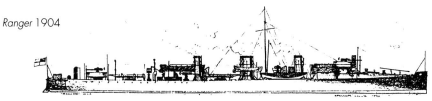
Ranger 1904

Opossum anchored, photographed in 1902, still without a topmast. (National Maritime Museum, London: N1980)

Cheerful 1897

Cheerful 1914

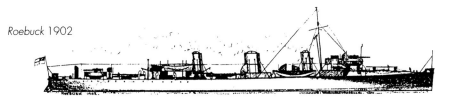

Roebuck 1902

Cheerful is shown here alongside in Victoria Dock, Dundee (this identification is thanks to David Hodge) in front of the shed where Scott's *Discovery* had recently been built. The picture would have been taken on a 'meet the navy' cruise in the early 1900s, which explains the crowd aboard her. An awning is spread aft. (National Maritime Museum, London: N2095)

30-knotters. 1896-1897 Programme

ORDERED: ? for delivery ?.

	Yard No.	Laid down	Launched	Completed
Cheerful	343	7.9.1896	22.2.1898	Jun 1899
Mermaid	344	7.9.1896	14.7.1897	Feb 1900

DIMENSIONS: 215ft oa, 210ft bp × 21ft × 13ft 1in+ 8ft 2in
DISPLACEMENT: 355 tons light, 400 tons full load
MACHINERY: 4 Thornycroft boilers, 220lbs, 6100ihp
FIRST COSTS: £54,509 and £53,935.

This design was to rival that of Palmer's for being the most popular and seaworthy of the 30-knotters. As usual the design seems to have been an enlargement of the builder's 27-knotter design with rather more power, but no radical alterations. It is not clear from the records consulted why *Mermaid* should be launched before, but completed after, her sister.

Both spent all their service lives in home waters except that *Mermaid* visited Gibraltar in 1910. *Cheerful* was mined on 30 June 1917 off the Shetlands. *Mermaid* on 23 July 1919 was sold to Ward, New Holland.

1897-1898 Programme design

In 1897 the firm tendered a design which was a repeat (though they did not point it out) of *Cheerfuls* – they proposed Thornycroft boilers but offered a rebate of £750 per vessel if boilers of the Yarrow type were fitted.[111] This must have led on to the acceptance of this design in the next programme.

1898-1899 Programme

ORDERED: 30 March 1899 (or April 1899?) for delivery in 15, 16 and 17 months.

	Yard No.	Laid down	Launched	Completed
Greyhound	377	18.7.1899	6.10.1900	January 1902
Racehorse	378	23.10.1899	8.11.1900	March 1902
Roebuck	379	2.10.1899	41.1901	March 1902

DIMENSIONS: 214ft 6in oa, 210ft 11in bp × 21ft 1in × 13ft
DISPLACEMENT: 385 tons light, 430 tons full load
MACHINERY: As *Cheerful* except: 4 Yarrow boilers
FIRST COSTS: £61,066, £61,068 and £61,032

On 25 July 1898[112] it was decided that as Hawthorn Leslie had successfully tried two vessels (for working though they had not yet reached contract speed), their name should be added to the list for invitations to tender and on 30 March 1899 their 'mixed' tender of 25 January 1899 was accepted. Three TBDs were ordered for £56,778 each (£21,200 for the hull and £35,578 for machinery). They were virtually repeats of the very successful *Cheerful* apart from using a different type of water tube boiler.

All three spent their careers in home waters. *Greyhound* after serving in the Dover Patrol was sold on 10 June 1919 to Clarkson, Whitby. *Racehorse* was sold on 23 March 1920 to M Yates who later re-sold her to Ward, who broke her up at Milford Haven in 1921. *Roebuck* was broken up in 1919 at Portsmouth Dockyard.

Left, Greyhound is shown at Portland in 1906 with a *Devonshire* class armoured cruiser in the background. (National Maritime Museum, London: N20856)

Below, Greyhound as built and as altered to 1908, then as altered to 1914. (National Maritime Museum, London: 22505)

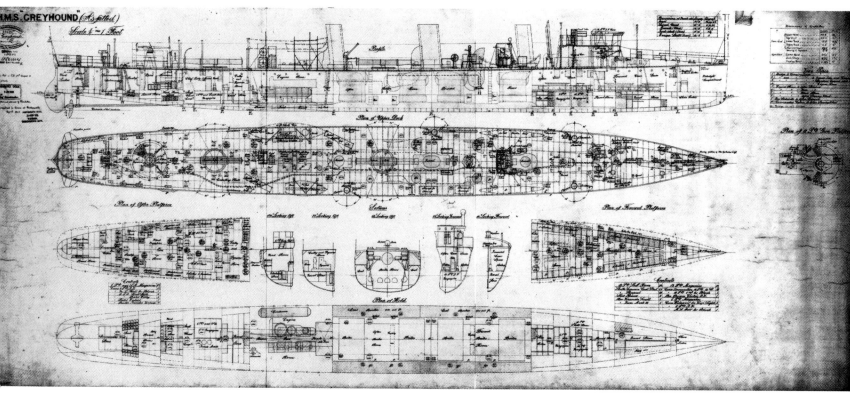

Part III:
TBDs in Service

Details and Fittings

Machinery and endurance

The printed conditions sent to the builders asked to tender for the 27-knotters give[1] a fair idea of the general parameters within which the machinery for all the TBDs was provided: 'The quality of the workmanship is to be in accordance with Admiralty practice and all the materials used are to be subjected to and are to stand the Admiralty tests and the work is to be carried out in accordance with the general conditions of the Admiralty machinery specification with which the firms are familiar and to the satisfaction of Admiralty inspecting officers. It is understood that the Contractors will be entirely responsible for the design of the machinery but all the arrangements are to be submitted to the Admiralty for

concurrence. The machinery is to be guaranteed for twelve months after the first commission of the boat for sea service.'

The operational trials of *Havock* gave a good idea of the abilities of the new type of vessel, essentially short-ranged and capable of high speed for only a short spurt, but better than anything that had gone before. Flaming from the top of the funnels, partly as the result of unskilled stoking, was a major source of preliminary discovery at night. To counter this menace the funnels of the earliest TBDs were raised and the later vessels of this type built with taller funnels from the start. Particularly significant were the following remarks in the report: ' . . . The highest working speed of the *Havock* may be considered as lying between 23 and 24kts – and her economical speed 12kts. The results of these trials show that she maintains the advantage over existing Torpedo Boats in "working speed" that she has in "Contractor's" trial speed . . . '[2]

After the 1895 manoeuvres, the first real service experience with a group of TBDs, the following remarks were made:[3] 'On the whole I do not think that the defects developed were of a serious nature taking into consideration the fact that these vessels had not been in commission before, and further I think that the longer the ships were in commission the less one would have to do to them and the fewer accidents would take place. Practice in craft of this sort is essential to efficiency and I believe that if a perfect vessel were constructed there would be still a fine crop of casualties if the crew were unaccustomed to the ship.'

Slightly later, the following significant remarks were made[4] about the first Palmer-built boats. *Janus* was one of those TBDs fitted with balance weights to her engines before official trials 'and she proved to be the most satisfactory vessel of those yet built as regards absence of vibration.' In several TBDs vibration had been greatly reduced by fitting balance weights, but as 'further and convincing proof' *Janus* had been tried with and without weights: 'In fact these experiments may be taken as demonstrating in a most striking manner the beneficial effects of a proper balancing of the engines in this vessel. With balance weights properly designed and properly adjusted, as in the present case, all feeling of distress or discomfort

disappears, the vessel being practically without vibration.'
Her sister vessel *Lightning* had just passed trials with
equally satisfactory lack of vibration.

By 1898 sufficient experience had been gained with the
30-knotters to make the following table possible:

*Typical 30kt destroyers' coal consumption in pounds per ihp
per hour*[5]

Name	At full speed for 3 hours	At 13kts for 12 hours
Quail	2.63	1.62
Fame	2.595	1.66
Foam	2.205	–
Mallard	2.08	–
Angler	2.347	–
Gipsy	2.45	–
Fairy	–	1.79
Bat	2.59	2.368
Chamois	2.42	1.84

The introduction of the Parsons steam turbine made for
greater reliability, smaller engine room crews, the ability
to sustain maximum speed as long as fuel (and, initially,
the endurance of stokers) held out, and reduced vibration
– but made less difference as far as endurance was concerned. The coal consumption trials[6] of the prototypes
show this:

Name	Speed (kts)	N. miles per ton	Bunkerage	Range (nautical miles)
Cobra	15.114	10.42	107 tons	1115/1070*
	15.01	12.21	ditto	1310/1265*
Viper	15.039	11.1	86	955/920*
	14.963	11.06	ditto	950/915*
	31.118	3.51	ditto	305/300*
Albatross	14.33	22.63	104	2355/2200*
	31.552	4.05	ditto	420/410*
Stag	13.081	32.03	78	2500/2240*
	30.156	5.63	ditto	440/430*

* = allowing 1 ton per day for incidental purposes

Clearly, reciprocating engines performed much better
than turbines at cruising speed – the latter would require
twice the coal capacity to cover the same distance. As
speed increased, however, the difference reduced. A major problem with turbines was that they could not reverse,
unlike reciprocating engines, and had to be fitted with
separate turbines for going astern. This initially caused
some problems with the *Viper* whose contract required
her to make 15½kts astern – but did not specify the time

The proposed arrangement of
machinery for *Racehorse* and
Roebuck can be taken as fairly
similar to that for most other TBDs,
with its details of engines, boilers
and shafting. (National Maritime
Museum, London: 97786)

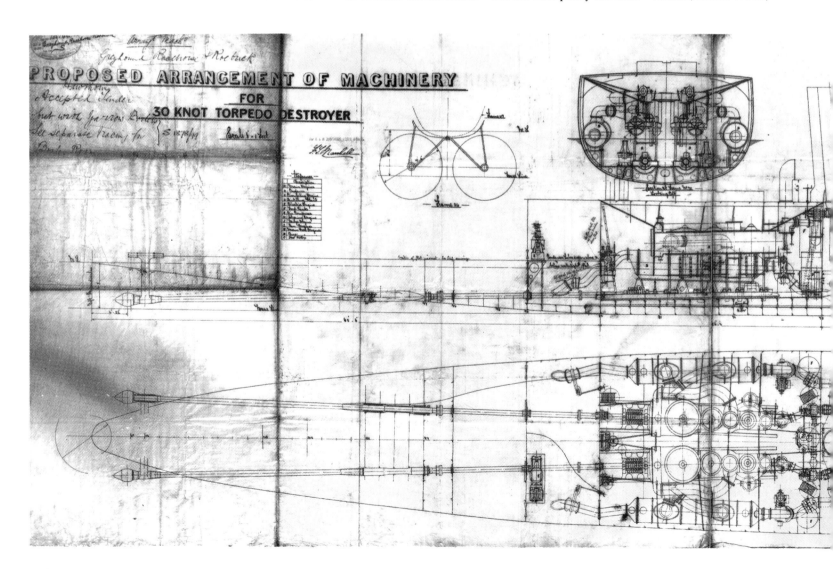

Hornet on trials, going flat out to make her 26kts, with mast, boats and armament not yet fitted. (National Maritime Museum, London: 3767)

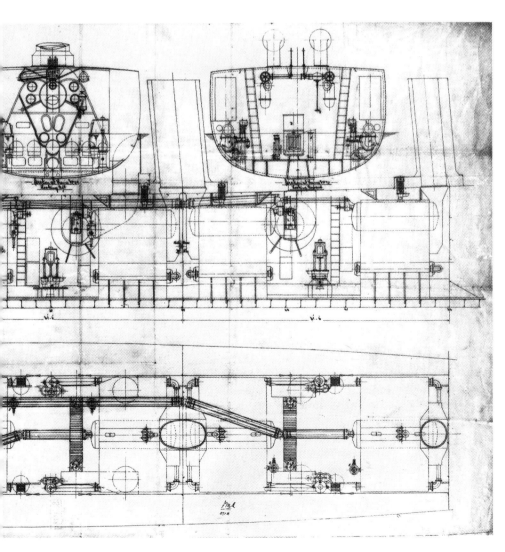

she had to do this for. She had not done this in a straight line astern – but had made sufficient revolutions astern for that speed whilst going round in circles. The steering engine needed to be strengthened and Parsons to continue to work on better astern steering.

On 28 February 1900 Commander Mark Kerr of the *Mermaid* submitted a report[7] after a year of serving as second-in-command and then in command of the Medway instructional flotilla, based on his observations and talking to the engineers of destroyers: ' . . . My personal opinion [is] that great improvements are of absolute necessity for even bare efficiency in wartime . . . The principal defect is a general lightness of machinery, the consequence being that the Flotilla rarely if ever go through a full speed trial without some boats breaking down. This is due to the Engines being cut down to save weight in order that speed may be got at the minimum expense. It hardly ever occurs that this Flotilla is at sea at its full strength on account of the constant breakdowns, all of which occur through want of strength in some part of the machinery and yet our cruises are only of three weeks duration and principally at moderate speeds. At present the [full speed] trial is run over the mile at a light draught, at which draught *the boat is never run on service*, consequently the Destroyers' *best lines are built at that draught and are never again utilised.* There is only one 30kt Destroyer – the *Ariel* – in this Flotilla which has ever run a distance of 28kts in an hour at her service trim . . . '

The development of a sturdier and more seaworthy vessel with the emphasis on sea speed rather than performance on trial had already begun with the design of the 'River' Class. Already in 1898 the First Lord had minuted: 'Personally I should prefer a 27kt ship which was less often in dock and less liable to accidents to a 30kt boat as liable to accidents as our boats have been. I do not propose this, but I am anxious about these accidents . . . '[8]

An enormous difference was made to the endurance of both ships and engine-room staff by the adoption of oil fuel. On 7–8 December 1904,[9] a vitally important series of comparative trials were run round the Isle of Wight by *Spiteful* and *Peterel*. The former had been fitted to burn oil (in this case obtained from Texas) – the latter was conventionally fuelled with coal. In trial No.3 the mean speed on the measured mile and consumption of fuel per hour were not wildly different, *Spiteful* obtained 22.27kts at 2.7 tons per hour, whilst *Peterel* did 21.5kts with 2.5 tons per hour – so far a fairly neatly balanced result. However, the significance of using liquid fuel showed in the other results: the oil-fuelled vessel had three men in the stokehold, the coal-fired ship six, whilst the time in preparing for sea was ten minutes instead of one and a half hours and ash and clinker overside nil as opposed to 1.5 tons. The labour-saving potential of liquid fuel was fairly obvious, the advantages in speed of reaction possibly less so, but the military benefits perhaps even greater.

The usual pattern with lightly-built steam-powered torpedo craft was that the boilers went first, then the hull (usually as a replacement set of boilers were coming to the end of their useful life), and finally the engines, which in the case of many of the earliest torpedo boats were removed from the scrapped hulls and went on to give many useful years of service as stationary engines in the Royal Dockyards. The TBDs had a shorter life, and by the time the earliest vessels of this kind had been in service for just over a decade both boilers and hulls were in need of replacement or at least serious repair. However, by this time they were considered obsolescent because of the rapid development of the type. In February 1908 the Admiralty declared: 'On the whole it is not recommended to spend the money on retubing the boilers of any 27kt destroyers nor on any 30kt destroyers which, at the time of retubing, have been 15 years in the service.'[10]

Armament

Originally the 26-knotters were intended to have two alternative armaments, one for the torpedo boat role, the other when acting as a destroyer or gunboat. The fixed bow torpedo tube was common to both roles. As gunboats they would carry this 18in fixed tube with two 18in torpedoes plus one 12pdr QF gun and three 6pdr QF (two mountings amidships, one each side, with another aft). One hundred rounds of ammunition would be carried per gun. The 12pdr gun was of 3in (75mm) calibre and was a larger version of the 6pdr (itself of 57mm calibre – just over 2in). Both were aimed by the gunlayer using the forward-curving shoulder rest which was such a visible feature of these guns. As torpedo boats the 18in fixed tube would be supplemented by a revolving mounting with two 18in tubes and a total of five torpedoes (three in the tubes and two spares). The 12pdr was retained but with only a single 6pdr, with 100 rounds per gun.

For the destroyer and self-protection roles the combination of one heavier weapon for hitting power and several lighter ones for volume of fire, and therefore an increased chance of achieving hits from a small, lively and fast-moving platform, was chosen. However the option of an even greater volume of fire from more, lighter and even quicker-firing guns (ie 3pdrs) was ruled out on the grounds that they would require too many gunners. The limits on the size of these small ships' complements determined the number of guns they could carry.

It was not proposed to carry a heavy armoured shield for the 12pdr, but 'a shield can be attached if [a] light pattern can be arranged hereafter'.[11] This appears to have been done for both the 12pdr and 6pdr mountings aboard all the TBDs. Shields could be, and were, carried for all of the guns, but by no means always fitted, being stowed in the mens' accommodation or elsewhere. The choice of whether to mount the shields or stow them seems to have been a matter for the destroyers' officers, which makes the careful notes compiled by collectors of photographs assigning dates to the times when the shields were fitted or not of less significance than they appear at first sight.

By the time the design of the 27-knotters was being discussed, it would appear that there were second thoughts about the suitability of having a fixed bow tube. Its removal would enable more ammunition to be carried for the gun armament, which was felt desirable to increase the ships' anti-torpedo boat capabilities. Furthermore, the heavy weight of the torpedo tube forward had an adverse effect upon seaworthiness. Despite arguments that the retention of a fixed torpedo tube gave the TBDs a defence

against larger vessels, the DNC W H White wrote on 7 October 1893 that the stem tube should be removed and a further two 6pdrs fitted amidships in future destroyers. J A Fisher, the Controller, noted on 10 October that he proposed to approve this suggestion. F W Richards, the First Sea Lord, agreed on 13 October: 'The object for which these vessels are required is to clear the Channel of the enemy's torpedo boats and they should have a clean sharp stem with no projections calculated either to check their speed or throw water inboard when in chase. They are 1st Class gunboats with auxiliary torpedo armament, the bow tube should not feature in the design.' Fisher added on the 20th that 'the above minute of Sir F Richards should guide future action' – and it did.

The torpedoes themselves were the longer versions of the 18in weapon provided by Whitehead and described[12] as '18in Fiume, long' (Fiume in Austria-Hungary being the base of the Whitehead company). The outfit of ammunition per gun, originally intended to be 100 rounds per guns, was later amended to 100 rounds per gun for the 12pdr and a total of 300 rounds for all the 6pdrs whether three or five were fitted.[13]

Following the initial trials of the prototype, *Havock*, W H White concluded: 'As regards armament it seems desirable to obtain further experience before a decision can be reached as to withdrawing torpedoes in favour of more guns or the opposite. For the vessels now in hand the balance of guns and torpedoes was most carefully considered, and at any time it is possible, if preferred, to remove the torpedo armament temporarily, mounting additional 6pdrs. But it will be noted that in preparing these designs one most important condition is the securing of *clear deck spaces* for the torpedo tubes: so that it is absolutely necessary to assume the necessity for carrying the torpedo armament at least occasionally, and arrange accordingly.'

From this first destroyer prototype right the way through to the destroyers of the Second World War there was intermittent debate as to whether these craft should carry heavier or lighter guns. Heavier guns offered longer range and greater hitting power, *when* they secured a hit, but lighter weapons could attain a greater rate of fire gun for gun, more of them could be carried, and they were easier to both load and fire. In retrospect, given the non-existent, or, at best, primitive fire control possible on such light and lively craft in that era it would seem that sense was on the side of lighter weapons with a higher rate of fire and a better chance of obtaining hits.

Meanwhile, the design of the larger and faster 30-knotters was being debated. There were suggestions for the fitting of larger numbers of lighter guns, 3pdrs and rifle-calibre Maxim machine-guns being suggested, but the perennial problem of restricted complements, the need to retain guns capable of dealing with torpedo boats and not least the logistical problems a change in destroyer armaments would cause meant that these suggestions were never acted upon. Therefore, the 30-knotters appeared with an armament of one 12pdr 12cwt gun on a P.1 mounting with 100 rounds, five 6pdrs with 300

This excellent bow shot shows *Lynx* at anchor in 1897 at Spithead. The cap to the bow torpedo tube is open, showing that the tube was of oval cross-section at its mouth (presumably to allow for a certain amount of downward angle when the torpedo was fired). Note the canvas dodger protecting the front of the 12pdr platform, the Diamond Jubilee Review berth number boards and the very restricted field of view possible from the conning tower under the 12pdr. The washing drying on the guy line would appear to be canvas covers stripped from the 12pdr. There are two long boat-hooks stowed sloping down forwards in front of the conning tower. (National Maritime Museum, London: G5299)

rounds per ship, and two 18in torpedo tubes with two long 18in torpedoes.[14]

The subsequent 30-knotters, the faster 'Specials' and the turbine boats all had this same standard armament. However, the two modified 30-knotters purchased from Palmer's and added in 1909 as *Albacore* and *Bonetta* had a different weapons fit. They carried three 12pdrs, two forward and one aft, plus the usual two 18in torpedo tubes, though the full outfit included four reloads (six torpedoes in all) but, 'only two of the six torpedoes are carried on board the vessel, the remainder being kept in depot as usual'.[15]

By the beginning of the new century destroyers were as a matter of course carrying a combined gun and torpedo armament,[16] though the usual procedure with 27-knotters was for the forward of the two torpedo tubes to be landed at the flotilla's base, or carried aboard the depot ship. This was, however, a temporary peacetime measure for increased safety and convenience. Should war come the intention was to replace the forward tube aboard. But when stability had sunk to such a level that topweight had to be removed permanently it was the forward of the two tubes that would be made the permanent sacrifice.

Top left, Amidships detail photo showing the 12pdr gun and its platform of *Tiger* taken in 1906. Notice the detail of the chart table. (National Maritime Museum, London: N8788)

Top right, Quail in dry dock with a mangled bow in August 1907 after a collision with the scout cruiser *Attentive.* The light structure of TBDs crumpled easily when in collision. Besides revealing some of the structure of the vessel this photograph shows an excellent view of a Berthon boat. (National Maritime Museum, London: B7673/G)

Left, this picture was taken at Foster's Pier, Esquimault, British Columbia, Canada (the base of the Pacific squadron) in January 1898 and shows the two TBDs on that station, *Sparrowhawk* and *Virago.* Both have awnings rigged and the nearer of the two (*Sparrowhawk*) has the Commander-in-Chief of that station (Rear Admiral H St L Palliser) aboard, as she is flying his Rear Admiral's flag at her masthead. Both ships have men over the side on what is probably a multi-hulled pontoon or 'balsa' – presumably painting ship. (National Maritime Museum, London: A2336)

By September 1904 double tubes had been removed from 'the *Havock* class' (in other words the six 26-knotters). In the cases of *Shark, Skate, Hardy* and *Haughty* both torpedo tubes and racers had been removed as well as the pivots as a result of inclining experiments showing how much topweight had accumulated. In all other destroyers from which torpedo tubes had been removed, the racers and pivots were ordered to be left and kept efficient so that the tubes could be replaced if necessary – whilst the question was raised whether the removal of these items from the four listed above should not be reconsidered.[17] However, Deadman noted that retaining the extra tube was only possible from the stability point of view if the original scheme of alternative armaments was adhered to. At this stage the 27-knotter vessels carrying only one tube were those built by Laird, Fairfield, Hawthorn, Doxford, Elswick (Armstrong), Vickers, Doxford and Brown (Thomson).

In February 1908 it was stated[18] that 26- and 27-knotters were by then generally made to carry combined gun and torpedo armaments as in the 30-knotters – except for *Banshee, Contest, Dragon, Sunfish, Opossum, Ranger, Handy, Hart, Hunter, Swordfish, Spitfire, Haughty, Hardy, Shark, Ardent, Boxer* and *Bruiser* in all of which it was undesirable for stability reasons to carry the additional top weight involved by the second torpedo tube and torpedo. The 26-knotters only had three 6pdrs (in addition to their 12pdr) and their single bow torpedo tubes instead of the two revolving tubes usually carried.

Late in their careers a number of TBDs had one of their two 18in torpedo tubes replaced by a 21in tube. The prototype installation, done in 1909, was in *Rocket* using a 21in tube taken from the 'River' class destroyer *Waveney.*[19] The heavier tube, torpedo, and larger davit plus separate winch added some 14 tons to topweight in this vessel.

During the First World War at least one TBD was actually fitted with the gun armament proposed during the design stage of the 27-knotters – two 12pdrs only (the second one replacing the after 6pdr).[20] Other vessels were fitted during the war for depth charges and with the 2pdr pom-pom.

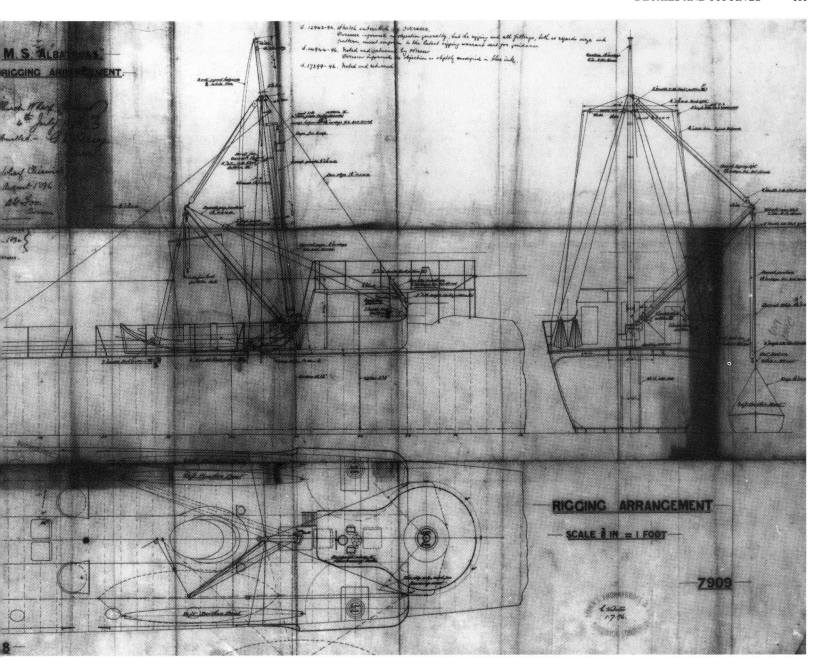

This rigging plan for the *Albatross* shows how the two Berthon boats were hoisted out by the derrick attached to the mast. Though a plan drawn by the builder, Thornycroft, it comes from the Admiralty Collection. (National Maritime Museum, London: 61278)

Boats

The following chronological list summarises the changes to the boat outfit of TBDs:

1892   Original outfit approved for 27-knotters – one 25ft whaler for general ship's duties, two 20ft Berthon boats (wood and canvas folding boats used as emergency lifeboats).

1894   Reindeer hair boats to be substituted for Berthons. These 'unsinkable dinghies', stuffed with reindeer hair, were built by Cunnah, Wright & Co., but proved unpopular in service. 13ft 6in skiff dinghy to be added to all TBDs, as ships' complements too small for effective manning of 25ft whaler for general ship's duties, although the whaler's greater seaworthiness meant it was retained. (? Decision probably taken at this stage – but evidence lacking.)

1895   Berthon boats to replace the reindeer hair boats in the twenty-four TBDs equipped with the latter (18ft for 27-knotters, 22ft for 30-knotters).

1895   First twelve of the 30-knotters ordered with one 18ft light gig, one 13ft 6in dinghy and two hair boats (the latter soon replaced by two 20ft Berthon boats)

1900   One 18ft gig rather than one 25ft whaler carried aboard *Desperate, Fame, Foam, Mallard, Quail, Sparrowhawk, Thrasher, Brazen, Electra, Virago, Recruit, Vulture* and *Havock*.

1900   *Albatross* as built carried one 25ft whaler, three (instead of two) 20ft Berthon boats and one 13ft 6in dinghy as did *Viper* (and probably the same obtained for the 'Specials', *Arab, Express* and *Cobra*, with their heavier complements of stokers).

1915   TBDs by now carrying two Carley floats, the standard British lifesaving raft of both World Wars, as well as their Berthon boats.

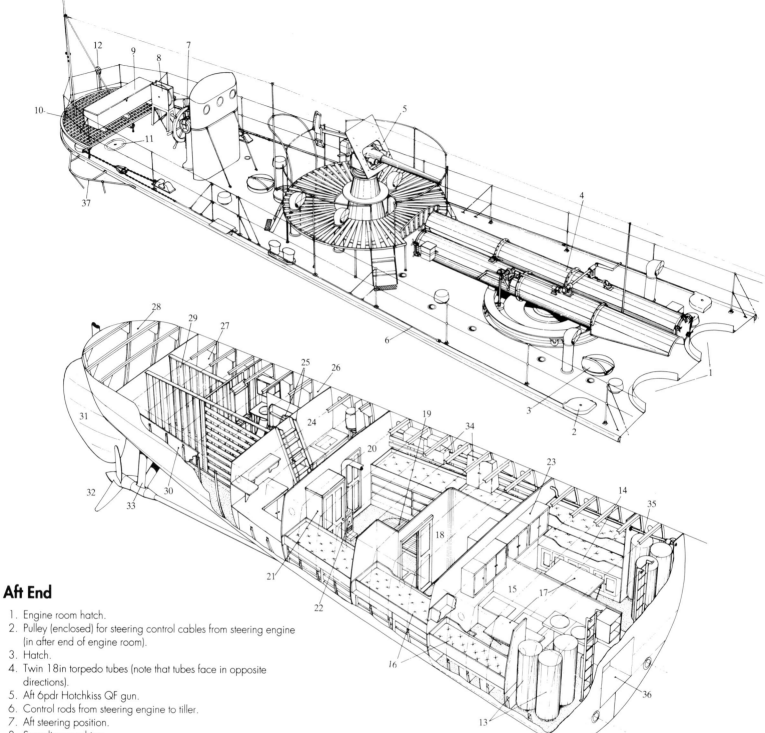

Aft End

1. Engine room hatch.
2. Pulley (enclosed) for steering control cables from steering engine (in after end of engine room).
3. Hatch.
4. Twin 18in torpedo tubes (note that tubes face in opposite directions).
5. Aft 6pdr Hotchkiss QF gun.
6. Control rods from steering engine to tiller.
7. Aft steering position.
8. Sounding machine.
9. Wash deck locker.
10. Raised platform (tiller under).
11. Scuttle to engineer's store.
12. Roller for sounding machine cable.
13. Fresh water tanks (port and starboard).
14. Engine room artificers' berth (small arms and 6pdr magazine under).
15. Chief stoker's berth (small arms and 6pdr magazine under).
16. Bed places.
17. Table.
18. Commander's cabin.
19. Table.
20. Ward room (including officers' berths – stores under).
21. Wardrobe.
22. Stove.
23. Mess cupboards.

24. Ward room pantry (pantry stores under).
25. Ladder.
26. Officers' WC.
27. Bread room (watertight compartment under).
28. Engineer's stores.
29. Wood battens.
30. Shelf (port and starboard) in bread room.
31. Rudder.
32. Port propeller.
33. 'A' bracket.
34. Cupboards.
35. Fire main.
36. Recess in after engine room bulkhead for steering engine.
37. Propeller guard.

HMTBD *Havock* 1895
Cutaway drawings by John Roberts

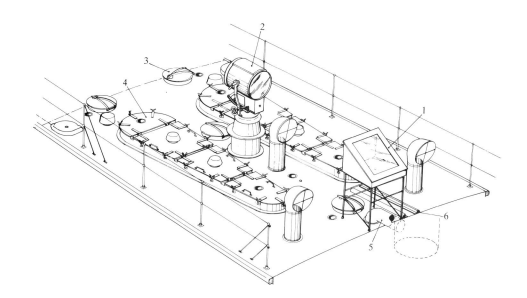

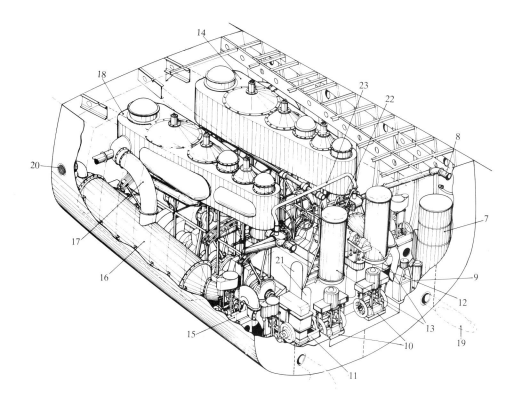

Engine Room Section

1. Chart table.
2. Searchlight.
3. Hatch.
4. Engine room hatch (port and starboard).
5. Vent to engine room from boiler room intake.
6. Torpedo trolley tramway.
7. Evaporator.
8. Main steam pipe.
9. Water distillation equipment.
10. Air compressors.
11. Steam driven dynamo.
12. Steam engine for aft boiler room fan.
13. Feed water tanks.
14. Port 3-cylinder, triple-expansion engine.
15. Steam driven centrifugal circulating pump (port and starboard).
16. Condenser (port and starboard).
17. Exhaust steam from low pressure cylinder to condenser.
18. Starboard 3-cylinder, triple-expansion engine.
19. Condenser sea water intakes.
20. Condenser sea water outlet.
21. Air vessels.
22. Ladder.
23. Main steam cross-connection pipe.

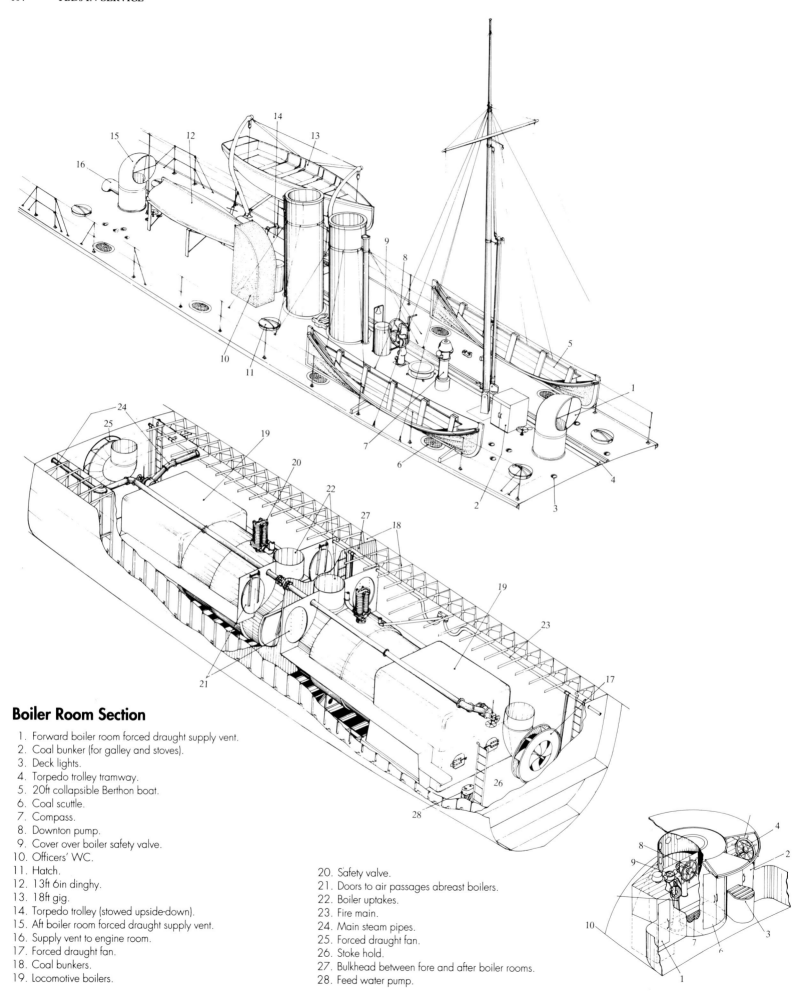

Boiler Room Section

1. Forward boiler room forced draught supply vent.
2. Coal bunker (for galley and stoves).
3. Deck lights.
4. Torpedo trolley tramway.
5. 20ft collapsible Berthon boat.
6. Coal scuttle.
7. Compass.
8. Downton pump.
9. Cover over boiler safety valve.
10. Officers' WC.
11. Hatch.
12. 13ft 6in dinghy.
13. 18ft gig.
14. Torpedo trolley (stowed upside-down).
15. Aft boiler room forced draught supply vent.
16. Supply vent to engine room.
17. Forced draught fan.
18. Coal bunkers.
19. Locomotive boilers.
20. Safety valve.
21. Doors to air passages abreast boilers.
22. Boiler uptakes.
23. Fire main.
24. Main steam pipes.
25. Forced draught fan.
26. Stoke hold.
27. Bulkhead between fore and after boiler rooms.
28. Feed water pump.

Fore End

1. Bow stoppers.
2. Chain pipe.
3. Riding bitts.
4. Capstan.
5. Anchor.
6. Cat head.
7. 12pdr, 12cwt QF gun on PI mounting.
8. 6pdr Hotchkiss QF gun (port and starboard).
9. 18in bow torpedo tube.
10. Cement.
11. Watertight compartment.
12. Cable locker.
13. Torpedo loading tray.

14. Stokers' berth.
15. Torpedo well (under).
16. Stores.
17. Bed places (note that on the lower berths the sides could be hinged down so that the berths could be used as seats).
18. Hatch.
19. Torpedo warhead magazine.
20. 12pdr magazine.
21. 6pdr magazine.
22. Naval stores (starboard), 12pdr shell room and slop room (port).
23. Seamen's berth.
24. Galley.
25. Fresh water tanks.
26. Engine for forced draught fan in forward boiler room.
27. POs' berth.
28. Table.
29. Hawser reels.
30. Ladder to conning tower and upper deck.
31. Lockers (under bed places).
32. Mess cupboards.
33. Steering control shaft.
34. Fire main.

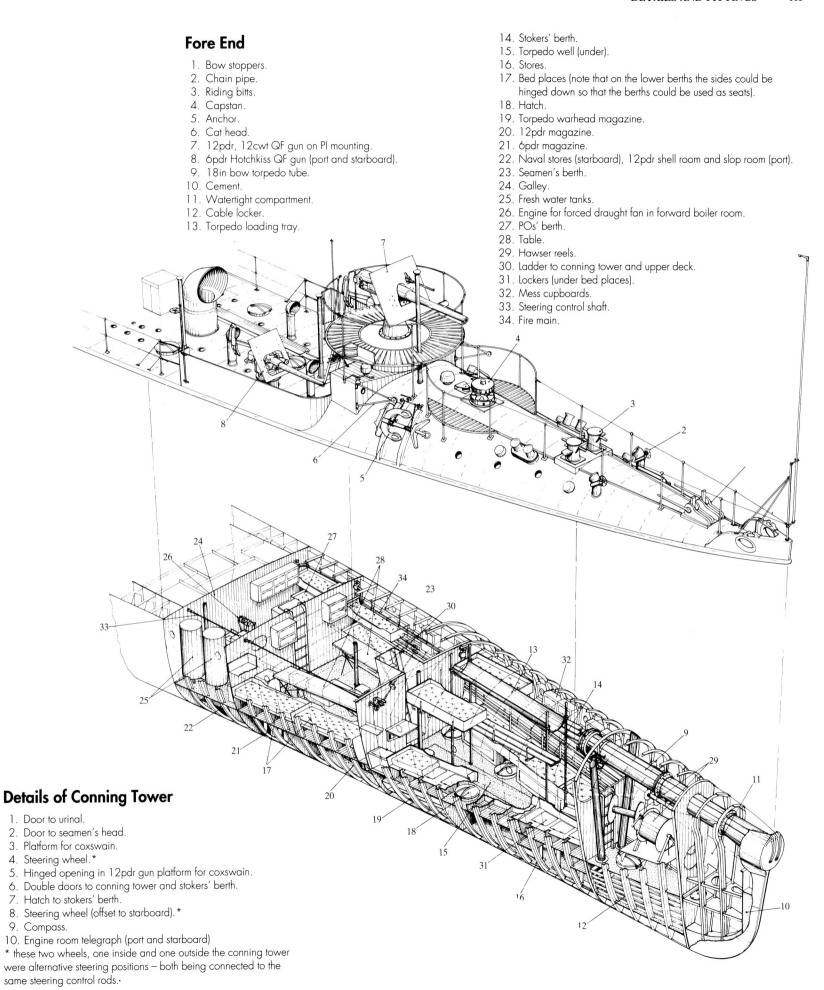

Details of Conning Tower

1. Door to urinal.
2. Door to seamen's head.
3. Platform for coxswain.
4. Steering wheel.*
5. Hinged opening in 12pdr gun platform for coxswain.
6. Double doors to conning tower and stokers' berth.
7. Hatch to stokers' berth.
8. Steering wheel (offset to starboard).*
9. Compass.
10. Engine room telegraph (port and starboard)
* these two wheels, one inside and one outside the conning tower were alternative steering positions – both being connected to the same steering control rods.

Accommodation and Habitability

The complement proposed for the 'Torpedo boat catchers' ordered in July 1892 was originally to be forty, including one Lieutenant (who was in command), one Sub-Lieutenant and a Gunner (who was a warrant officer) with eleven more men as deck complement and an engine room staff of twenty-six.[21] Then (15 September 1892) the Engineer Committee reported that they thought that the design with eight water tube boilers would need a total of twenty-seven engine-room staff at the minimum: 'The very high speed of revolutions of these engines will necessitate very careful supervision. Consider Engine room complement cannot possibly be reduced without materially impairing their [ie the TBDs] efficiency as steamers.' As a result on 11 November 1892 it was approved to add an extra stoker (as a spare) to the complement. On the 17th[22] of the same month the official scheme of complement for the 26-knotters was settled at two officers (Lieutenant and Sub-Lieutenant), one Gunner, three Petty Officers, seven Able Seamen, one Signaller, one Chief Engineer, one Chief Engine-Room Artificer, five Petty Officer ERAs, three chief stokers, three leading stokers and seventeen stokers (with no 2nd class stokers carried at all), making a total of forty-two in all.

The 27-knotters ordered under the next year's programme (1893-1894) had an enlarged deck complement to cope with the effective increase in the armament of these ships, though retaining the engine room complement of twenty-eight, a total of fifty in all.[23]

With the ordering of the first 30-knotters the question of whether extra stokers were needed was raised. A J Durston (the Engineer-in-Chief) minuted on 27 September 1895 that the proposed engine room complement was based on that of *Havock*, which provided for short bursts of full speed with the engine-room staff working watch and watch. With the *Boxer*'s (27-knotters) 'IHP [was] raised but not number of stokers on account of the strong desire to keep the numbers as low as possible.' In a 30-knotter at full speed stokers would be more on watch than off watch. With two separate stokeholds it was unlikely that full speed would be kept up for more than 4 hours continuously. 'If the highest possible speed is required for a longer period it will be necessary to clean fires and the labour of the men in the stokeholds will become very arduous . . . Having in view the distressing conditions under which the men will work it is considered that Engine Room complement as s[uggested?] is on the lowest possible scale.'

The early designs for the 30-knotters produced a couple of departures from the norm. The arrangement of accommodation shown in one of the tender designs involved messing and sleeping of some of the crew in the engine-room, whilst another design placed the wardroom and captain's cabin so that the officers were berthed forward and crew aft. It was decided that the first should only be considered if absolutely necessary and, fortunately for the crews concerned, was never adopted. Interestingly it was ordered that the proposal to berth officers forward should be favourably considered, though it was not in fact adopted until some fifty years later.[24]

As might be expected the greater power and size of the high-speed 'specials' (32 and 33-knotters) meant that more stokers were needed. A rule of thumb was suggested: 'to be to allow one man additional for every 250ihp actually found necessary to guarantee full speed over a three-hour trial and therefore to allow 72 rather than 68 originally provided for in conditions of tendering.' On 4 February 1898 it was decided to give *Express* (which was intended to reach 33kts) a complement of seventy-three – five more stokers than that allocated to the *Arab* (which was supposed to reach 32kts).[25]

In fact the problem of inordinate numbers of stokers would soon solve itself. The increased reliability and reduced levels of noise, vibration and generally nasty conditions in the engine-rooms produced by the replacement of reciprocating engines by turbines made a small saving in engine-room staff possible – which mainly explains the fact that the modified 30-knotters purchased from Palmer's, which were turbine-powered, had a total complement of fifty-six.[26] Had these vessels also had oil fuel the numbers would have been considerably less, and it was the adoption of liquid fuel which enabled the engine-room component of the crew to be cut considerably from its original dominant position. Yet another major step had been taken in reducing the role of human muscle-power in moving ships.

The general instructions[27] for building 27-knotters give a graphic picture of the physical surroundings in which these men lived: 'The mess fittings consist of a cupboard and plate rack for each seamen [sic] and a bread tray for every two men. Lockers of special pattern are fitted so as to be readily removed, one for each man. No provision is made for ditty boxes or bags. Hammocks are stowed overhead on the hammock beams. The fittings in the Ward room take the form of a wardrobe with separate compartments, one compartment for each officer, and two lockers for each Officer and Waterproof [ie for oilskins] and Seaboot racks are provided. The Officers sleep on horsehair cushions placed on the lockers. Both cushions and bolsters are provided by the Contractor [ie the shipbuilder]. All lockers both for Officers and men are provided with lee boards and used for sleeping purposes, the men sleeping on lockers being provided with cork mattresses which are stowed overhead on hammock beams. The cork mattresses are supplied by the Government . . . Sanitary arrangements consist of WC for Officers aft, fitted to pump direct from the sea, a sea-cock being fitted. The closet adopted has generally been obtained from the Firm of Beresford. For seamen a WC and urinal are fitted forward abreast the conning tower. These are flushed by means of buckets . . . The firehearth is of a special pattern and made by Pascall, Atkey & Co. of Cowes. Fresh water tanks are placed so the water can be drawn from them into a bucket. No lift pumps are fitted. These tanks are connected to the distillers. No watertight doors are to be fitted for passage between compartments, but doors placed well up on the bulkhead have been fitted for passing food from the Galley to the crew space. Where the Galley is aft these doors are not required . . . All provisions are stowed in tins, so that the provision spaces need only be battened and cork cemented.'

So much for the intention, but what was living aboard these small, lightly-built craft actually like? The sea trials of the first of them all, the *Havock*, gave an early idea.[28] The commanding officer (Arthur W Torlesse) commented as follows: 'The complement . . . seems sufficient for the purpose and admits of every one being told off in three watches, unless under steam for more than three hours, when coal trimmers would be required . . . The behaviour of the ship and the accommodation is such that no one gets undisturbed rest at sea even in fine weather and in bad weather of course there would be very little rest for any one so that I should (except in very exceptional circumstances) recommend a limit of five nights at sea . . . '

The main report added: 'The manoeuvring power of the *Havock* is equal to that of a modern Torpedo Boat – the life on board is easier and more comfortable in moderate weather, *but very little better in bad weather.*'

As the TBDs grew older so the discomfort became even greater. The crews of small craft generally had an extra allowance of pay – known by the splendidly graphic title of 'hard lying money' – and some crews really earned it. One thing that does seem true is that most early destroyers were 'happy ships' with a more relaxed attitude to discipline and standards of turnout than 'big ships'. Small ships, then as now, tended to breed a cheerful spirit of camaraderie and shared hardships. Certainly one gets that impression from the written memories of officers like Lionel Dawson and 'Taffrail'. One must not exaggerate the degree which the class boundaries between officers and men were crossed in the more intimate context of the 'small ship navy' – and some destroyer captains were martinets and sticklers for uniform appearance. However the general impression from the little hard evidence available seems to show that ratings as well as officers tended to enjoy their time in destroyers and torpedo craft, and there was more comradeship and less discontent.

Colours and visibility

The original colour scheme for the new TBDs was to be the same as the smaller torpedo boats that they were to supersede: 'The outside of the vessel, deck fittings, funnels &c. should be painted black. The fittings in Officers' cabins are usually polished, the panelling being painted in a light colour. The crews' quarters are generally painted in a light stone colour. All steel work in living and store spaces &c. should be cork painted, the cork being in the form of dust. The cork is not painted over.'[29] The cork painting was intended to combine a degree of insulation with a surface which prevented condensation.

In 1898, after experiments with searchlights in the North Sea it was decided that all destroyers in home waters were to be painted in the following scheme: 'Turtle back grey (black and white mixed) up to underneath side of 12pdr platform, also coamings of the hatchways and cowls for 2ft from the deck. Rubbing strake to be unpainted and scrubbed or painted grey, insides of the smaller cowls as a rule to be painted vermilion and hatchway covers (galvanised iron) to be kept plain – remaining portion of weather work (*ie* parts of ship exposed to the weather) black.'[30]

On 22 November 1899 the Admiralty wrote to all Commanders-in-Chief stating that the home waters scheme should be used for all destroyers 'except white to be substituted for black if the heat of the climate justifies . . . ' This was as a result of the Commander-in-Chief, Mediterranean asking if he could paint his destroyers Brunswick green. In effect he was being told to use white instead, as was the Commander-in-Chief, China.[31]

The protective compositions applied below the waterline of destroyers at this time seem usually to have been black in colour For example, in March 1899 Hayes' black protective composition was used on *Teazer*, *Wizard* and *Conflict*.[32]

Black was to remain the main colour of TBDs for many years, though there was a continuing discussion on the best (*ie* least visible) colours to use for flotilla craft, which

Whiting in China Station white, moored, possibly, at Hong Kong, between about 1906 and 1914. (National Maritime Museum, London: 63/158)

had started at least a decade before the first TBD came into service. In 1900 'Jackie' Fisher – at that stage, Commander-in-Chief, Mediterranean – was conducting exercises which produced relevant evidence. Captain Jackson of the torpedo craft depot ship *Vulcan* conducted these exercises with his own ship and her own, small 'Second Class' torpedo boats, plus the TBDs – *Griffon*, *Earnest*, *Foam*, *Boxer* and *Dove*, four 140ft TBs, three 125-footers, one 113ft boat, the 'torpedo ram' *Polyphemus*, the small cruiser *Barham* and the torpedo gunboats *Speedy*, *Hazard* and *Sandfly*. A precis of Jackson's report indicated that: 'as regards invisibility in the day time there is no doubt that it is harder to see the grey colour . . . against the sea than any other – the white being especially conspicuous.' However, in discussing a night attack by eight torpedo boats and two torpedo gunboats on *Vulcan* and *Barham* in Marsa Scirocco, Malta with the torpedo boat destroyers used to patrol the entrance and four of *Vulcan*'s Second Class torpedo boats assisting in defence, the following points were brought out. The small and almost invisible Second Class torpedo boats were of great value in guarding the narrow entrance in fine weather with a fairly powerful vessel to distract the enemy's attention and blind him with searchlights. The Second Class boats could not be seen from *Vulcan* whilst the destroyers and '90' class torpedo boats (the 140-footers) were plainly visible at treble their distance of 800 yards. 'The increase in size of torpedo boats militates against them making sneaking attacks in restricted waters . . .'

Conclusions included the fact that the '40' class (125ft torpedo boats) 'possess neither the speed nor invisibility (one of which is a *sine qua non*) essential for their protection. [TB] No.21 is the most invisible, probably due to her rounded contours . . . sharp outlines are much more easily caught by the eyes than rounded or uneven ones in the dark, or in an uncertain light . . . ' It is interesting

(but should scarcely come as a surprise) that the Royal Navy of a century ago was interested in what we would now call 'Stealth'. Fisher summed up the report: 'a dull light grey appears to be the best colour as regards invisibility.'[33]

However, not everyone agreed with Fisher's conclusion on grey being best. Less than a year later the Commander-in-Chief, Portsmouth – Admiral Charles Hotham – wrote (19 January 1901) to the Admiralty: ' . . . destroyers should be painted same [?] colour and bottoms black before delivery from contractors. *Myrmidon* arriving here from Jarrow had a broad white waterline which had to be scraped out – Some three years ago after experiments with Search Lights in the North Sea I recommended that destroyers should be painted dead black throughout as the most suitable colour for night work . . . ' The captain of *Vernon* agreed with him. 'The service colour, black with grey upperworks and red inside of vents gives lines which are conspicuous under Search Lights. Gray is also an elastic colour for officers to play with, changes can be rung on it from nearly white to practically black. I think a dead black boat looks very well and serviceable . . . ' However, a shining black band looked like ice under a searchlight beam – so gloss black was not a good idea.

Admiral W H May considered that all destroyers should be dead black, whilst Deadman (the constructor responsible for destroyer design) agreed: ' . . . until about two years ago all destroyers delivered by contractors were painted black throughout, when on the representation of the Commander-in-Chief, Portsmouth, it was ordered that in peace time vessels should be painted in a more ornamental manner.' This explains the grey turtleback and red cowl scheme.

In response to a question whether that decision should be extended to their respective commands, the Commander-in-Chief, China thought it undesirable in

This photo shows *Hunter* leaving Portsmouth in 1898 – with the Union flag at her masthead. The figure '2' in a white diamond is presumably a flotilla marking. The contrast between the turtleback, presumably in light gray, and the black hull is striking. (National Maritime Museum, London: N1941)

peacetime – when absent from the parent ship destroyers should carry enough black to repaint quickly in case of outbreak of war; whilst the Commander-in-Chief, Mediterranean indicated his chosen scheme was that the funnels, all upper works and boat screens were to be Admiralty Colour (yellow ochre) – the hull otherwise white to the waterline. The bottoms to be black antifouling (Rahtjen's or Stephenson's). The whole above water scheme could be repainted as black in six hours.[34] That white and buff scheme was indeed the one used on both the Mediterranean and China stations.

The question came up again in 1907 when, on 23 May Lewis Bayley, Commodore (T), requested that destroyers should be painted same colour as their 'scouts' (light cruisers built as flotilla leaders), which were grey. At night, Bayley reported ' . . . the destroyers are extremely easily seen from *Attentive* on account of the colour of their paint and that the destroyers have found it very difficult to see the *Attentive* even when close to her – as an example of which I would refer to an occasion during the night attack by torpedo boat destroyers on the 13–14 May, when I had to use my syren to avoid colliding with the *Swale*. In my past experience of many years, I have always found that black was only the next worst colour to white, and since torpedo boat destroyers are intended in every way to be ready for war, I would submit that their colour should be such as the necessities of war demand, which in my opinion is not black but grey.'

The Secretary of the Admiralty wrote to the Commander-in-Chief, Home Fleet about this divergence in opinion: 'The probable reason for this is the varying nature of the conditions of attack as practised by the different fleets and flotillas. It would appear that while grey is the better colour in moonlight, or when searchlights are not in use, black is the more effective in keeping the boat invisible when in the beam of a searchlight at long distance . . . ' He concluded that experiments were

needed – half of the boats were to be painted grey and night attacks tried both with and without searchlights. A report should be made after six months.

The Director of Naval Ordnance (R H Bacon) minuted that the fact that the tendency had become not to reveal position of a ship by using searchlights until she had definitely been sighted made grey the better choice.

By late 1908 the relevant trials had been made and H F Oliver, then the captain of HMS *Achilles*, reported on destroyer visibility trials: 'The black destroyers were very difficult to make out in the searchlight, the first thing seen was the white bow wave and wake and then the hull, the wet portion near the waterline shining and catching the light and showing up before the dry portion, as the boats got closer the upper works and funnels came into view . . . The grey boats were shown up at once by the light very distinctly . . . you see the whole boat at once . . . They appear almost white in the beam and are a splendid target. A weak beam which will not pick up a black boat at all will show up a grey boat.' He suggested black hull and light grey upperworks for the Scouts.

Bayly reported that destroyers were best sighted from a viewpoint low down on the target ships. Grey boats only suffered in comparison with black ones when searchlights were on them. It was worth noting that destroyers were often sighted by eye and then lost when a searchlight was switched on, until caught fully in its beam.

Admiral Bridgman added the remark that his experience showed grey to be the best day colour and black the best night colour and both should be of a dull finish.

Apparently in December 1908 trial was to be made of a yellowish-green colour on one destroyer – if this was done it appears to have left no trace in the record. In the end it was, after 1916, to be grey that would be the wartime colour for destroyers, and black that was to be abandoned. Probably that was a sensible decision.

This picture of *Dasher* passing Clarence Pier, Portsmouth, was taken in 1898. The white funnel bands are probably a temporary recognition feature to distinguish her from her sisters. (National Maritime Museum, London: N1965)

Operational Factors

Trials of the prototype

The *Havock* was rushed into service as rapidly as possible to enable the Admiralty to experiment with the new type at the earliest possible opportunity. Her trials took place between Portsmouth and Portland from 4 to 9 June 1894, under the aegis of HMS *Excellent*, the Royal Navy's gunnery school. These entailed a series of exercises 'with the object of testing the enduring power of crew, coal and stores while employed in carrying out the work which would probably fall to the share of such a vessel under war conditions', consisting of simulated attacks on torpedo boats and pursuits of the *Havock* by a 'Torpedo Catcher'.

The following conclusions were submitted to the Admiralty on 22 June 1894:[35] 'From the foregoing and other trials, which we have carried out at various times to test the fitness of *Havock* as a Torpedo Boat Destroyer we have drawn the following conclusions and upon these we beg to offer some general observations –

The highest working speed of the *Havock* may be considered as lying between 23 and 24kts – and her economical speed 12kts.

The results of these trials show that she maintains the advantage over existing Torpedo Boats in "working speed" that she has in "Contractor's" trial speed.

The manoeuvring power of the *Havock* is equal to that of a modern Torpedo Boat – the life on board is easier and more comfortable in moderate weather, *but very little better in bad weather.*

Her ability, when at high speeds, to stop for some time or start again readily, without inconvenience is a most important and valuable quality.

The quickness with which she can give chase at her highest speed well adapts her for catching Torpedo Boats – economises coal and so enables her to remain longer on her station. Broadly speaking, she can, within three hours, catch any Torpedo Boat that she sights, but that should be the limit of her spurt.

Her means of offence as regards the 12pdr is very good, and as regards the aft 6pdr is good, the two other 6pdrs are not of great value.

If it was possible to arm the after position with a 12pdr gun mounted in the same way as the foremost one, it would be a very good exchange for the two deck 6pdrs, and any of the other weights that could be spared.

The tactics of the Destroyers when chasing to windward should be to approach to 600 yards, stop one minute to fire and then overhaul again – if passing to obtain the weather gage, and a range of 4 to 500 yards, and if the Torpedo Boat turns to turn too.

The one great risk is being approached by a Cruiser – considering the chances of meeting at night or being chased in rough weather, the danger is a very real and

important one against which the Destroyer has no protection.

We are therefore strongly of opinion, that they should, when on destroyer duty, retain two Torpedo Tubes with the Torpedoes in them, if necessary, at the sacrifice of some other weights such as the Search Light, Dynamo and one anchor and cable – a Cruiser who knew the Destroyer to be armed with Torpedoes would hesitate to approach her at night, and would have much more respect for her in the day – on Destroyer duty, the Torpedoes would be for the purpose of defence only.

Experience shows that the outside steering position forward cannot be used for a chase to windward or for manoeuvring at high speeds on account of the blinding spray thrown in the eyes of the helmsman. Nor is the position right aft suitable in such circumstances as the whole length and high bow of the vessel intervene between the helmsman, who is only at the deck level, and the chase, and he is too far from the Officer who would conn from the 12pdr Platform.

The conning tower as now fitted does not give a sufficiently wide or clear view, and we do not hesitate to say, cannot be used either by day or night either for chasing or manoeuvring.

Top, Havock as reboiled with water tube boilers. There are canvas covers on the three funnels now fitted, and there is a bridge semaphore. The photo was taken in 1904 when she was moored to a buoy at Spithead. Her dinghy is alongside. (National Maritime Museum, London: N1974)

Above, Banshee in a gale, a photograph published in the *Navy and Army Illustrated* for 1899. One of the few photographs showing an early TBD in adverse conditions. Conditions aboard, particularly for the stokers, cannot have been comfortable. Destroyer crews certainly earned their aptly-named 'hard lying money' – an extra allowance of pay for serving in smaller ships or other difficult circumstances. She is painted in the Mediterranean white scheme. (National Maritime Museum, London: 59/1944)

It is probable that if a 12pdr is mounted in an elevated position aft it will also afford the best all-round position for a steering station, but apart from that it seems to us very important that for purposes of attack the Conning Tower should be made capable of use as a Conning and steering station at least in the daytime.

We are of opinion that the trials of the *Havock* are very satisfactory as proving her suitability for this special service, implied in the name of a Torpedo Boat Destroyer; but we beg respectfully to say that we are confirmed in the opinion which we gave in a former Report, that to require her in addition, or combination, to accompany Squadrons of ships to sea, is incompatible with the highest development of her qualities as a Destroyer.

We desire also to point out that the great merit of the *Havock* lies in the fact that during the various incidents of such service as the last trials have illustrated, her Commander has never been hampered in her movements or tactics by the necessity to consider the state of the Boilers or Fires, and that this may prove to be an advantage not obtainable with other types of Boilers.'

The problems that were later to arise with the TBDs, such as seaworthiness, the suitability of the steering position in the conning tower, and the fundamental question of the balance of their armament between guns and torpedoes were already identified in the trials of the first ship of this type.

Seaworthiness and handling

It rapidly became apparent that the bow tube in the 26-knotters was a handicap. As early as 27 October 1892 the Controller was obviously having doubts about this feature, as he asked[36] for the bows to be filled out as much as possible in its neighbourhood so that there was as little as possible projection to throw off spray.

The early trials of the *Havock* produced the following remark:[37] 'the boat behaved well in the sea way, steers well, lurching but very slightly when helm is put hard over. The vibration was exceedingly slight and chiefly horizontal. No signs of straining were observed.'

Once the prototype was in service other modifications were seen to be desirable. The captain of *Hornet* made suggestions[38] for fittings which he recommended should apply to all vessels: 'A conning position to be built before the funnels high enough for seeing over the 12pdr gun, with telegraphs &c. If the galley is fitted on the upper deck the top could be utilised and steering wheel &c. put there. This conning position is necessary for the following reasons: (a) The position inside conning tower is most difficult to see from even under favourable circumstances and I do not think it could be used efficiently by the officer conning the ship, either when working in close water or in action, except perhaps when making an actual torpedo attack on a big ship. It would be out of the question to chase a torpedo boat from that position. (b) The wheel outside the conning tower is very useful for going in and out of harbour but becomes untenable when steaming fast against the sea or wind owning to the force with which the spray strikes the helmsman, and of course the Officer at the Con has to use the 12pdr gun platform so that this position is cut off on service.'

The 1895 manoeuvres produced further comments on the conning tower and steering:[39] 'Protection for the Helmsman is not worth thinking about as any QF shell must be able to penetrate any protection that could be given, whilst it is essential that every facility should be given to get a good view and as much protection from spray etc. as possible, keeping of course the rigidity of the foremost gun platform well in view . . .'

The armoured conning tower was a regular feature of all warships at this time, but was already beginning to fall

Havock photographed in No 3 Basin at Portsmouth on 30 October 1895, tiny compared to the battleship *Revenge* behind her. (National Maritime Museum, London: G10206)

into disfavour, as experience came to show that the visibility given by a bridge was of far greater operational importance than the largely illusory protection given by the cramped and visually restricted confines of a conning tower. However, it was not until after the last 30-knotters had been ordered that the decision was made to drop this feature, and it was only the two modified designs purchased a decade later from Palmer's as *Albacore* and *Bonetta* which had proper bridges from the start.

Much was learned about the seaworthiness of the new type when the first TBDs were steamed out in company with larger ships to foreign stations, as the following extracts from *Ardent*'s Commander's letter on her voyage from Portsmouth to Malta show:[40] 'With wind abeam and on quarter she rolled her gunwales under once or twice . . . the heat below gave me a bit of a headache . . . rolls very quickly and with very little swell aft the screws race and the ship in my cabin feels as if she was falling to pieces, the vibration is great. No trouble either with engines or boilers on the passage out.'

The DNC had already indicated the precautions to be taken on such voyages:[41] ' . . . [it] will be advisable to remove torpedo tubes, torpedoes and torpedo stores. Limitations on amount of coal to be carried in some vessels are in ships' books and should be strictly adhered to. For similar stability reasons depth to which vessels should be loaded should be restricted.'

In 1898 it was stated[42] approvingly: 'As regards the hulls, experience has shown that the structural strength is adequate under all circumstances, although many cases of collision or grounding have occurred in which the vessels have necessarily received extensive damage, they have in every case retained their powers of flotation and their mobility and have safely reached port and been repaired at moderate cost. Several have made long ocean passages and have passed through very severe weather, and the reports upon their behaviour and seaworthiness have been most satisfactory.' However, it had already been noticed[43] that: ' . . . Again it is now a matter of experience that, under working conditions at sea, where dead smooth water is but seldom met with, the higher contract speed of two knots is not associated in practice with an equal gain in sea-speed. In fact the limit of speed attainable is very commonly fixed by the condition of the sea rather than by the power available in vessels.'

The one 'Sailing Qualities Report' that survives in the Ships' Covers for the TBDs gives the following information about *Orwell*:[44] 'Rides easily at anchor – rolls easily in the trough of the sea – lying too, she rolls very heavily – under ordinary circumstances she steers very well. With strong beam wind and heavy sea (5 to 6 wind force and heavy swell) steers unsteadily, mainly due to racing of propellers.- in similar conditions with following wind steers very unsteadily, yawing as much as 1½ points off course, as sea catches quarter. Best steaming trim is light fwd, deep aft - she is generally well built.'

As the TBDs got older so the reports of damage in rough seas accumulated. On 1 April 1902 a report was made by Deadman[45] on damage to *Fervent* and *Zephyr*

Angler leaving Portsmouth in 1898. (National Maritime Museum, London: N8800)

resulting from severe weather in the Channel. Deadman noted that the damage was peculiar and almost unique in character. When the 26- and 27kt destroyers were first brought into service it was found that when forced against a head sea, the bows above water were liable to damage and these and eleven succeeding boats had been stiffened to meet this contingency. The bows below water generally proved satisfactory. In the cases now under consideration no damage whatever had been sustained by the bows above water: 'but the bow plating below water on the starboard side only for from 20ft to 30ft longitudinally, has been more or less severely punished. The plates being bent in between the frames causing . . . leaks . . . ', rivets being broken off. *Zebra*, which was in company, reported no hull damage: 'There is nothing in the construction of these vessels to indicate that one is more able to meet the ordinary circumstances of sea service than the other two.' The Surveyor's report indicated that the damage occurred when the boats were amongst waves of approximately their own length which were striking on the port bow. The vessels rolled heavily to starboard but only slightly to port.

In January 1905 the commander of the China Station sent a report on the state of the destroyers on that station:[46] ' . . . It will be observed that whereas the engines and boilers of these destroyers are generally speaking in good order, the hulls, which are the more important matter of the two [*sic*] in the China stormy seas are bad. I have always been of the opinion that the life of the destroyers has been overestimated. They should be capable of doing three to five years' good service as originally constructed. After, at most, five years, it would be a good policy to reconstruct them, making them stiffer and stronger by broad steel plates along their whole length, and let them take a place in Reserve, with an accepted speed of 5kts or so less then that for which they were originally designed . . . destroyers are nursed in peace time to avoid continual repairs and consequent expense.' The China Station report reached these conclusions: '(1) It is a matter of common knowledge and of experience that these destroyers cannot be freely handled at high speed in a rough sea without probable damage. (2) At their age and in their present condition this practically amounts to a certainty. (3) War service would not allow of their being nursed. (4) Damage to hull would necessitate docking, or if neglected would lead to total disablement or loss, as the strength of a destroyer's hull depends on its being intact.'

The remains of the wreck of *Viper* on the rocks in August 1901. This photograph is taken from the *Navy and Army Illustrated* and gives a good view of two of the quadruple shafts with their installation of two propellers each. This was an attempt to minimise cavitation and maximise power at the very high speeds of rotation necessary with turbines. Improvements in propeller design, and also the development of geared turbines with a corresponding slowing down of rpm would enable a more conventional arrangement of propellers to be used. (National Maritime Museum, London: 59/1794)

The following 1911 report[47] shows what happened when a 27-knotter was exposed to a Mediterranean storm. Almost the first trip *Banshee* took after being inclined 'was to accompany part of the Fleet to Platea; when she left Malta it was already blowing hard and soon afterwards it worked up to a heavy *gregale* [a Mediterranean gale] to which she was fully exposed when near Sicily . . . [forwarding the captain's report] . . . it being about the nearest approach to a loss that I am acquainted with. By coming through *Banshee* has I think provided good evidence as to the values of GM [metacentric height] and maximum GZ's that may be taken as satisfactory in a vessel of her type . . . *Banshee* . . . was rolling very heavily and at times put her davit heads in the water, her commanding officer kept her head slightly off the direction of the sea to avoid having his bridge carried away and she was constantly swept fore and aft by the seas. The water that found its way below came partly through the cowls but chiefly through one of the bunker plates on the upper deck, one of the lockers that broke adrift smashed the nut fastening the securing dog and the plate was washed away by the next sea, so permitting the water to have free access to the bunker and the machinery space. She had her total allowance of coal on board when leaving Malta and this with the large amount of water shipped must have produced at times in the heavy sea a large sagging moment. As soon as she was in dock her bottom and deck were carefully examined for defects or straining. The stringer and next deck strakes were uninjured and only one deck plate, a thin one on the middle line at station 60, was found to be crumpled between the beams, this has been renewed . . . the bottom . . . gave no indication of straining, but after . . . the ship had been in dock for a couple of days thin white lines appeared in the black paint at all the garboard butts and at several butts in the keel and the strakes above the garboards . . . in my opinion they were due to the caulk [caulking] having been slightly disturbed by the working of the ship, making a microscopic crack the water in which evaporated in dock and left its salt on the edges of the crack . . . there were no

leaky rivets or other defects anywhere. There is no doubt that *Banshee* had a very narrow escape, the *Cornwallis* which stood by her during the night expected to see her founder and was devising means for saving her crew if she did so, the condition of her butts shows that there was some risk of her breaking her back; fortunately we have in the last year or two replaced many worn plates in the bottom, doubled the garboards, and introduced extra stiffening on the deck, and the fact that she came through at all is I think largely due to this; even with the additional doubling the keel and garboard appears to be weaker than the deck, but the large quantity of water shipped amidships necessarily made the sagging moment acting on the ship larger, and correspondingly increased the stresses in the lower parts of the ship . . . '

In 1907 a lively debate about the seaworthiness of these craft had been caused by a letter to the First Lord[48] from a Mr W A Jenks of Catford quoting a correspondent of his aboard one of the ships of the Mediterranean fleet about the Malta flotilla, complaining that the destroyers on this station were in a dangerous condition due to their constant exposure to conditions for which they had not been designed, and that the authorities were failing to take action. As part of this debate, the DNC wrote,[49] quoting the TBD Committee report, apropos of the 27-knotters that: 'The original idea was to build torpedo boats of a larger, faster and better-armed type than any other then existing which would be able to keep the sea under less favourable conditions of weather than the French *hautemer* boats of the time. The ascertained capabilities of the vessels when built led gradually to their extended use at sea under less favourable conditions than those originally contemplated. It is fully recognised that vessels of the 27kt and 30kt type when employed under the conditions stated above, are peculiarly liable to damage, but the fact that special care and attention has been bestowed upon them is clear from the fact that of the 113 vessels of the class only six (including the *Cobra*) have been lost and one sold out of the service after being used as a target. Additional evidence in this direction could be obtained from the expenditure in making good the defects of these vessels, as well as the fact that surveys of the hulls of destroyers are made at much more frequent intervals than in other vessels. The *possibility* of an accident such as described . . . [in the correspondence] cannot be disputed but its *probability* can be to some extent estimated from the fact that (omitting the *Cobra*) there have been 112 of these vessels serving for periods of from five to thirteen years in Home and Foreign waters and not one has yet "broken up".'

In spite of this problem the TBDs still in service in 1914 survived the war years with some losses to the enemy and others to collision, but, perhaps surprisingly, none to stress of weather. Their builders had done well.

Alterations

Inevitably, discussions on alterations and amendments to the TBDs began as soon as they entered service. Mostly these were initiated by suggestions or actual modifications made by the commanders of individual boats or flotillas. As will be seen from the files summarised below the DNC and the Admiralty were usually reacting to rather than initiating such initiatives.

Right at the start of these vessels' service the perennial problem of the increase in topweight, to which destroyers were particularly prone, had appeared. In 1895 and 1896 the Commanders-in-Chief at Portsmouth and the Mediterranean were informed of the importance of keeping weight down in destroyers.[50]

The *Coquette*, one of the Mediterranean Fleet destroyers, had been inclined in 1901 and found to have a metacentric height of 1.18ft with her bunkers full. Somewhat later Deadman wrote: 'The loss of stability which has occurred can only be accounted for by the extra fittings which have been considered necessary for service in the Mediterranean – the raising of the searchlight from the deck to a platform over the conning bridge, &c.' – one small engagement in the long battle of the naval constructors against the (often very necessary) build-up of small alterations which threatened the stability of such weight-critical ships as destroyers.

Another example of an improvised modification was put forward by the Admiral Superintendent (whose name was Holland) at Chatham as a measure to be made official.[51] The forward (12pdr) gun platform was a grating and much discomfort was caused to officers (and presumably the men) on the forward gun platform the by the sea and a rush of cold wind coming up through it. Covers of corticene were tried and found very satisfactory. Admiral Holland stated that the submission arose from conversations with commanding officers of destroyers and was 'concurred in by all who have sea experience in Destroyers: Their efforts to obtain bits of corticene to cover these platforms show how necessary they find it.' W H May (the Controller) noted:[52] 'This seems to be a necessary fitting for the comfort of officers – returns from various dockyards indicate it has already been done in numerous vessels in an extempore manner.'

In early 1904 Deadman once again raised[53] the matter of the build-up of topweight with the DNC: ' . . . It has been ascertained by experiments with a number of destroyers that their displacement has increased on an average about 10 per cent since they were first completed and in most cases . . . this has been accompanied by a reduction in metacentric height . . . it is desired to secure the cooperation of officers in command of destroyers and torpedo boats in reducing weight wherever practicable and in avoiding any increase whatever after the vessels have been delivered by the builders.' W H May[54] added a note to the Senior Naval Lord: 'weights . . . are generally added without the knowledge of the Admiralty, considering the great importance of speed in this class of vessel I propose to inform the fleet of the total weight that has been added and urge upon the Officers in command of Destroyers, the absolute necessity of not allowing any extra weights, and if possible to reduce those at present carried.' The speed loss with an addition in displacement which increased draught by 10in was approximately 1kt.

By the beginning of the new century, weakness in the bow structure of some of the 27kt TBDs had appeared and been cured by the addition of some stiffening. The changes made were summarised on 24 April 1901 as: *Havock* and *Hornet* two web frames and longitudinal girder; *Ardent* and sisters ditto; *Contest* and *Beacon* two web frames added; *Janus* and sisters three web frames and longitudinal girder added; *Handy* and *Hart* three web frames added and brackets at the heels of several frames stiffened; *Skate* brackets at the heels of frames stiffened. Nothing had been done to the remaining twenty-nine vessels. 'The arrangements provided in the vessels built by White, Brown, Doxford and Hawthorn Co may possibly be regarded as efficient, a vessel of each class having reached a foreign station without damage.' More information was needed from the builders of the others on framing.[55]

There were problems with some of the earlier 30-knotters as well. A 1901 report on *Crane* and *Vulture* in dry dock – stated that they should be stiffened: 'They are not quite so strongly constructed as many (particularly the later ones) designed and built by other firms, and it is desirable to consider how some additional strength to the top and bottom can best be given if these vessels are

Wireless Telegraphy (W/T) rig for *Velox*, showing the array of aerials needed for an early wireless installation. (National Maritime Museum, London: 24229F)

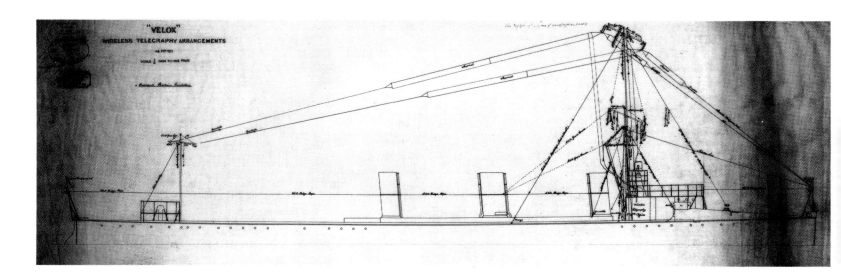

Above, the reason why the fore funnel looks particularly far aft in this TBD is that she is the originally three-funnelled *Wizard* as reboilered with only two funnels. The photograph was taken in 1912 and also shows the wireless aerials, enlarged conning platform and other modifications made by this date. (National Maritime Museum, London: N1962)

Below, this shows *Boxer* towards the end of her career as the added topmast and extended 12pdr platform show – the picture was taken in 1913 passing Clarence Esplanade approaching Portsmouth Harbour. (National Maritime Museum, London: N1949)

required to keep the sea for lengthened periods under all conditions of weather.'[56]

The beginning of the end for the earliest TBDs is marked in a letter[57] written on 20 February 1908 by the Controller, H B Jackson, to the Admiral Superintendent, Chatham about: ' . . . the necessity for very critically examining all 27kt destroyers in future when these vessels are in hand for survey, as it is considered that on account of their age there is possibility of their being structurally weak and not fit for service except with very large repairs. In any future case instructions are to be sought before putting the work in hand . . . ' The sense of this was shown by a series of reports on these ageing craft, for example in the same month *Lynx* reported that her lower deck plating and bulkheads were rusted through in places.[58]

As an example[59] of what then happened we can take one of the prototypes. On 23 February 1909 the report on a survey of the *Hornet* stated that the outer bottom plating was in a generally deteriorated condition near the waterline, and there was a considerable amount of buckling in the three top strakes of plating, flat keel plates between stations 59 and 78 were found to be buckled and there were a series of buckles in the upper deck plating from the fore mess deck to the after end of the after boiler room. A proposal was made to stiffen keel plates and also to fit girders to stiffen the upper deck. The boiler tubes were given another three years to last from the previous November. Repairs and alterations would cost £4050. The Controller was asked whether he would approve the spending of this, in view of his minute. He replied: 'Repairs proposed for the older boats are now carefully considered before approving them, but up to the present it has not been considered necessary to propose to condemn any, and I think as long as the hull repairs do not exceed say, 10 per cent, of the original cost of the hull they are worth repair.' As *Hornet* was sold within the year it would appear that she had not been considered worth further work.

The 30-knotters were also becoming obsolete. An April 1909 proposal[60] to reposition searchlights was decided not to be done in 30-knotters because of their age. On 28 July 1911 the First Sea Lord (A K Wilson) minuted: 'Alterations and additions should not be carried out in any 27kt Destroyers in view of their age.'[61]

The records of inclining experiments made in September 1918[62] show how the armament of TBDs had altered by the end of the First World War. *Fervent*'s armament now consisted of one 12pdr, one Hotchkiss 6pdr on a high-angle anti-aircraft mounting aft and two 6pdr Hotchkiss guns on their normal mountings en echelon amidships. A 2pdr pom-pom on a platform had been added between the first and second funnels, though she retained her two 18ft torpedo tubes. Two Thornycroft depth charge throwers, twelve depth charges, and one Lewis gun (0.303in machine-gun) had also been added. She still had her searchlight (between the fore funnel and the pom-pom). All this meant an increase in complement of twelve and a considerable growth in topweight. It is interesting, and a tribute both to the original designers and commanders, that none of these craft actually capsized.

Comparisons

This section represents a selection of the remarks made about the different builders' TBDs as a result of experience in service.

The 1895 manoeuvres caused the following remark: 'Structurally both Laird's and Thomson's boats have shown themselves weak in the forward compartment. Heavy seas striking them have bulged in their sides breaking away mess fittings in some of the boats.'[63]

At the beginning of October 1895 the DNC noted[64] that the following firms had completed one or more TBD satisfactorily: Thornycroft, Yarrow, Laird, Thomson, Palmer's, Naval Construction & Armament, Fairfield and Earle's. The last two were annotated: 'The vibration in these boats is not yet satisfactory but this will be overcome.'

Deadman's 1897 notes[65] on the TBDs intended for, or on, foreign stations is a significant indication of those boats which were considered seaworthy, sturdy and reliable.

Bermuda	*Quail, Sparrowhawk, Thrasher, Virago* – 'Good sea boats for Atlantic passage' (having ample stability)
Pacific	*Haughty* and *Hardy* (preferred by engineers) or *Salmon* and *Snapper*
Malta	*Contest* (sister to *Banshee* and *Dragon* on station), *Desperate, Fame, Foam, Mallard*
Cape	*Swordfish* and *Spitfire*
China	*Hunter* (sister to *Handy* and *Hart* on station), *Whiting, Bat* (good, reliable boats), *Crane* (?last doubtful if ready in August, but Laird's will no doubt have another delivered which could be [substituted?])

Another hand noted that this list was submitted at the request of the Controller for the most notable boats – subsequently *Janus* and *Lightning* (good stable boats) were substituted for *Haughty* and *Hardy* for the Pacific Station in consequence of their greater radius of action and *Rocket* and *Shark* (good reliable boats) for the Cape for similar reasons.

Further comparisons of seaworthiness and habitability could be made once the TBDs had voyaged out to these stations, and extracts from reports of such voyages were sent to the DNC: ' . . . *Earnest* rolls easily – steers well except with following sea when steers wildly. *Griffon* steers well, rolls easily . . . *Quail*; during passage from Trinidad to Bermuda heavy weather was experienced – heavy gale bringing speed eased to 10kts and ship rode more easily, sea increasing caused ship to vibrate in such a manner as to lead us to believe engines were racing excessively, but was caused by heavy seas shaking her. The CO cannot speak too highly of the seagoing qualities that this ship displayed [?]. No sign of strains or leaks . . . *Ardent* – rolls easily but very quickly – with wind abeam or on quarter rolled her gunwale under once or twice. *Handy* and *Hart* – behaved exceedingly well and appeared to make as good weather as *Flora* [an *Astrea* class Second Class cruiser].'

In 1901 a general survey was made of those boats which had required structural reinforcement, which included the following, slightly grudging, words of praise: 'The arrangements provided in the vessels built by White, Brown, Droxford and Hawthorn Co may possibly be regarded as efficient, a vessel of each class having reached a foreign station without damage.'[66] However, in the same year it became apparent that the early Clydebank 30-knotters required stiffening, producing the following report from Deadman: 'Although these five (J Brown) vessels are among the later ones brought into service they were among the earliest 30kt destroyers ordered, having taken many years to deliver owing to the contractors (Messrs Brown & Co) failing to obtain the contract speed. They are not quite so strongly constructed as many (particularly the later ones) designed and built by other firms, and it is desirable to consider how some additional strength to the top and bottom can best be given if these vessels are required to keep the sea for lengthened periods under all conditions of weather.'[67]

In 1905 the Rear Admiral (Destroyers) S Winsloe reported[68] that alterations costing large sums of money on *Ranger, Sunfish, Opossum, Swordfish, Spitfire, Hardy, Salmon,* and *Snapper* 'should be suspended . . . in my opinion every shilling spent on these old 27-knotters is a waste of money. They are all worn out, and whatever they make a run of even 200 miles with the flotilla, they at once break down, and they are as fighting machines not worth the cost of their upkeep . . . I strongly recommend paying them all off and using the best as tenders to Gunnery and Torpedo Schools or as torpedo boats, but those which continually break down and cost much for repair should be got rid of. I endeavoured some months ago to get *Skate* and *Shark* condemned, but money was spent on them both, and I am sure that they are not worth it, because if it came to use in time, they have neither speed to catch any torpedo boat, or to run away from a cruiser or destroyer.' The Controller (H B Jackson) noted that he did not propose to take special action: 'I have not approved of the alterations to boiler in which this question arose. Those named . . . are amongst the worst of our Destroyers, but many of the 27-knotters are still capable of doing good service . . . [each vessel was to be dealt with on its merits when the question of expenditure arises] . . . The case of the early torpedo boats is really much worse than this and they are still kept efficient.'

At much the same time *Ferret* was considered the worst for stability of the 26-knotters whilst *Banshee* was the worst and *Janus* the best (1.74ft compared to 2.64ft as metacentric heights) of the 27-knotters – the two worst being Laird boats, the best built by Palmers.

In 1908 Captain Charles Corbett included the following assessment in his paper on the best craft to use attacking the German coastline:[69] 'In my opinion among the best of the 30kt TBDs were Palmer and Hawthorn Leslie boats. They were good seaboats and steamed well. Fairfield, Brown, Laird and Doxford boats I think were also good sea boats. Earle, Naval Construction & Armament Co and Thornycroft's probably not so good, as their forecastle were generally lower . . . ' Another officer, the Captain (D) at Plymouth, commanding *Leander* (a cruiser used as a depot ship), considered ' . . . little difference exists between the various types of 30kt destroyers, but if any preferences should be given, I should classify them as follows: (1) Hawthorn Leslie's *Roebuck* class. (2) Palmer's *Kangaroo* class. (3) Fairfield's *Leven* class. (4) Doxford's *Sylvia* class. (5) All other 30-knotters. (6) Oil TBs.'

Captain Tyrwhitt, who had started this particular discussion, had his own opinion of the seagoing capacities of the TBDs: ' . . . My remarks are based entirely on observation and personal experience. Hawthorn Leslie: *Cheerful, Greyhound, Mermaid, Racehorse, Roebuck* and *Velox*, are, in my opinion, far superior to any [other] 30kt type of destroyer. They are fine sea boats, combining strength, economy of coal consumption, and seagoing qualities besides being fast, when required, and reliable steamers at all times. Palmer's and Doxford – are both good types and have a great advantage over other types in the shape of a forward thwartship coal bunker, holding about 15 tons of coal. This coal, when expended, as it always is, as soon as possible, raises the forward freeboard and leaves the remainder of the coal equally divided in the Stokeholds. They are rather slightly built and vibrate considerably but are fast and reliable steamers. Laird's . . . [list of that firm's TBDs with *Express* noted as 'Freak'] . . . are

strongly built craft, and considering their low freeboard are good seagoing vessels and reliable steamers up to 24–25kts. Fairfield . . . are good strong sea boats but are, unfortunately, unreliable steamers. Vickers . . . are bad sea boats, very weakly built and most unreliable steamers. They are always to be found in the Dockyards undergoing extensive repairs. Thornycroft's . . . are good [in] <u>fine</u> weather and reliable steamers, but are unfortunately indifferent sea boats. They are the only destroyers built with "falling home" sides, which not only makes them very wet but reduces their accommodation and cramps their Engine Rooms. They are very low forward and have double rudders which make them liable to broach to in a heavy following sea. This is an important point as a Destroyer will, when chases, invariably run downwind, and a boat which is constantly yawing 5 and 6 points each way must lose a great deal of speed.' He considered that the oil TBs (Coastal Destroyers) 'are certainly better sea boats than the Vickers and Thornycroft type of TBDs, but inferior to the other types'.

It is most interesting to see the general opinion (confirmed in other sources) was that the TBDs built by the north-eastern builders, Palmer's, Hawthorn Leslie and Doxford, were the favourite ships. A combination of hull sturdiness and machinery reliability seems to lie behind this reputation.

Thornycroft's *Daring*, or possibly her sister *Decoy*, moored on the upper Thames near Chiswick, with guns, masts and torpedoes not fitted for trials. Amongst the handsomest of the TBDs because of their twin slab-sided funnels, they performed well in light conditions, but their semi-tunnel stern caused 'slamming' in heavy conditions. (Author's Collection)

Part IV: Foreign Comparisons

As one might expect, the three nations other than Britain who built their own torpedo boats did the same with TBDs. Although the Germans did have one prototype built in Britain, this was the exception which proved the rule, and it was France, Germany and the USA which built vessels notably different from the standard British-designed TBD type. All three navies went their own way, building vessels of a recognisably national stamp, especially the French and Germans, both of whom also successfully sold their designs abroad. The Americans had not yet reached the level of industrial development when they could successfully compete in the export market for warships with the three main players, Britain, France and Germany.

A group of navies were in an intermediate position, having their prototype TBDs built by one of the specialist builders in Britain, France or Germany, but building others themselves usually to foreign designs. These included Russia, Italy and Japan. Portugal could also be counted in this group, as her one TBD was built in the country, but to a Yarrow design. Details of destroyers built for foreign navies by British firms are to be found in the specific builders' chapters.

Spain and the South America countries relied entirely on foreign builders, whilst other navies did not go in for TBDs at all, continuing to rely on torpedo boats entirely, as in the case of the Dutch and the Danes.

Germany

Roughly contemporary with the first British TBDs were the Schichau-built 'Division Boats', enlarged TBs with extra accommodation and improved seaworthiness, designed as flotilla leaders.

'Division Boat' *D 9*: commissioned 29 December 1894.
DIMENSIONS: 206ft 10in oa x 25ft 3in x 12ft 3in
DISPLACEMENT: 249 tons
BEST TRIAL SPEED: 23½kts
ARMAMENT: 3–50mm, 3–450mm torpedo tubes
NOTES: Raised forecastle

Although this class of vessel (of which nine were built between 1886 and 1894) had the size of the TBDs, they lacked both their speed and their gun power.

Germany's first true TBD was built by Thornycroft's in 1898. *D 10* was a duplicate of the British 30-knotters

with the armament of, and classed as, a 'Division Boat' (see chapter on Thornycroft for details), and Schichau followed this with twelve further ships.

S 90–S 101: built between 1898 and 1901.
DIMENSIONS: 206ft 10in x 22ft 11in x 9ft 4in
DISPLACEMENT: 310t
BEST TRIAL SPEED: 26½kts
ARMAMENT: 3–50mm, 3–450mm torpedo tubes
NOTES: Raised forecastle, with well between that and
      bridge

German destroyers continued to be referred to as 'Torpedo Boats', and emphasised the torpedo weapon at the expense of gun power. They were certainly well adapted to the German Navy's still largely defensive requirements for North Sea and Baltic warfare. The addition of a short raised forecastle in the later German TBDs certainly seems to have improved their sea-keeping ability, and was a feature that was generally copied later. However, one wonders whether a confrontation between British and German TBDs in the early 1900s would have produced the same result as the clash between German and British destroyers at Jutland a decade or more later. In 1916 it was the British destroyers with their heavier gun armament which broke through their opponents and were able to attack the enemy battle line with torpedoes, whilst fulfilling their other duty of preventing their opponents bringing their heavier torpedo batteries within range of the British battleships.

In the journal *Engineering* of 27 January 1899 there was a report of the destroyers building in Germany for China

Taku at Hong Kong in 1904 showing the characteristic cambered hull shape of a Schichau-built vessel, visually very similar to her contemporaries built for the Imperial German Navy, painted in the white with yellow funnels scheme of the China Station. (National Maritime Museum, London: N1948)

Taku 1904

Design for a TBD for Italy by Thornycroft's. This was never built, though the firm was later to provide many designs to Pattinsons of Naples who were to build them for the Italian Navy. This design is unusual for placing the 12pdr aft and all the 6pdrs closely grouped at the end of the forecastle firing forward. (National Maritime Museum, London: HO 6237)

reaching very high speeds on trial. Schichau reported the attainment of 35.2kts with the trial load of complete armament plus 25 tons coal. With bunkers full (67 tons coal) the claim was that they had steamed at 33.6kts 'for several hours' and with 67 tons coal but with natural draft between 30 and 31kts were claimed. However 6000ihp and 280 tons displacement were incompatible with a speed of 35kts.

Although these claims were quite rightly doubted, there was considerable interest in finding out what the performance of these vessels actually was. This was made possible when all four of these destroyers were captured from the Chinese during the Boxer Rebellion by the British destroyers *Fame* and *Whiting* under the command of Roger Keyes. One of them (it is not entirely certain which) was taken into the Royal Navy under the name of

Taku and was thenceforward available for close examination and comparison.[1]

Taku: built Schichau, Elbing, Germany (as *Hai Nju*?). Launched 1898, delivered 1899, captured 17 June 1900.
DIMENSIONS: 198ft 6in oa, 194ft bp x 21ft ext x 10ft 5¼in + 5ft 10in (mean)
DISPLACEMENT: 305 tons light, 334 tons full load
MACHINERY: 6000ihp
ARMAMENT: 6–47mm guns, 2–14in torpedo tubes
COMPLEMENT: 58

Trials at Hong Kong found her speed to be significantly below that claimed by the builders, and it was reported that her crew accommodation was 'generally not so good as British 30kt destroyers'. Five years later, the Commander-in-Chief, China, reported that[2] '[*Taku*'s] present structure is only suitable for speeds up to approximately 24kts, in smooth water, and that if continuous steaming at higher speeds is required it will be necessary to strengthen the hull, though this action will again increase her weight and draught'. *Taku* spent her career on the China Station and was sold on 25 October 1916 at Hong Kong.

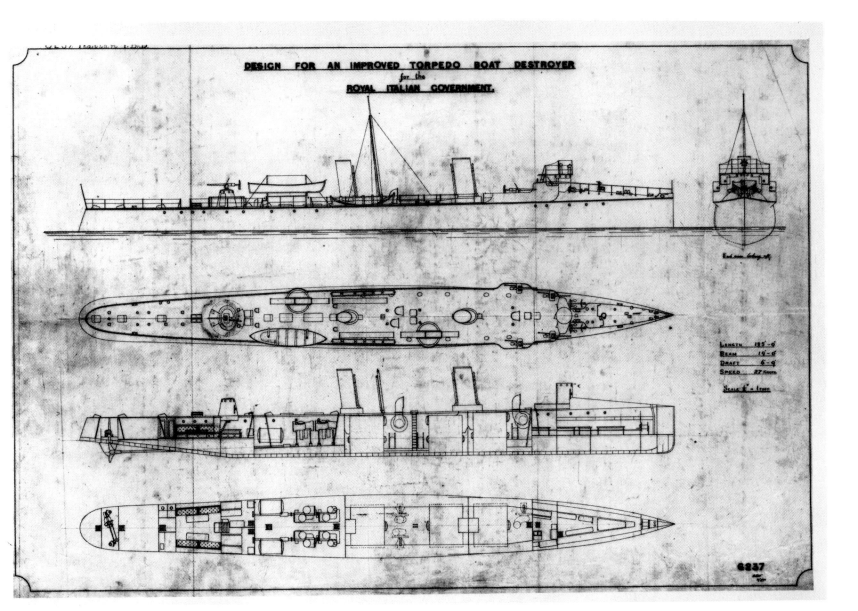

France

The somewhat belated French response to the TBDs was to enlarge their best builder's torpedo boat designs.

Durandal class (4 boats): ordered from Le Normand on 25 August 1896.
DIMENSIONS: 188ft 8in x 20ft 8in x 10ft 5in
DISPLACEMENT: 296t
BEST TRIAL SPEED: 26kts
ARMAMENT: 1–65mm, 6–47mm, 2–15in torpedo tubes

The Le Normand type was excellent for its time, sturdy and relatively seaworthy, but it had little potential for enlargement and development as time was to show.

The *Durandal*s were followed by the four ships of the *Framée* class (launched 1899-1900), the four *Pertuisane* class (launched 1900-1901) and the twenty-strong *Arquebuse* class (launched 1902-1903), all little changed from the original French TBDs, carrying the same armament.

A comparison between British and French TBDs is in the former's favour as far as speed is concerned. Interestingly the French carried more guns and lighter torpedoes, despite their keenness for torpedo attack. It is difficult to compare the British, German and French vessels for seaworthiness, though none of them put enough emphasis on this quality by later standards, and all were marred by too much attention to trial speed.

Russia

Russia was the first foreign power to build a TBD, which had the prototype built in Britain by Yarrow's, and then built similar vessels in her own yards.

Sokol (later *Pruitki*): completed 1 January 1895.
DIMENSIONS: 190ft oa x 18ft 6in x 7ft 6in
DISPLACEMENT: 220 tons
BEST TRIAL SPEED: 30.2kts
ARMAMENT: 1–11pdr, 3–3pdr, 2–15in torpedo tubes

She was followed by twenty-six broadly similar vessels built by several Russian builders, laid down 1896-1900 and completed 1898-1903.

A noticeable feature of the Russian TBDs is that they carried lighter weapons than most of the rest – with 15in instead of 18in torpedoes and 3pdrs rather than 6pdrs, also that most were fitted to carry a few mines. The experience of action in the Russo-Japanese War resulted in the survivors substituting two 11pdr guns for the smaller guns carried hitherto, and also 18in torpedoes instead of 15in ones.

Thornycroft design for a TBD for Brazil (never built), to be armed with 37mm pom-poms (an enlarged version of the Maxim machine gun), of which five are grouped to fire forward. (National Maritime Museum, London: HO 6800)

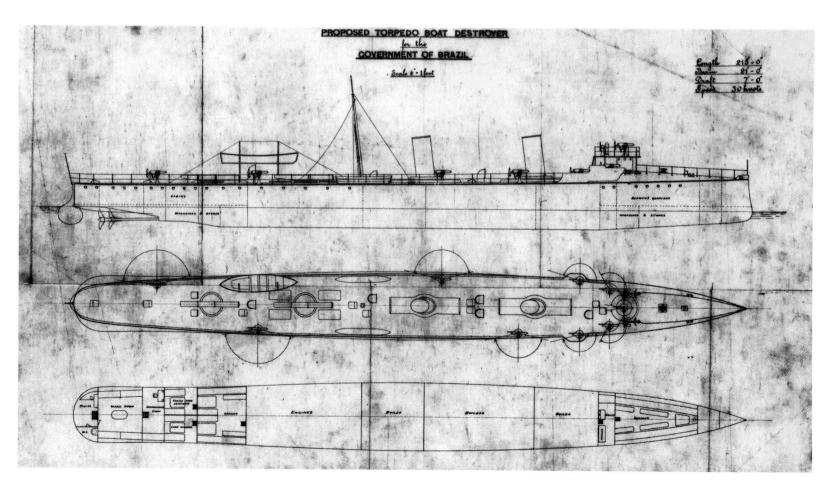

United States of America

The Americans began by enlarging their own torpedo boat designs, though clearly influenced by the British developments.

Farragut: ordered from Union Iron Works 10 June 1896, commissioned 22 March 1899.
DIMENSIONS: 214ft oa x 20ft 8in x 6ft
DISPLACEMENT: 279 tons
BEST TRIAL SPEED: 30kts
ARMAMENT: 4–6pdr, 2–18in torpedo tubes
NOTES: Classed as a TB

America began early to build destroyers to suit her own requirements, introducing the raised forecastle, and building larger and more powerful craft than anyone else, in the '400-tonners', none of which made their design speed of 30kts, but were the first real step forward in design, as with the British 'Rivers' (much later in conception), representing the step from TBD to Destroyer.

Bainbridge class (4 boats): commissioned May-November 1902.
DIMENSIONS: 250ft oa x 23ft 7in x 6ft 6in
DISPLACEMENT: 420 tons
BEST TRIAL SPEED: 29kts
ARMAMENT: 2–3in, 5–6pdrs, 2–18in torpedo tubes
NOTES: Introduced raised forecastles.

Hopkins class (2 boats): laid down February 1899, commissioned 20 May and 23 September 1903.
DIMENSIONS: 248ft 8in oa x 24ft 6in x 6ft
DISPLACEMENT: 408t
BEST TRIAL SPEED: 29kts
ARMAMENT: As *Bainbridge* class: later fitted with 4–18in torpedo tubes

Lawrence class (2 boats): commissioned 1903.
DIMENSIONS: 246ft 3in oa x 22ft 3in x 6ft 8in
DISPLACEMENT: 430 tons
OTHER DETAILS: As *Bainbridge* class
NOTES: Gun armament later reduced to 7–6pdr

Paul Jones class (3 boats): commissioned 1902-1903
DIMENSIONS: 250ft 7in oa x 23ft 6in x 7ft 3in
DISPLACEMENT: 480 tons
OTHER DETAILS: As *Bainbridge* class

Probably the comparatively large American 400-tonners were the most useful of all the TBDs listed here, as much because of their size as for any other reason, though certainly the ones which had raised forecastles scored on seaworthiness.

Conclusions

The British vessels had one enormous advantage over all their rivals. They were first. First to be ordered, first into service, and there in much greater numbers than the TBDs of any other navy. By the time other navies were getting their roughly comparable vessels into service the British were already working towards the next stage in destroyer development. By the time the American 400-tonners were entering service in numbers, the first 'River' class were appearing, considerably bigger, more powerful and more seaworthy than the destroyers that any other navy would build for some time to come.

Plans

This is a listing of the main TBD plans held in the Admiralty Collection at the National Maritime Museum (NMM). That Museum also holds numbers of relevant plans of TBDs in the Thornycroft Collection.

The list given here does not list all TBD plans held in the Admiralty Collection, there are a number of detail construction and fittings drawings as well. This list is only of those plans considered to be of major interest to historians and modelmakers.

The TBDs' names are given in alphabetical order in the *first column*. Those for which there are no major plans have been omitted, but look under sister ships for relevant drawings. The *second*, *third* and *fourth* columns give the details of the main general arrangement drawings showing side and plan views. These normally come as either profile, decks and cross section plans (**P&D&S** – the *second column*) or two separate plans, the profile and top deck(s) (**P&TD** – the *third column*) plus the bottom decks and cross sections (**BD & S**, the *fourth column*). The latter plans usually bear the same number as the profile and top decks plans, but are differentiated by the addition of an (A) or other letter. The *fifth column* (**Dates**) refers to the plans whose Admiralty numbers are noted in the previous three columns, and indicates the original dates on which those plans were prepared; most often on completion – showing the vessel 'as fitted' (**A/F**) but sometimes produced, or just modified in one or more later years – as shown here.

The next type of plan is the **Lines** plan, indicating the shape of the hull and the reference numbers of these are given in the *sixth column*. These plans were normally drawn up at the design stage, but sometimes another lines plan would be drawn up after completion, and details are given if this is the case. The following column (*column seven*) indicates whether the document known

as a *specification* (often printed, though sometimes typewritten or manuscript) exists for this vessel. This will lay down thickness of framing and plating, quality of material and fittings to be used, etc, and is usually highly detailed. Some of these have Public Record Office document numbers (in the ADM 168 or ADM 170 series – the NMM acts as an outstation for public records such as these and the plans and Covers), others have Admiralty plan numbers. Some are described as 'Contracts' because they are the contract specifications, but very rarely do they have financial information in them, bar perhaps a schedule for making payments. They are technical not financial documents.

Column eight indicates when there is a constructional **midships cross section** (**MX**) plan available and *column nine* if there is a **shell expansion** (**SHE**) plan – showing the side plating as if it had been ironed flat, a very useful plan for the modelmaker who wishes to make a realistic model. The last type of plan to be listed is the **rigging plan** in *column ten*, usually in these cases a plan which shows only the mast and its rigging, not a complete side view of the vessel in question. The final column (*column eleven*) is for notes on the foregoing types of plans, or about other plans or documents which might be of interest.

The standard scale of nearly all these plans is ¼in to 1ft (1:48), though lines plans and midships sections may be at multiples of this, either ½in or 1in to 1ft (1:24 or 1:12). The plans themselves are either on cloth lined cartridge paper or on tracing linen. A few are prints of one kind or another made from the tracings. 'As fitted' plans are usually finely coloured, and when they are altered at different times the allocations are made in coloured ink, a different colour being used each time alterations are made. This will be seen on a number of those plans reproduced here.

Admiralty Collection

Name	P&D&S	P&TD	BD&S	Dates	Lines	Spec	MX	SHE	Rigging	Notes
Albacore	154210*	125517	(A)/A/F – 1910-1913		113394		15210A			*= dated 1908, also for *Bonetta*
Albatross	11474			A/F	64040			4701	61278	
Arab		39113	(A)	A/F	104708	170/11	105485	33838	6637	
Ardent	58586	52444*		A/F – 1896	52859					
Avon		103877	(A)	1909-1910*	59146		59532	101694	62264	
Banshee		60677	(A)	A/F						
Bonetta		125666	(A)/A/F – 1910-1913		115186			1255669		1916 modifications to upper deck – Fly to 125666. 1916 modifications to lower deck – Fly to 125666(A)
Brazen					59058	A57915				Capstan plan 58564. Spec in bad condition.
Bullfinch	24490			A/F – 1907	63952		103512			103512 is port side of SHE – (A) is starboard side – a separate plan
Cheerful	4301			A/F – 1905-1914	60251A	60766	60256	105276	244076	
Contest							180358			
Coquette								99494		
Crane	6122			A/F – 1914						
Cygnet	105492			A/F – 1917						
Daring	49376*				75015	56840				
Decoy	64135			A/F						

Name	P&D&S	P&TD	BD&S	Dates	Lines	Spec	MX	SHE	Rigging	Notes
Desperate		94419	(A)	A/F			57301	60556	59834	
Earnest		94451	(A)	A/F – 1907-1909				127698	60274	SHE dates from 1909
Electra	14677			A/F – 1905				4568		
Express	62529*	32260	(A)	A/F	63294	62114C		29822	88803	
Falcon		19958	(A)	A/F – 1905-1914	2146	C101733	161730	12709	244206	
Fawn	5337					170/117				
Fervent	55832*	5285	(A)	A/F – 1905	59076		53142	53144		
Gipsy					61514	A61255		98088	63122	
Greyhound	22505			A/F – 1908-1914	104059	170/131	103461	20320	9052	
Handy					54775		54778	138103		
Hasty	64328	15431*	(A)*	A/F						
Haughty		62651	(A)	A/F – 1905	58752	170/311	No.No.	119729		
Havock	60932	16189*	(A)*	A/F	Partial	170/310	50187			* = 1904-1907. GA 50728 dated 13.6.1892 is design for 'High speed seagoing Torpedo Boat'
Hornet	93674			A/F – 1905-1906						
Hunter	64301			A/F – 1906					12505*	* = 1901
Janus	53239*	60682	(A)	A/F – 1900	53087		52855			* = design, 1894 – no Sx. Also Torpedo loading 55805
Kestrel	8453			A/F	89835	89834	60585	3309		1908 alterations 383556
Lee	17358	90453*	(A)*	A/F	90451		A90452	10906		*= design. Turtle deck plating 91027
Leopard		103874	(A)	A/F – 1903-1914				103396		
Leven		104523	(A)	A/F		170/174				
Myrmidon		103056*	(A)*				103057			* = 1899
Orwell		7786	(A)	A/F – 1906-1909		170/212	62258	964		
Osprey		102858	(A)	A/F – 1914-1918						
Otter						60262	62257	2176		
Peterel	19620			A/F – 1913				19620F		
Quail		94440	(A)	A/F – 1898-1909						MA 27629 (1905)
Recruit					105278					
Rocket	53384*				No.No.		53393	No.No.		* = GA (design, 1894)
Salmon		62227	(A)	A/F – 1902-1906	53238			52939		Also lines plan as taken off 1902 – 32027
Sparrowhawk		89402	(A)	A/F – 1898						
Spiteful	10191	90552*	(A)*	A/F – 1905	90550	90581	90551	No.No.		* = 1897 design
Spitfire								43243		SHE is dated 1903
Sprightly		27871	(A)	A/F -1906						
Stag					92551	A3421	90591		95202	1897 design – Profile 90547/TDS (A)/LD & Sections (B)/Hold and Hold Sections. (B)
Star					45550			64166	60273	
Starfish	104793			A/F	58537					

Name	P&D&S	P&TD	BD&S	Dates	Lines	Spec	MX	SHE	Rigging	Notes
Sturgeon		53292	(A)	1894, design	53298		53295	No.No.	54736	Another midsection dated 1909 – 142952
Success		26096	(A)	A/F	103547		103550	17994	43	An un-numbered rigging plan is from 1914. 103530 is a design P&TDS of 1899
Sunfish		62657	(A)	A/F-1900-06 – 08 – 17	58676				56244	Conning tower 55878–1in
Surly		60246	(A)	A/F						
Swordfish	52867*	89066	(A)	A/F	58742		53228	53537		* = design GA Nov 1893. An earlier (1894 instead of 1896) lines plan is No.53150. Midsection A52866 dates from 1902
Syren		24429	(A)	A/F – 1906-1913					24229F	Rigging plan is W/T rig for 1913
Thorn		14956	(A)	A/F – 1914		170/311		12716		
Thrasher		95481	(A)	A/F – 1906						
Velox		57821	(A)	A/F – 1913	37337	170/369			41565	Rigging 1913 – 57821 fly
Vigilant		A14961		A/F -1906						
Violet				A/F – 1908-1909	ʋ4050					GA, design, 1896 – 61028
Viper					104992?			7757?	9913?	
Virago		9445	(A)	A/F – 1898						
Vixen		24436	(A)	A/F 1914				102909	20345	Conning Tower – 105023
Vulture	8443			A/F	90061		32267B	89843		GA – 1897 design – 90018
Wolf		102952	(A)	A/F – 1906-1909						
Zebra		103307	(A)	A/F – 1905-1906	59075	170/379	53376	89492		1894 design: Profile/Upper deck/LD/Sx – all numbered 53575

Thornycroft Collection

Name	Lines	P & UD	P & LD	Sections	Dates	Rig	Fittings	Boats	Documents	Notes
Daring & Decoy	5473						Propeller 6022		Trial reports/ report from Engineering on boilers	
Ardent, Bruiser, Boxer	6336						18in torpedo tube			
Desperate, Fame, Foam, Mallard	7054			Midships 7077					Trials	
Angler, Ariel	7054								Trial/ specification	
Coquette, Cygnet, Cynthia	8635								Trial sheets	Also stern lines 7766
Stag	8837								Trial/ specification	
D 10	7847		7007 B	Midships 8578B	May 1895				Trial/ specification/ contract	
Murakumo class		9394A		9394A					Trial	

Name	Lines	P & UD	P & LD	Sections	Dates	Rig	Fittings	Boats	Documents	Notes
Kagerou, Usugumo			7958B							Trial
Shirakumo, Asashio	9522A			Forward 10734A engine room 10734B: aft 10734C		10605	Deck fittings 10630: conning tower & chart house 10268: searchlight platform 10813: compass platform etc 10665			
Magne	11529C (proposed)	10822A (as fitted)	14171 (as fitted)	Midships 12529B		14171A (as fitted)	Upper deck fittings 12708: searchlight platform 2291: bridge, deckhouse, conning tower 12779			

Notes

Introduction

1. The 'sea-going' in all these varieties of title is a clear reference to the French *Haute Mer* torpedo boats, whose introduction into service was the direct reason for the British developing their new type. However, Theodore Ropp's statement that ' . . . the English had developed the destroyer directly from the successful French high-seas torpedo boats . . . ' in his *The Development of a Modern Navy* (Annapolis 1987) gives entirely the wrong idea.
2. Cover 128/5.
3. Cover 128/8.
4. Cover 128/12.
5. Cover 128/76.
6. Ruddock Mackay, *Fisher of Kilverstone* (Oxford 1973) quoting Bacon's life of Fisher and F Manning's life of White for the two different versions. Either is possible and I have seen nothing in the Covers or elsewhere which gives any indication of which is the correct version.
7. Cover 128/20.
8. Cover 142/25.
9. Cover 142/33.
10. Cover 142/97.

Part I: Development

1. The author has given several papers on this subject. See, for example: International Commission on Military History – 1980 Proceedings (Bucharest) – 'Theory and practice of Torpedo Warfare' and 'The Impact of the Torpedo' in H D Howse (ed), *Five Hundred Years of Maritime Science*, NMM 1981.
2. Quoted in Mackay, *Fisher*, pp200–201.
3. Mackay, *Fisher*, p205.
4. Cover 128/2.
5. Cover 128/5.
6. Cover 128/14.
7. Cover 128/44 (draft by DNC).
8. Cover 128/36.
9. Cover 142/1. Note also signed by Dunn and Durston (DNO) as well as the DNC.
10. Cover 154/28.
11. Cover 154/30.
12. Cover 160/22B.
13. Cover 165/1.
14. Thornycroft Document J/6.
15. Thornycroft Document D/18.
16. Cover 160/233.
17. Cover 160/299.
18. Cover 160/322.
19. Cover 160/331.
20. Cover 154/3a.
21. Cover 154/22.
22. Cover 154/39.
23. Cover 154/49.
24. Cover 154/5.
25. Cover 154/92 dated 8 February 1900.
26. Cover 154/93 signed by Deadman 12 February 1900. W H White concurs.
27. Cover 154/1 28 March 1899.
28. Cover 154/30.
29. Cover 154/21.
30. Cover 154/57 – made from Pethick's rough notes and sent to Deadman who was staying at the Pier Hotel, Southsea at the time.
31. By D K Brown, Royal Corps of Naval Constructors. See his article on the TBD enquiry in . . . ???? . . . I am very grateful to David Brown for not only providing copies of this and many other research papers over the years, but also in discussing this and many other such issues with me.

32. Cover 154/36.
33. Cover 154/48 Parsons, Turbinia works Wallsend on Tyne to Admiralty on 25 October 1901.
34. Cover 154/148 unsigned and undated but early November 1901.
35. Cover 154/50 dated 25 November 1901.
36. Cover 154/52.
37. Cover 154/54a.
38. Cover 154/58.
39. Cover 154/59.
40. Cover 154/64.
41. Cover 154/71.
42. Cover 154/73.
43. Cover 154/76.
44. Cover 154/124.
45. Cover 154/116 dated 18 October 1907.
46. Cover 154/130.
47. Cover 165A/72.
48. Cover 165A/19.
49. Cover 165A/18A.
50. Cover 165A/19.
51. Cover 165A/117.
52. Cover 165A/121A.
53. Cover 165B/36.
54. Cover 165B/40.

Part II: Builders

1. Thornycroft Document BH/1 p11.
2. In Thornycroft Document A/4.
3. Thornycroft Document A/4.
4. Cover 128/73.
5. Cover 128/9.
6. Cover 128/99.
7. Thornycroft Document D/14.
8. Thornycroft Document D/12.
9. Thornycroft Document A/4.
10. Thornycroft Document A/4.
11. Thornycroft Document D/13.

12. Cover 128/31.
13. Cover 128/47.
14. Thornycroft Document D/13.
15. Thornycroft Document D/13.
16. Cover 142/1.
17. Thornycroft Document BA/5.
18. Thornycroft Document D/14.
19. Cover 142/31 – 30 January 1895.
20. Cover 142/28.
21. Cover 160/298.
22. Cover 160/298.
23. Cover 160/22B.
24. Cover 165/1.
25. Thornycroft Document D/14.
26. Thornycroft Document BC/1.
27. Thornycroft Document D/18.
28. Thornycroft Document D/18.
29. Thornycroft Document D/18.
30. Thornycroft Document D/18.
31. Thornycroft Document A/4.
32. Thornycroft Document D/19.
33. Thornycroft Document A/4.
34. *Plans*: General Arrangement – in. *Documents*: D/13.
35. *Plans*: General Arrangement – in.
36. Cover 128/2.
37. Cover 128/5.
38. Cover 128/11.
39. Cover 128/75.
40. Cover 128/15.
41. Cover 128/189.
42. Cover 128/72, preliminary trial dated 23 February 1894.
43. Cover 128A/178.
44. Cover 128/44.
45. Cover 128/31.
46. Cover 128/47.
47. Cover 142/4.
48. Cover 142/1.
49. Cover 142/7.
50. Cover 142/9.
51. Cover 142/31.

52. Cover 142/30.
53. Cover 165/1.
54. Cover 128/2.
55. Cover 128/5.
56. Cover 128/7.
57. Cover 128/14.
58. Cover 128/74A.
59. Cover 128/71.
60. Cover 128/112.
61. Cover 128/43.
62. Cover 128/69.
63. Covers 128/157 and 128/186.
64. Cover 142/4.
65. Cover 142/9.
66. Cover 142/31.
67. Cover 142/28.
68. Cover 160/22B.
69. Cover 128/5.
70. Cover 128/7.
71. Cover 128/14.
72. Cover 160/22B.
73. Cover 128/2.
74. Cover 128/2.
75. Cover 160/22B.
76. Cover 128/43.
77. Cover 128/60.
78. Cover 165/1.
79. Cover 142/30.
80. Cover 165/1.
81. Cover 128/43.
82. Cover 160/258.
83. Cover 160/22B.
84. Mr William Donald, grandson of one of the partners of the firm, very kindly sent me his account of the ordering and reboilering of these two destroyers, in which he made use of surviving papers from that firm. He did this because of an inaccuracy in my account of these destroyers in *Conway's All the World's Fighting Ships 1860-1905*, and I am very happy to withdraw the suggestion, taken from earlier accounts, that the prolonged problems with *Fervent* and *Zephyr* drove the firm into bankruptcy. However, I regret that I must continue to pain Mr. Donald by considering that the firm was, when

considered in the context of the successes and failures of the other shipbuilders constructing TBDs, one of the least successful and least competent in the field. Whatever the role of the Admiralty in the failure of both the original locomotive boilers and of the reboilering with water tube ones, it does not seem reasonable to absolve the firm from any responsibility at all for this regrettable series of failures.
85. Cover 128/2.
86. Cover 128A/212.
87. Cover 128/2 – May 1892.
88. This point is from Cover 128/11 and it is uncertain whether it applies to the original 1892 design, though it probably does.
89. Cover 128/5.
90. Cover 128/7.
91. Cover 128/14.
92. Cover 128/47 – dated 3 November 1893.
93. Cover 142/30.
94. Cover 165A/40.
95. Cover 165/1.
96. Cover 128/43.
97. Cover 128/47.
98. Cover 160/300.
99. Cover 165/1.
100. Cover 128/41 Pledge (probably, the document is initialed 'HP') to Deadman, who concurred and sent the note on to DNC.
101. Cover 128/86.
102. Cover 128A/101.
103. Cover 160/22B memo dated 6 September 1897.
104. Cover 128/74 – acceptance letter of 7 February 1894.
105. Cover 142/30.
106. Cover 160/22B.
107. Cover 165/1.
108. Cover 128/43.
109. Cover 128/43.
110. Cover 128/60.
111. Cover 128/22B.
112. Cover 165/1.

Part III:
1. Cover 128/2.
2. Cover 128A/257.
3. Cover 128/214 F Hervey to 'Dear Sir John' (presumably Fisher).
4. Cover 128A/49 – comments by Deadman and by Ellis.
5. Cover 160/42.
6. Cover 154/51.
7. Cover 160/237.
8. Cover 165/1.
9. Cover 165/251.
10. Cover 165A/66.
11. Cover 128/12.
12. Cover 128/56.
13. Cover 128/60.
14. Cover 142/19.
15. Cover 165A/137.
16. Cover 128B/64 (January 1903).
17. Cover 128B/130.
18. Cover 165A/66.
19. Cover 128C/20.
20. Cover 128C/62 – the vessel in question was *Ranger*.
21. Cover 128/8 – memo dated 30 July 1892.
22. Cover 128/16.
23. Cover 128/78. Complement for *Boxer* etc 7 March 1894.
24. Cover 142/13 – memo dated 27 November 1894.
25. Cover 160/32.
26. Cover 165A/121A.
27. Cover 128/46.
28. Cover 128A/257 – report on trials of *Havock*.
29. Cover 128/46, Instructions to Overseers for the first 27-knotters.
30. Document S.5765–98 quoted in Cover 142/218.
31. Cover 142/218.
32. Cover 128A/228.
33. Cover 142/225. The Fisher quote is dated 19 March 1900.
34. The whole of this discussion is in Cover 165/118.
35. Cover 128A – Enclosure at folio 257.
36. Cover 128/16.
37. Cover 128/189 – 3-hour trial 28 October 1893.
38. Cover 128/119A – Arthur W Torlesse to Admiral Fisher, mid-September 1894.
39. Cover 128/214 – F W F Hervey to Fisher (?).
40. Cover 128/179.
41. Cover 128A/131 – dated 13 August 1896.
42. Cover 165/1 – Note by DNC and Engineer-in-Chief dated 9 August 1898.
43. Cover 160/22B – DNC's note dated 6 September 1897.
44. Cover 160/239 – for April to July 1900.
45. Cover 128B/1.
46. Cover 128B/145 – Vice Admiral Noel, 27 January 1905.
47. Cover 128C/41–26 April 1911 letter W J Berry to Mr. Champagnes (written from Malta Yard).
48. Cover 165A/63.
49. Draft initialled HRC – signed P Watts 14 November 1907.
50. Cover 165B/71.
51. Cover 165/100. Holland's memo dated 25 June 1901.
52. 6 July 1901.
53. Cover 128B/96 – on 26 February 1904.
54. On 30 March 1904.
55. Cover 128A/259a.
56. Cover 142/249, Deadman reporting on 23 October 1901.
57. Cover 128B/193.
58. Cover 128B/227.
59. Cover 128C/2.
60. Cover 165A/143.
61. Cover 128C/45.
62. Cover 128C/69.
63. Cover 128/214.
64. Cover 142/30.
65. Cover 142/76 – to Engineer-in-Chief.
66. Cover 128A/259a.
67. Cover 142/249.
68. Cover 128B/163.
69. Cover 165A/102.

Part IV: Foreign Comparison
1. Covers 128A/255, 128B/255c.
2. Cover 128B/145.

Index